'A major contribution to the emerging literature on the future of capitalism. Joe Zammit-Lucia shows how business and markets necessarily operate within a social and political context – and demolishes the statist/neo-liberal dichotomy.'

Professor Sir John Kay, London School of Economics and Political Science. Fellow, St John's College, Oxford

'In *The New Political Capitalism* Joe Zammit-Lucia explains why the currently dysfunctional relationship between politics and business is holding us back. From the climate crisis to growing inequality to supply chain disruption, none of the complex, multi-faceted challenges that the world currently faces can be addressed by politics or business acting alone – the two must work in partnership. *The New Political Capitalism* is essential reading for all who are seeking to build more resilient societies based on better political and better business cultures.'

Helle Thorning-Schmidt, Prime Minister of Denmark, 2011–2015. Member, European Council on Foreign Relations. Board Member, Vestas Wind Systems A/S

'*The New Political Capitalism* is a book for our times. Never in our contemporary history have the links between the world of business and the political environment been so close. This is the case in our democratic Western societies, but also in the Eastern autocracies. In France, we have seen a young man, Emmanuel Macron, move directly from an investment bank to the state palace of the Elysée, first as deputy secretary general in charge of the economy, then as president. What we needed was a comprehensive framework for the links between politics and business to give us a better understanding of the world around us. As an enlightened observer of the world of politics as well as business, Joe Zammit-Lucia gives us a landmark book. I advise all those interested in political science to read it.'

Renaud Girard, Grand Reporter and Foreign Affairs Columnist, Le Figaro. Professor of International Strategy, Sciences Po, Paris, France

'*The New Political Capitalism* identifies and explores the crucial, necessarily interdependent relationship between business and government. The simplistic elevation to dominance of de-regulated, financialized markets generated the Global Financial Crisis and the populist threats to the democratic order that followed. Now Joe Zammit-Lucia examines the intricacies of political economy in the digital age. *The New Political Capitalism* is an essential guide for establishing a stable and sustainable future out of the incoherent chaos that surrounds us.'

William H Janeway, Managing Director, Warburg Pincus Private Equity, New York; Faculty Member, University of Cambridge; Member, Board of Governors of the Institute for New Economic Thinking

'Timely, highly relevant, insightful, useful and readable are the words that come to mind as I read *The New Political Capitalism*. I heard some of my own frustrated comments mirrored in the scripts. Getting to win-win with other sector partners is hard work and I so enjoyed the many examples Joe uses to illustrate the simultaneously connected yet disconnected realities that business and politics need to navigate together. Building trust and this win-win muscle is essential if we are to address the societal challenges and business opportunities that are so often two sides of the same coin.'

Gail Klinsworth, Inter alia Board Chair, Globescan, Toronto, Canada and Chair, Board of Trustees, The Shell Foundation. Chief Sustainability Officer, Unilever 2012–2015

'Joe brings together a rare combination of strengths: he has a nose for new trends; he is a critical thinker; and his writings are lucid and with wit. *The New Political Capitalism* reflects all these strengths. The book captures a seismic change in the relations between politics and business. The reinvigorated force of geopolitics, the failings of neoliberalism, and a quest for identity during uncertain times have re-inaugurated the primacy of politics, in small and large. Joe captures this trend, illustrates it with examples from the corporate world, and indicates how we can make the best out of it. Spoiler alert: the answer can neither be to go back to "we just make money", nor should we fuel the quest for belonging with superficial marketing tricks.'

Leon Wansleben, Max Planck Institute for the Study of Societies, Cologne, Germany

'Those of us who have spent time in the worlds of politics and business often struggle to define the differences and overlaps between the two. Joe Zammit-Lucia's book is an impressive analysis of that relationship. The book is well written and the author, as both a successful entrepreneur and deep thinker, has many important insights. Business schools, in particular, will benefit from this analysis of the politicized environment within which business currently operates.'

The Rt Hon Sir Vince Cable, UK Secretary of State for Business, Innovation and Skills and President of the Board of Trade, 2010–2015. Professor in Practice, London School of Economics and Political Science. Former Chief Economist, Royal Dutch Shell plc.

'This book's insights on the changing competitive landscape should be required reading for all senior executives facing a new-game environment in which the model for customer value creation is changing – a scenario facing virtually all industry sectors today. Joe Zammit-Lucia has consistently been one of the most astute observers and predictors of the core issues senior executives must master. This book is a must-read for understanding why some companies are leaders and others laggards in leading the customer experience revolution.'

Dr Lynn Phillips, Faculty Member and Professor of Marketing, Stanford Graduate School of Business, 1983–1996. Managing Director, Reinventures, California.

with best wishes

The
New
Political
Capitalism

How businesses and
societies can thrive in a
deeply politicized world

JOE ZAMMIT-LUCIA

BLOOMSBURY BUSINESS
LONDON · OXFORD · NEW YORK · NEW DELHI · SYDNEY

BLOOMSBURY BUSINESS
Bloomsbury Publishing Plc
50 Bedford Square, London, WC1B 3DP, UK
29 Earlsfort Terrace, Dublin 2, Ireland

First published in Great Britain 2022

A catalogue record for this book is available from the British Library

Library of Congress Cataloguing-in-Publication data has been applied for

ISBN: HB: 978-1-4729-9021-1 eBook: 978-1-4729-9019-8

2 4 6 8 10 9 7 5 3 1

Typeset by Deanta Global Publishing Services, Chennai, India
Printed and bound in Great Britain by CPI Group (UK) Ltd, Croydon CR0 4YY

MIX
Paper from
responsible sources
FSC® C171272

To Astrid and Mario

'The good life is one inspired by love and guided by knowledge.'
Bertrand Russell

Join the discussion

visit

www.newpoliticalcapitalism.com

Acknowledgements

This book draws on the work of many who have addressed similar issues in the past and who have reported and provided insights on events from around the world. My thanks to them for their valuable work, without which this book would not have been possible.

My thanks to the many friends, colleagues and acquaintances, too numerous to list, who, through countless discussions and conversations, have continually challenged my thinking and helped improve my understanding of the topics I have tried to address. Particular thanks to Richard Galea Debono, Paul Goldsmith, William H Janeway, Gail Kintworth, Rick Smith, Mike Tuffrey and Leon Wansleben for generously agreeing to read early drafts of the manuscript and devoting their time to providing valuable comments that I have tried my best to incorporate.

All remaining errors of fact or judgement are entirely my own.

'It is not the most intellectual of the species that survives;
it is not the strongest that survives; but the species that
survives is the one that is able best to adapt and adjust to
the changing environment in which it finds itself.'

Leon C Megginson (1963)[1]
paraphrasing Charles Darwin's *Origin of Species*

Contents

Preface

Business and politics are inseparable. The relationship is as complex as it is dynamic. And it is becoming ever more relevant to sustainable business success.

These are the central messages of this book.

It is often thought that 'political' equates with partisan politics, or with the increasingly grubby nature of political campaigning, or with the shady world of lobbying for self-interest. Yet politics is not that. Politics is the mechanism by which we all decide what kind of society we wish to live in. That is something in which every one of us has an interest and about which we have views – often visceral and strongly held. Politics is 'a great and civilizing human activity', as Bernard Crick put it in his seminal work *In Defence of Politics*.[*] He goes on to argue that establishing a functioning political order that recognizes different views, different preferences and even different truths marks the birth, or the recognition, of freedom.

The relationship between politics and business has always been, and will remain, complicated. For the last several decades a school of thought has prevailed that business is driven purely by commercial logic. That political issues had little place in business management. And when they did, they were often viewed as irritants getting in the way of 'doing business'. That perspective has always been a simplistic one that didn't stand up to the most cursory of scrutinies.

Things have changed. As I explore in the examples examined in this book, considerations that are political in nature now permeate almost

---

[*]Crick, Bernard. *In Defence of Politics*. Pelican Books, 1964

every aspect of corporations' operations. We shall see how Google and Microsoft employees intervened in their employer's ability to provide services to US immigration and defence authorities because they were not in agreement with public policy in these areas. How, by following a purely commercial logic, Harley Davidson management demonstrated a set of values that were at odds with those of their employees. How the nature and shape of globalization is changing in the face of realigning geopolitical forces. How political failures have contributed to significant scandals and damage for Wirecard, Volkswagen and Boeing.

From issues related to climate change and environmental degradation, to political expectations of what the multinational model should deliver, to investors' increasing focus on ethical behaviour, sustainability, and the long-term social value-added of corporations in which they invest, political issues have now become a core driver of future commercial success and corporate valuations. Some have argued that political logic is overtaking commercial logic in shaping how markets operate.

In other words, we have entered a new era – The New Political Capitalism.

This is not a superficial development that will pass. It is rooted in the belief that our system of political economy is now failing too many. Large swathes of the population see the social contract breaking down with ever more people being left behind and environmental damage increasing even as the amount of financial wealth being created continues to soar. The inter-relationship between business and politics is in the eye of that storm – what some have labelled 'Angrynomics'.*

The New Political Capitalism is reflected in the emerging 'Cornwall Consensus' that followed the G7 leaders' meeting in Cornwall in 2021. It is starting to replace the longstanding Washington Consensus of globalized, *laissez faire* neoliberalism. Instead, the Cornwall Consensus prioritizes a politics that moves proactively to shape markets to deliver a better political economy. It recognizes the central role of politics in the construction of functioning markets.

How can businesses adapt to this new era?

Success will come to those who develop a deep understanding of how politics and the constant contestation of political ideas work, how they

---

Angrynomics is the title of a book by Eric Lonergan and Mark Blyth. Agenda Publishing, 2020.

drive as well as follow contemporary culture, and how to embed these understandings into the core of their business models.

The world is changing – fast. The shape and nature of that change will have the characteristics of politics, not business. Volatile, emotional, complex, multi-directional and multi-dimensional, not comfortably linear. Full of the unexpected. As in politics, businesses must now look at their addressable market as a coalition of customers that share values and political outlooks. Outlooks that change more rapidly over time making the market fluid and only manageable and somewhat predictable if looked at through a political lens.

To thrive in this world, business thinking will move on from traditional approaches. Business leaders that will navigate the new era successfully are those who develop and hone the skills to think, act and structure their business politically as well as they have, to date, honed their skills to think and act commercially and financially.

This is not a technique. It's a frame of mind.

As we shall see, a number of brands – like Benetton and Patagonia – have always had political issues as a core part of their brand identity. Others such as Nike have dived into the Black Lives Matter movement. Yet others are now exploring how to integrate their customers' increasing, and ever more passionate, engagement with political issues – from climate change to diversity to environmental sustainability and to many others – into their value propositions and customer experiences. How to behave in a world where businesses' understandable desire to be liked by everyone and disliked by no one is becoming increasingly hard to sustain in a world that is progressively more polarized on political issues.

The shouty world of social media is yet another major political issue to be addressed – both for social media companies themselves and for business and for politics in general.

Even in the time it has taken to move this book from a final manuscript to a published book, events have moved on significantly – all in the same direction: an ever-increasing impact of political considerations on corporations' performance. We have seen an aggressive Chinese crackdown on commercial interests that were claimed not to be in the wider societal interests – however financially successful they may have been. Governments' agents such as central banks have been struggling with how to manage monetary policy in a way that balances political imperatives and the needs of capital markets. 'Selective decoupling' driven by ever increasing concerns around national security, commercial production processes, energy security, and trans-national debt as countries have found themselves dependent on geostrategic rivals – a state of affairs that may deliver short term financial benefits but is politically unsustainable.

We have seen financially efficient but clearly non-resilient supply chains that seemed to have weathered the COVID-19 pandemic break down to near collapse as demand started to recover. An energy crisis that sent the price of natural gas soaring. A widespread shortage of skills came to light. All of which was met with loud demands from business and from citizens for governments to intervene just as they did to support businesses during the pandemic and, before that, in the financial crisis. The usual business mantra of 'politics should keep out of our way so we can continue to do business' was nowhere to be seen.

A senior businessperson I was speaking to worried that the development of the New Political Capitalism could destroy a significant amount of value creation. At the time of writing, the China crackdown had reduced valuations by some $2 trillion. But we need to look at developments through a different lens if we are really to understand them. What is happening is a societal re-evaluation of what 'value' they expect business to deliver. The late twentieth-century financialized capitalism where the conception of business was that its primary, and for some its exclusive, role was to make money and deliver shareholder value; that the only 'value' that matters is that which can be measured in financial returns, is well past its sell by date. Today, that is seen as far too blinkered a definition of the role of business in our societies.

Business is part of our panoply of political institutions. Corporations are political and social actors. They play a significant role in employment, consumption patterns, environmental sustainability, national security, market structures and regulation, and even in the election process itself in those countries that have elections. In that context, there is a growing consensus that the role of business is broader and fuzzier – to help create a better society. That is the 'value' that citizens everywhere now want to see business deliver – not just financial returns and stock price performance. What constitutes 'a better society' is, of course a purely political question placing business right at the core of political debate.

By the time you read this book, events will have moved on even further. Exactly how cannot be perfectly forecast. But one thing is certain. With every passing week, month and year, we will see headlines in every newspaper and business magazine that further highlight the increasingly political nature of markets and the increasing importance of political considerations in business success. We will also see a widening in the performance gap between those businesses that understand these issues and incorporate them into their purpose, strategy and operations, and those that do not.

I hope that the examples I have examined in this book can help further understanding of the intimate and ever-dynamic relationship between business and politics and help management and executives enhance their success in the new age of political capitalism.

I

Bridging the Cultural Divide

'Politics is pervasive. Everything is political and the choice to be "apolitical" is usually just an endorsement of the status quo and the unexamined life.'

Barbara Solnit
American author and activist

A friend, a chairman of a major multinational, was relating some discussions he had been having with his peers at a business event:

'We were discussing politics. We came to the conclusion that politics operates to a totally different logic from business. And, quite honestly, we don't understand it.'

Business and politics do operate to different thought processes, a different culture and different perspectives. And many in business wrestle with a framework so fundamentally different to that which they are used to – and which they need to run their businesses successfully.

My friend's words put me in mind of C.P. Snow's renowned 1959 *Rede Lecture* on the divide between art and science:

I felt I was moving among two groups – comparable in intelligence ... who in intellectual, moral and psychological climate had so little in common that instead of going from Burlington House or South Kensington to Chelsea, one might have crossed an ocean ... They have a curious distorted image of each other. Their attitudes are so different that, even at the level of emotion, they can't find much common ground.[1]

This book is intended to make some contribution towards bridging that cultural divide. To provide a framework for how businesses can enhance their success in the new age of political capitalism through an understanding of political rationality, the development of effective political antennae within their organizations and adapting their operations to the ever-increasing impact of political considerations on business performance.

When I was working in business, neither I nor my colleagues nor those in more senior positions really understood political culture. We had very little interest in taking the time to understand it. The general feeling about politics was one of frustration. If only politics would just keep out of it, we would be able to get on and run our businesses properly. That was the prevailing discourse.

Neither are such divides limited to business and politics. During the COVID-19 crisis, I was having a repeated ping-pong conversation with a friend I have known since we were at school together. He, too, was totally soured on politics except that, in his view, it was science, not business, that should reign supreme.

'*Science is humanity's best hope for advancement and indeed survival into the future. From pandemics to the existential threat to our species of climate change, science is the one shining hope. Politics and politicians can be enablers of scientific progress. More often than not, they are* disablers *and contrive to muddy the waters of rational thought and decision making,*' read one of his emails. He goes on to say that scientists are human exemplars '*compared to the narcissists and ego-centred individuals in the political and business fields.*'

None of this is surprising. We all have a tendency to be tribal. To believe that our tribe is somehow different – and better. Locked in our bubbles of friends and colleagues who are like us, our biases tend to grow rather than wane, leading to a collective belief in the essential righteousness and superiority of our own perspectives.

We also tend to empathize more easily with those of our own tribe. Through repeated email conversations, another friend, an accomplished surgeon, would repeatedly stress the impact of the COVID pandemic on healthcare workers. One of his emails concluded, '*Pity about healthcare staff!!!'* I felt compelled to respond that maybe some pity should also flow towards those who had passed away and their families. I thought it would, maybe, be trying to push his empathy envelope too far also to suggest sympathy with those who had lost their businesses and livelihoods, with the politicians and policymakers who had to make impossibly difficult decisions daily, and all the rest.

It's not that my friend is an unsympathetic person, just that it is much more natural for all of us to sympathize with those whose situation we understand and feel close to. With those who are one of us – the in-group.

Then there is the human tendency to create binaries and put them in conflict. It soon becomes 'business vs politics'; or, as one sociology professor recently put it to me, 'capitalism vs humanity'; or, as we saw during the COVID-19 pandemic, 'saving lives vs the economy'; or whatever else we can put in opposition. All false binaries that create conflict, close people's eyes to alternative perspectives and to the fact that everything is interconnected. It ensures groupthink with ever-rebounding echoes of a constricted language where dissent and fresh ideas struggle to find an opening. Yet, nothing is an either/or. Most things are also/and. We need different disciplines, different sets of responsibilities and different lenses through which to see the world we all live in. Diversity of thought, of political views, of ideas, of business models, of ways of seeing the world – that is what drives progress and innovation and provides resilience. We can see it in the beautiful and highly effective diversity of the natural world – a diversity that we are, sadly, destroying. Through that wonderful diversity emerge functioning ecosystems that are self-sustaining, resilient and able to evolve – without anyone needed to manage them. Indeed, any attempts at human 'management' usually result in disaster.

This came home to me while hiking in Japan. We were on a ridge. To the left was a pine plantation managed for logging. Zero diversity. A monoculture of pine trees. To the right, the hill fell off more steeply making it unsuitable for commercial exploitation. It remained wild and diverse. As I stood on the ridge, I could hear to the right of me the sounds of life – birds, creatures rustling in the undergrowth, bees and butterflies, the lot. To the left was total silence. The lack of diversity had killed life. Just like tribal belief systems that become monocultural, trotting out the same old mantras to the exclusion of looking beyond the tribe for different ideas and approaches, end up killing those very systems and leaving devastation in their wake.

Having spent many years first working in the medical/scientific field and then in business, I too was locked into my own tribal beliefs. Since then, I have spent a number of years in the political world. This has helped me look at things through a political lens as well. It has improved my understanding of both the differences and the essential complementarity of business and politics, the positives that emerge from some of the inevitable tensions between the two and the importance of building political perspectives into business organizations and business decision making.

This book is not yet another diatribe pitting government and the private sector against each other. The world has had to suffer through enough of that claptrap and nonsense for decades. It is, instead, based on the indisputable fact that politics and business are essential and important components of our society. That improving the interaction between the two will yield substantial benefits. That businesses that are able to look at the world through a political lens as well as the commercial one will do better – better for themselves, and better for how our societies function. But for diversity of thought and perspective to flourish, we need a common language and minds that are open to listening to, and capable of understanding, other perspectives. The ability to see diversity as enriching. The willingness to change our entrenched views in response to alternative ideas without fear of disapproval from our peer group because we have dared to challenge received wisdom and tribal beliefs. Otherwise, diversity, as well as that other fashionable if more unwieldy term 'multi-disciplinarity' become a Tower of Babel; all of us locked into our own way of seeing the world, our own set of acronyms that lock others out, remaining unable even to start to comprehend what others are saying, never mind learn from them.

And, maybe above all, we need some humility.

But, it seems, these are still minority views. Speaking to a senior Apple executive recently and relating the 'Why doesn't politics just keep out of it so we can do business?' attitude that I mistakenly imagined had become obsolete, her response was 'Sounds familiar.'

Some time back, I wrote a paper on corporate governance,[2] including how to address the incendiary issue of executive pay. Another chairman of a major multinational told me that he disagreed with everything I had written in the paper – except for one useful insight: that many of the issues raised were purely political in nature. This should have come as no surprise, seeing as the paper was targeted at policymakers. But it was clear that the chair in question saw the term 'political' as interchangeable with 'irrelevant', or 'irritating', even, maybe, illegitimate in a business context.

The flipside of this emerged when Boris Johnson in an unguarded moment well prior to his elevation to the office of UK Prime Minister, blurted out 'F**k business!' – a moment of frustration at a business establishment that sought to thwart his Brexit campaign. At the time, many of my business friends were shocked by an outburst that they considered nigh on sacrilegious. It is not clear why they should be so offended when, not infrequently, they express similar sentiments about politicians, occasionally in equally florid language.

The cultural gulf between business and politics remains wide and persistent. *'Business is business and politics is politics and never the twain shall meet,'* according to American journalist Suzy Welch.

The premise of this book is that such attitudes are not only mistaken, they are also damaging both to those businesses whose leaders and executives hold such views and to the fabric of our societies. Here, I shall explore how and why business and politics are not only related but are vital, inextricably linked and interdependent parts of our complex social systems – what used to be called the political economy. It's a term that seems to have fallen out of favour except with a few academics such as the late Alberto Alesina (1957–2020), who kept the concept alive in the face of decades of academic economics that, remarkably, had seen fit to set to one side issues relating to trust, moral values, beliefs, and norms – the bread and butter of politics. Neoclassical economics *'abstracts from social, political and institutional aspects of real markets which cannot be dismissed as "exogenous" factors but are inherent, and indeed may be essential, characteristics of the functioning of markets in the real world,'*[3] as we shall see in Chapter 3.

If nothing else, the 2008 financial crisis, the COVID-19 pandemic, and the perceived success (at least for now) of China's state-directed economy have all put paid to any credibility in the idea that business and politics are separate. Businesses of all shapes and sizes held their hands out for government bailouts that, all told, ran into the multi-trillions.

They saw central banks buy their bonds in vast quantities and even start accepting junk bonds as collateral. All deep and wide interventions by public institutions to prop up business when needed. Where was the 'Keep out of my way so I can get on with my business' mantra then?

Not to mention how Western business leaders, attracted by China's economic potential, seem happy to co-operate with the political establishment and, as we shall see later, when investing in the country even let themselves be subjugated to highly onerous political demands. Yet in their own countries they kick, scream and express dismay at government action that doesn't come anywhere near being as intrusive. Eventually they will be faced with the question: why is it that you seem happy to sign up to highly restrictive conditions to access the China market but not the US or EU or other markets where any restrictions actually have democratic legitimacy and therefore represent, as best possible, what our societies wish?

COVID-19 has changed, perhaps permanently, the perceived role of government in the economy and in its relationship with commercial enterprise. Interventions on a scale previously unseen maybe even in wartime have placed government action at the centre of commercial enterprise and it remains unclear when, how and if government will, once again, retreat. The pandemic, coupled with the changing geopolitical landscape, has also emboldened government intervention in the nature and shape of globalization, broadening the definition of strategically important industries and opening further discussion on the role of self-sufficiency as opposed to globally dispersed supply chains focused on short-term financial efficiency.

Both the financial crisis and the pandemic, piled as they were on top of growing awareness of ever-increasing environmental and social breakdown, accelerated an already existing significant change in thinking about the relationship between business and politics and the role of business in society. Many businesses stepped up during the COVID-19 pandemic to protect their workers, change production lines to produce products and equipment needed for the crisis, and to start re-thinking their role in society. Sadly, a number did not. While readily pocketing the government's shilling, they soon reverted to their old habits of believing that they had no other duty to society except to maximize financial returns to which their own remuneration was linked. Highly damaging to people's trust in, and respect for, business and its leadership. And frustrating, to say the least, for those business leaders who did step up.

There are, today, plenty of business leaders who recognize the significant political power that they have (and I shall explain in Chapter 2 what I mean by 'political') and choose to use that power to improve the societies in which we live. From McDonald's to Patagonia, to several others around the world, successful businesses have embarked on a journey that does not put their business into conflict with wider social and political imperatives. Rather, they are making tremendously important contributions to the wider social order.

Of course, the relationship between business and politics is dynamic. It changes across time and between cultures and countries, and never reaches a stable equilibrium. That relationship is widely different in the US than it is in Germany, Japan, or China. But it is important everywhere. A 2019 survey of asset managers conducted by UBS, a Swiss bank, found that 66 per cent of fund managers believed that politics, rather than economic fundamentals, was the primary mover of market performance.

We all operate as part of the political economy and businesses that can look at themselves through a political lens as well as a financial one are more likely to have sustained success. I hope that executives will therefore find some usefulness in the discussions, controversies and polemics raised in this book, allowing them to manage their businesses more effectively and more sustainably. Less prone to being taken by surprise by political actions that affect their business, yet which are often fairly predictable – directionally if not in the details of specific policy initiatives. Some might find it helpful also to explore how their own actions have political impact, an issue explored later in Chapter 2.

Issues taking up a huge amount of senior management time and corporate resources – from Environmental, Social and Governance (ESG) questions, to the relationship between data and privacy in a digitized world, to the impact of artificial intelligence (AI) on our whole social fabric, to the regulation of financial markets and the search for financial stability, to supply chain structures, to very many others – are all driven by the prevailing political climate and the political way of thinking. These developments increasingly require senior executive teams to have a deep understanding of political thinking. They cannot easily be dealt with by delegating them to departments of public affairs or corporate social responsibility. The issues are core to the very functioning of the business.

> Companies used to avoid political issues at almost any cost. But those still relying on a strategy of abstention and neutrality are quickly learning that it no longer works the way it once did. Sometimes it leads to more harm than good.[4]

Nor is it sufficient to reduce corporations' position on issues of political importance to box-ticking exercises – like spending resources on filling in forms to achieve some kind of positioning on the ever-multiplying generic indices of corporate sustainability or ESG performance – if these exercises are not intimately linked to corporate purpose, strategic objectives and operational performance. In other words, to the role of one's business in our societies.

As Jane Fraser wrote on her first day as CEO of Citi:

> "Our ESG agenda can't just be a separate layer that sits above what we do day-to-day. Our commitments to closing the gender pay gap, to advancing racial equity, and to pioneering the green agenda have demonstrated that this is good for business and not at odds with it. And we will continue to be part of the solution to these challenges and enable others to do so as well."[5]

On the other hand, we must not take it all too far. While business has a vitally important positive role to play, private enterprise cannot be expected to solve all of today's social and political issues. Rather it's a question of ensuring that business practices are aligned with societal expectations rather than engaging in business practices that make things worse. Ensuring that businesses and societies can thrive as the world becomes increasingly politicized.

When preparing this book, I spoke to a few literary agents. Explaining the project to one of them, he told me that he was particularly interested in business books, having just completed his MBA at Imperial College, London. I asked whether there had been any politics classes as part of his course, whether the interrelationship between business and politics had been discussed. It will come as no surprise to anyone that the answer was negative. As Tom Peters put it in an article relating how he was 'angry, disgusted and sickened' at how McKinsey & Co., his first employer, and its army of clever MBAs ended up paying nearly $600 million for their part in the US opioid scandal: '*business schools typically emphasise marketing, finance, and quantitative rules. The "people stuff" and "culture stuff" gets short shrift in virtually all cases.*'[6] It is time to plug that gap and to recognize that politics is what people stuff and culture stuff is all about. I hope that this book might stimulate others to bring their own experiences and insights to bear on a subject the importance of which to the business world – and to our societies – is only matched or exceeded by the lack of attention it seems to receive.

Ludwig von Mises – one of the thinkers behind what was later to become known as 'neoliberalism' – expressed his views as follows:

The mixing of politics and business not only is detrimental to politics, as is frequently observed, but even much more so to business.[7]

That formulation has merit, but, as tends so often to be the case, the words of a thoughtful man have been misinterpreted and taken to unreasonable extremes.

Von Mises' observation is quite correct when one looks, for instance, at those countries where business and politics are so incestuously intertwined that democracy in any meaningful sense is impossible, leading to a descent into plutocracy or oligarchy. Or when business uses its financial heft and lobbying power to exercise excessive influence for narrow self-interest rather than broad societal benefit. Or when politics itself descends into the narrow defence of powerful vested interests and clientelism.

South Korea is a relatively young democracy, having moved towards full democracy in the late 1980s and the 1990s. Yet power remains concentrated. The presidency has substantial, some might argue excessive, powers. Samsung is the largest and most powerful of the Korean *chaebols* (conglomerates) that more or less control the country's economy. The pride of the nation, Samsung accounts for 13 per cent of South Korea's GDP. The scandal involved Lee Jae-yong, Samsung's chief, and the country's former (and first female) president, Park Gyun-hye. It started with Lee's efforts to secure his position as heir apparent to his father at the head of the conglomerate. Bribes in the tens of millions of dollars flowed from Mr Lee to President Park through a confidant – Choi Soon-sil.

As the scandals came to light, millions protested in the streets, President Park was impeached, convicted, removed from office, and eventually sentenced to a total of 35 years' imprisonment for multiple offences. Mr Lee was also tried, convicted, and sentenced to two and a half years in prison.

All these activities were illegal. They highlight the dangers of a deep incestuous relationship between business and politics. And particularly so when power is excessively concentrated – what one commentator called the 'gangsterism' that can arise in the nexus between politics and business.

But beyond the clear societal menaces posed by plutocracy, oligarchy, other forms of concentrated power and embedded corruption, we should also recognize that the positive interdependence between business and government runs deep in democratic societies. Workers are educated through public education programmes, they travel to work and deliver goods on largely government-built or subsidized infrastructure, their health is looked after by healthcare systems that are, to a greater or lesser extent, government-funded. Some of the world's most successful companies – Google, Amazon, Uber and many, many others – as well as our whole current way of life – would simply not exist if they were not free-riding on a huge government-built infrastructure: the internet. Pharmaceutical companies regularly draw on basic science emerging from academia, the National Institutes of Health, and other public bodies to bring us innovative medical treatments. Almost the whole defence industry is government-dependent – and we rightly worry when arms are sold to non-government actors. So it goes on, and on, and on. But most important of all is the understanding that markets are primarily political constructs, not business or economic constructs. Without political institutions, markets as we know them – whether local (Chapter 3) or global (Chapter 4) – cannot function, or even exist.

This book argues that politics and business, two important pillars of our democratic system, are joined at the hip. Because business is central to how our societies and our economies function, it is inherently political. Senior business leaders cannot be 'apolitical'. They may choose to be non-partisan in a political party sense (at least publicly), but that does not make them apolitical – because nobody who has any views at all on how the world should function – and the role of business in that

– can legitimately describe themselves as apolitical. In fact, taking the trouble to declare oneself 'apolitical' is, in itself, a political statement.

That business and politics are intertwined is clearly stated by economist and journalist Anatole Kaletsky: *'The economy of the future will be explicitly a mixed economy, in the sense that both the public and private sectors will play an important role.'*[8] What Kaletsky is writing about has always been true. But he is right in that we have entered a new era – what I describe as the new political capitalism. An age where, with increasing polarization, ever more people are becoming politicized in the sense that they have, and increasingly express, strong views about how our societies should function – and the role that business must play. This offers huge opportunities for those businesses that develop effective political antennae. From why businesses exist at all, to how they are run, to the importance of diverse thinking, to what they stand for, culturally and politically. All of which offer positive prospects for those business leaders who have the capability to effect a change in mindset and to embrace the new political capitalism (*see* Chapter 5).

In Chapter 6, I examine how the new era is also visible in the surge in the number of political brands. Brands and companies that take a long-term, values-based approach to how they approach customers rather than a purely functional approach that is easily superseded. Some, like Patagonia, are authentic and successful. Others have committed missteps as they, and their advertising and branding agencies, misread the political and cultural runes.

Companies such as Facebook (now Meta) can be reasonably reclassified from technology companies to political corporations. All aspects of Facebook's business – from its fundamental business model to issues surrounding privacy, the influence on elections and the impact on social values to its attempt to set up Diem (previously Libra) as an alternative global currency – are almost purely political issues resulting in Mark Zuckerberg and other Facebook executives spending significant time facing lawmakers across the world.[*]

Some will continue to argue that the role of business is purely financial – to make money – and that everything should be looked at within that framework. Even if one were to accept that premise, which

---

[*]At the time of writing, the name 'Meta' was being contested by Meta PCs.

I don't, we need to acknowledge some fundamentals – like asking the question 'What is money?'

> Take a dollar bill and look at it carefully. You will see that it is simply a colourful piece of paper with the signature of the US secretary of the treasury on one side, and the slogan 'In God We Trust' on the other. We accept the dollar in payment, because we trust in God and the US secretary of the treasury. The crucial role of trust explains why our financial systems are so tightly bound up with our political, social and ideological systems.[9]

Or, to put it another way, *'In all modern economies the government defines money by choosing what it will accept in payment of taxes.'*[10]

Even the act of 'making money' is therefore intricately bound with our political and social systems because money itself must be so bound if it is to have any value. We shall see whether the movement to 'privatize' money through the launch of cryptocurrencies and other non-government-backed money will be successful and to what degree – especially if no major government will ever accept such currencies as acceptable for paying taxes while governments themselves launch central bank digital currencies.

Here I argue that we have entered a new era – what I call the New Political Capitalism. A period that meshes socio-political trends with business purpose, strategy and operations. It affects businesses top to bottom – from who is willing to work for them to how productive and innovative they can be, to the basis on which they acquire and retain customers. It represents the antithesis of the late twentieth-century culture of financialized capitalism with its exclusive focus on short-term financial performance at whatever cost and, for some, the insidious and corrosive separation of business activity from social context.

Of course, financialized capitalism itself is not separate from politics. Its rise was enabled by state action (e.g. the Greenspan put[†]) combined with state inaction in other parts of the political economy. All of which was part of the political ideology that flourished at the time, much

---

[†]Refers to former Federal Reserve chair Alan Greenspan's monetary policy response to financial crisis that came to be seen as encouraging extreme financial speculation and the creation of unsustainable asset bubbles.

of it encouraged by financial and business interests. Politically, that perspective is changing. And more rapidly than many of us imagined.

In the closing chapter, I bring together the various threads explored in the book to describe the change from financialized to political capitalism, what that means and how that progression is coming about in fits and starts – as is inherent in the nature of all social change.

Businesses, politicians and policymakers all face the same twenty-first-century set of radical challenges. Change is happening at a much faster pace. The issues faced are not linear, they are less predictable; they are not easily resolved within the confines of existing structures and institutions. Problems are more complex. They are structural and systemic in nature, not easily soluble with minor tweaks to the established order. This makes everything inevitably much more political.

Conventional tools may no longer work. As Jean-Claude Trichet, then President of the European Central Bank, put it in the wake of the 2008 financial crisis: '*As a policymaker during the crisis, I found the available models of limited help. In fact, I would go further. In the face of the crisis, we felt abandoned by conventional tools.*'[11] The same is true for business – in the aftermath of the COVID pandemic, the complexity of the necessary response to climate change and environmental degradation, for how we deal with the world of social media, the changing geo-political landscape that affects everything from supply chains to the impact of business activities on national security and the many other political issues that have started to envelop business practices. Well-established models and conventional approaches are no longer as effective in the twenty-first-century world of political capitalism.

As the new political capitalism continues to develop – and the indications are that it will accelerate rather than slow down or stall – we will see a clear divide between those who embrace it and ride the wave to sustainable success, and those who cling to the late twentieth century way of thinking even as the world moves on.

Which do you want to be?

2

What is Politics?

'What we mean by "politics" is the people's business – the most
important business there is.'

Adlai Stevenson
American lawyer, politician and diplomat
Democratic presidential nominee, 1952 & 1956

For many, the first thing that 'politics' brings to mind is the electioneering process. A process that may seem grubby and fundamentally dishonest.

That's hardly surprising. For a large proportion of the population, it is the showbiz nature and the sheer intensity of the electoral process that fleetingly focuses their mind on what they perceive as 'politics'. The rest of the time, most people are busy getting on with their lives, running their business, earning a living, putting food on the table, looking after their family, enjoying their holiday, or whatever else. Politics seems – only 'seems', mind you, as we shall see later – to play a small and intermittent part in their lives. Those who spend much of their mental and physical time focused on the political process are unrepresentative outliers.

Today, the electoral process seems even grubbier and more dishonest than it has for some time. This, in some part, is due to the activities of business. The rise of an uncontrolled and seemingly uncontrollable social media environment has not only degraded any concept of truth and honesty but has had a big cultural impact, positive and negative. Positively, it has given voice to many who previously had no discernible political voice. Through the creation of echo chambers and the erosion of basic civility between people who hold different views, it has also enabled greater political and social polarization. The increasing scrutiny and media coverage of political campaign financing and lobbying for narrow self-interest has also added to the feeling of grubbiness in the electoral and governance processes. The premise of this chapter is that the idea that politics is just about elections, that it plays a small part in people's personal and business lives, is fundamentally mistaken.

Some weeks ago, I went to another of those weekend friends and family gatherings we are all familiar with. As we sat down for dinner, our host opened the proceedings: 'Please let's not talk politics at the dinner table.' He wanted to keep the peace.

And in business?

> Most of us know that [politics and religion] should absolutely be avoided in business settings. After all, project teams have enough trouble meeting deadlines and keeping the peace among stakeholders. Why borrow trouble by getting into arguments about politics or religion?[1]

People want to avoid political discourse in these settings because it arouses deep passions. Because it affects every aspect of our lives. And nothing that arouses deep passions is unimportant or marginal in people's lives.

You may be glad to know that I am not about to argue that the workplace should become a free-for-all of loud political debate – though it might, whether we like it or not, as we shall see later. But what I do argue is that this reasonable desire to keep largely unresolvable political arguments out of the workplace setting is all too often translated into the falsity that business is therefore apolitical. Something that is clearly not the case when we see how overtly political issues like board representation and equal pay and status for women and minorities, environmental and climate impact, even day-to-day operational issues like whether one should have gender-neutral bathrooms have come to occupy so much management time.

To what extent have individuals been able to bridge the gulf between business and political cultures? The results are mixed. A number of successful business leaders did not get much traction in the political realm: Ross Perot, Steve Forbes, Carly Fiorina, Meg Whitman, Herman Cain, Morry Taylor.

Others went on to achieve political office.

Donald Trump achieved what many consider the highest, most important political office on the planet. Michael Bloomberg was elected Mayor of New York City. Other businessmen successfully became US State Governors – Rick Snyder (Michigan), Kenny Guinn (Nevada), John Hickenlooper (Colorado).

Outside the US, Jair Bolsonaro in Brazil, Andrej Babiš in the Czech Republic, Silvio Berlusconi in Italy, Saad Hariri in Lebanon, Piñera Sebastián in Chile, and others, are businesspeople who also achieved high political office. In contrast to the many politicians (including, for instance, David Cameron, Emmanuel Macron, George W. Bush, Theresa May) who are primarily political creatures but have had business experience in their youth.

Whatever one thinks of the performance of these businesspeople in office, the question is whether their success was driven by an intuitive understanding of political culture and a natural aptitude for turning their skills to politics, or that business had, in and of itself, prepared them especially well for political office.

Most businesspeople who achieve political office are usually elected on the basis of two premises. The first is a positioning as 'outsiders' from the political class, ready to shake the tree and change an entrenched culture that many voters have come to regard with suspicion at best, repugnance at worst. Of course, once there, changing politics is not as easy as it seems. '*Most of the folks who come in have little understanding of how things work but are arrogant enough to think they can change 200+ years of American governing*,' according to Eric Herzik, political scientist at University of Nevada-Reno.[2]

The second is the promise that their business experience will make them good administrators. There may well be some truth to that. In the UK, for instance, the government appointed Kate Bingham, a businesswoman and venture capitalist specializing in biopharmaceuticals, to manage the COVID-19 vaccine procurement process with great success.

But politics is not primarily a managerial or administrative job. As we shall see later, it's the job of making moral and ethical trade-offs, representing as well as leading the national culture and bringing a large proportion of the population willingly along with you. Administration is the job of civil servants, not politicians. Even basics like accounting rules are different for government and for business. It is a gross misunderstanding to believe that politics is about 'managing the economy' in the same way one manages a business.

> Eisenhower, the man, enjoyed from the first tremendous popularity. Eisenhower, the President, did not really become effective until he had lost Sherman Adams and John Foster Dulles, his two 'theater commanders' or 'general managers'. Their loss forced him to become a political leader instead of the non-political administrator he had tried to be.[3]

Understanding the difference

The nature of the gulf between business and politics can maybe be better understood by taking a flight of fantasy. How would management behaviours change if CEOs ran companies along the following principles:

- You would have to be voted into your CEO job every four or five years by your workforce (with any employees who have left or whom you have fired still having a vote);
- You could only choose your board of directors from people also elected by the workforce (as is the practice in some democracies);
- In parallel, the workforce would elect a shadow CEO and a shadow board, whose only jobs were to scrutinize and be publicly and loudly critical of what you and the Executive Team were doing in the hope that, a few years down the road, they would be chosen to take over;
- Any decisions you take would, before implementation, have to be approved by a large body of individuals whom you do not have the power to fire, who are also elected by the workforce and approximately half of whom would have an interest in seeing you fail;
- That your relationship with your workforce was not limited to employees delivering to a defined contractual agreement for which they got paid, but extended to carrying responsibility for the health services they could access, the education of their children, the building and maintenance of roads, transport links and all the other infrastructure necessary for the workforce to turn up and

actually do their work, how your employees would survive when made redundant, how you were going to protect your workforce from hostile foreign forces, etc., etc., etc.

I think you get my drift. Most businesspeople would, quite reasonably, run a million miles from such responsibilities. It is hard to imagine being able to run a successful business in such circumstances.

Then there is culture and perspective. A.G. Block, former editor of the *California Journal* and associate director of the UC Center Sacramento put it like this:

> Businesses tend to be dictatorships, where the edict of the CEO is carried out by an army of minions. Governance is a messy process, where coalition-building is required, and governors need to be good listeners willing to compromise. Goals also have social implications that business executives often do not consider when making business decisions. And their constituents in the business world – their stockholders – tend to be, for the most part, a homogenous group with one common goal: profits. [For politicians], the constituency is a varied mishmash with a variety of goals.

In short, continuous contestation of views and opinions is the foundation of democratic politics. Without continued, vociferous, public disagreement, democracy dies. Agreement, efficiency and practical effectiveness, on the other hand, underpin business.

Businesspeople are trained in problem-solving skills that they hone over the course of their career. Not so in politics.

> [The President's] job is not to 'solve' the new issues. It is to make us start to work on them. Above all, he has to create understanding, and this requires dissent and controversy as much as it requires support and approval.[4]

It is therefore unsurprising that business leaders reaching elected office often find difficult the constant bickering, endless opposition to what they do, being constantly pilloried in the media and swapping the deference surrounding a CEO for becoming every voter's convenient punch bag.

Through a businessperson's lens, it's also hard to fathom why on earth politicians do what they do:

> What's it all for, though?... you sacrifice your best years, your family, your friends, even your health — and for what? A portrait on the stairs? The opportunity to spend the rest of your life with your bodyguards? The rare privilege of having people shout abuse at you wherever you go?[5]

I guess it's a bit like asking why some people have a passion for collecting stamps, others for extreme sports. There is no 'reason' – it just is. And we should be grateful that some want to do the largely thankless job of politics.

I put all this forward not as some sort of simplistic guide for businesspeople wanting to enter politics. Rather, I suggest that going through this mental exercise and really spending time trying to imagine how one would conduct oneself under these circumstances is a good first step to starting to develop a worldview through a political lens.

LET'S GET BACK TO 'WHAT IS POLITICS?'

Hopefully, the previous section has convinced some readers that my friend was right when he claimed that he and his colleagues saw politics operating to a totally different logic than business. I also hope that I may have started tentatively to explore both why the logic is different, and that this different logic, let's call it political rationality, is both reasonable and understandable. Now I want to get back to the question posed as the title of this chapter: What is Politics?

This is a question that has occupied many for centuries. I don't pretend to be able to answer it in any way comprehensively – if anyone can. My aim is to help readers look at political thinking and political behaviour in a way that helps start to build a political lens through which they can look at their own business and their own business behaviours, thereby strengthening both.

Politics is a battle of ideas, in which participants attempt to control the narrative through tapping deep-rooted values and beliefs, rather than invoking objective self-interest.[6]

Let us parse the above statement for a moment. First is the statement that politics is about deep-rooted values and beliefs. These, of course, take many forms. As the author also points out in the same piece, it's primarily about identity and culture. People develop political allegiances based on their own vision of themselves – much as they choose some brands in an attempt to make a statement about who they are rather than for the brand's functional value.

Successful political parties are those that manage to capture the spirit of the times. Those that are in tune with the prevailing popular concerns and the predominant cultural mores. Unsuccessful parties are those that remain stuck within their narrow ideological frameworks irrespective of changing cultural expectations.

In the UK, for example, the Conservative Party has developed a chameleon-like capability to change its electoral programmes in tune with the prevailing mood and values. It broadly maintains an ideological belief in market economies and rewarding individual effort, but how that becomes expressed in its electoral platform changes significantly over time.

The 1970s saw the Party adopt a paternalistic 'One-Nation Conservatism' platform that resonated then. That political positioning ran out of road as the UK sank into prolonged economic downturn in the late 1970s, culminating in the Winter of Discontent in 1979 under a Labour government. The election of Margaret Thatcher in the UK and her soulmate Ronald Reagan in the US saw a swing towards what we now call neoliberal ideology: a small, non-intrusive state with private enterprise and the efforts of the individual as the cultural protagonists and drivers of the economy. It was a political revolution that revitalized Britain at the price of significant social unrest and much personal and community hardship in previously industrialized regions.

Thatcher read the mood. The experiences of the winter of 1979 left many ready for big change to get the country out of its funk: Britain was broken and needed fixing was the prevailing attitude.

The Thatcher revolution highlighted the key characteristic of politics – that it is all about moral choices:

Neoliberalism is not merely a policy agenda, but also a moral framework that teaches individuals to conceive of themselves not as, say, wage earners, but rather as risk-taking entrepreneurs who should expect to shoulder the financial risks of their participation in higher education, the credit system and deregulated labour markets.[7]

The author should have gone further. Politics, and political philosophies, are primarily about setting a moral framework and appealing to people's sense of identity. Do I like to think of myself as a low-risk wage earner or a risk-taking entrepreneur? Different people will have different responses to that question. And, of course, there are many in our societies who are simply unable to carry such financial risks even if they were so inclined. What of them?

Policies flow from that overarching framework. They are simply the practical means of putting it into practice. The development of a set of policies without a clear, overarching moral framework and worldview is a hollow exercise.

When business leaders declare any particular policy initiative to be 'anti-business', what they are mostly saying is that they are operating within a moral framework regarding the role of business in society that is different to that being put forward by the policymakers. Yet they rarely articulate it as such. Most often they express it only in operational terms; how the new policy might change how they run their business and possibly make it more challenging to do so. It would be more useful if the conversation were to shift up a gear or two to a discussion of the ethical, moral and ideological frameworks at play.

As with all change programmes, many did not get on board with the Thatcher revolution. Largely because they saw themselves as being at the losing end of the new order. With any political decision, there are always winners and losers; those who buy into the moral framework and those who don't. Politicians do not delude themselves that everything, or maybe anything, can be a win-win-win. They understand that all decision making is based on a *balance sheet of comparative potential losses and gains.*'[8] To govern is to choose, to choose is to divide.

The Thatcher period was marred by social unrest and violence in the streets. But, for all that, with her 'Iron Lady' brand and helped along by success in the Falklands War that overshadowed the social unrest at home, Margaret Thatcher remained Prime Minister from 1979–90, making her the longest-serving British PM of the twentieth century. Eventually, she was sunk when her success led to an ever-increasing belief in the unchallengeable righteousness of her own views (don't we all recognize that?), an inability to listen, and consequent increasing detachment from the public mood. It might be argued that sustained success tempted her to forget that she was Prime Minister – a politician and first among equals, not a chief executive commanding obedience.

She was removed by her own Cabinet.

Fast forward to 2020 and a world reeling from the COVID-19 pandemic. Overnight, Prime Minister Boris Johnson ditched what might be considered the Conservative religion of fiscal rectitude and small government to cushion the economic damage by mounting one of the largest exercises in public spending, soaring public debt and monetization ever seen. The Conservative Party chameleon once again changed colour, better to deal with contemporary necessities.

Like businesses, political parties have no inherent right to continue to exist – even less to be consistently successful. In the 2017 French presidential election, Emmanuel Macron built a brand, captured people's imagination, built an electoral campaigning infrastructure and won the presidency in a few short months from a standing start. Candidates for political parties that had had an incumbent position in French politics for decades were swept aside. These parties collapsed in the subsequent parliamentary election, where Macron's *En Marche* (later, *La Republique En Marche*) swept the slate on the coattails of his presidential success.

It is also notable that Macron's real opponents that year were not the traditional, incumbent parties but other insurgents: Marine Le Pen's *Front National* (National Front), running on a patriotic, nationalist platform and Jean-Luc Mélenchon's *La France Insoumise* (France Unbowed), running on a socialist, redistributive political platform.

Unlike incumbent parties steeped in their traditions, their ways of doing things and, maybe, a sense of entitlement, the insurgents read the spirit of the times – a desire for radical change. In the end, Macron won out for reasons I will not go into here except to say that the two-round French electoral system tends to favour candidates that lie more towards the mainstream. Fast forward a short three years and a large group of elected representatives defected from his party. Before the end of his term, his party suffered humiliating defeats in the 2021 regional elections. At the time of writing, it was doubtful whether he would win re-election – an outcome that would likely depend on who ended up as his main opponents.

Why am I writing all this and what on earth does this have to do with business?

Business, too, operates within the prevailing culture. Developing a political lens through which one can look at the world is one way in which businesses can understand the spirit of the times. Successful politics both follows and drives contemporary culture. It can therefore provide business leaders with insights into the social mores of the time – and, maybe more importantly, the direction of travel.

Rather than resisting political action that may be perceived as being against individual corporations' narrow interests, looking through a political lens enables business leaders to ask productive questions. Why are politicians behaving in this way? What does this tell me about the social and cultural norms in which we are now operating? What does all this mean for how I should be running my business? It requires looking at political action with curiosity and a wish to learn rather than reaching judgements based on self-focused perspectives. We call this approach 'Cultural leadership' and I shall explore it further in Chapter 5.

Important in this analysis is the role of what have come to be known by many as 'populist' political parties. Many dismiss 'populism' as some kind of political aberration to be condemned simply because it does not fit with their own worldviews. Yet the successful among these parties have a particular skill at tapping into people's grievances as well as their hopes. The leaders in question may often turn out to be unable to deliver on their promises. But lack of delivery capability – which happens for a whole host of reasons – does not mean that such parties are not politically savvy, or that they are not tapping into the spirit of the times.

I prefer to call these parties insurgent rather than the dismissive 'populist' label that seems to me to be simply a head-in-the-sand excuse for not engaging with why they are successful. Insurgents tend to ride a wave of popular discontent that leads voters to adopt a quasi-revolutionary mindset – that things have become bad enough that they want political leaders willing to tear down the existing order and replace it with something new. And they don't much care about what that 'new' might look like – as long as it's different from the old and as long as 'the old guard' is overthrown in an 'off-with-their-heads' moment.

Business leaders tend to abhor such insurgency. Their preference is for the stability of the status quo. That which has made them successful, that with which they are familiar and around which they have painstakingly structured their business. They hope for the continuation of established political forces with which they have built a position of influence.

Revolution is bad for business.

When established business leaders do call for change, it tends to be incremental and driven by business priorities – deregulation, lower corporate taxes, subsidy regimes for the favoured, etc., rarely from a desire to change market structures fundamentally.

In business terms, insurgents can be seen as the political equivalent of entrepreneurs. Dissatisfied with the status quo, they can imagine new models that upend how business is done. They proceed to create something that disrupts the system – even though the path to getting there is always fraught, uncertain, convoluted and rarely succeeds at the first attempt. It is not surprising that many entrepreneurs identify with political insurgents while leaders of long-established businesses tend to identify with established parties. It is also not surprising that most insurgent political parties end up failing – just like entrepreneurs.

To take one example, many insurgent parties have taken a stance against the current model of globalization (I'll address the politics of globalization in Chapter 4). This makes political sense in a world where the faults of our current model of globalization are becoming clearer and where it is seen as the cause of many communities and regions being decimated. Culturally, globalization is an increasingly dirty word – further sullied by the effects of the COVID-19 pandemic.

Business is usually horrified by such talk. The multinational business model depends on it. And many large businesses have managed to shape global trade to their advantage – an advantage they are unwilling to lose. Yet that model of globalization is more or less over.

Is it more productive for business leaders to resist these developing social mores because they may damage their business model? Or would it be preferable to be able to develop a deep understanding of the drivers of this cultural change and how best to think about one's own business model in this changing context?

Many businesses do both. They show a willingness to adapt (at varying speeds and with good or bad grace) while trying to delay change as much as possible to allow adaptation to take place. Others resist tooth and nail. Others still can see how more rapid change can give them a competitive advantage.

Making these choices requires a good feel of how and over what period the political climate will change. In politics, such change can be predictable and gradual, or it bubbles for a long time below the surface until it suddenly takes off when many disparate factors happen to come together to create the tipping point. Much like the process of innovation. Or, as Rudi Dornbusch put it in the context of economics, *'things take longer to happen than you think they will, and then they happen faster than you thought they could'*.

One such example is the issue of banking secrecy on which almost all the highly successful Swiss banking industry was based for decades if not longer. At some point it became clear that banking secrecy as practised was not going to remain politically viable. When I spoke to Swiss bankers at the time, they understood this perfectly. They knew full well that it was a dying business model and that no amount of lobbying would work because the underlying narrative no longer had political resonance. That the beneficiaries of the system had poor and eroding political standing. Rather than digging their heels in, resisting, and trotting out the same old mantras about wealth creation and all the rest, they pragmatically started to adapt. Their main political intervention was to seek to ensure that the process was gradual enough that it would give them time to change and develop new business models. Politicians were receptive to that in a way they would not have been receptive to the idea that the system had to be maintained. The industry changed and many players survived and prospered with new business models.

The danger comes when we start to believe that tipping points can be postponed forever. Or pushed so far into the future that we really don't need to worry about them now. Businesses then get taken by surprise with significant consequent disruption. Such misjudgements are often the result of insufficiently developed political and cultural antennae within organizations.

Another example is President Trump's war on climate change mitigation and environmental protection. Some in the business world cheered his executive orders, seeing them as a licence to carry on with business as usual. But it was always clear that Trump was pushing against the evolving cultural winds. That his actions would turn out to be a mere blip in the continuum of mounting concern, and increasing state action, around these issues. The wisest saw them as a welcome pause that would give them more time to adapt and change. Others truly believed he had turned the tide and that they could continue to obstruct further progress indefinitely. For that misjudgement they may pay a price in declining performance.

When it comes to climate change, there are also bigger tipping points to consider. Many businesses have now embraced the imperative to reduce carbon emissions. Others are piling on. The new fad around mining for cryptocurrencies uses up huge amounts of energy with consequent negative impact on the climate. This is leading major economies such as China to add climate impact to questions of financial stability and money laundering as a reason to crack down on the use of these assets.

What hasn't yet been talked about enough is that should severe climate change and critical ecosystem degradation come to pass, this will interact with other factors to change dramatically the whole geo-political landscape. From conflict due to food shortages and mass migration, from water poverty to national security, from the impact on human health to the increasing ineffectiveness of established institutional structures, politically, climate change and ecosystem degradation will upend everything. They will upset the political balances within which businesses have become used to operating: 'Climate impacts are manifold, diffuse and of systemic consequence in the aggregate... the more intangible third-order socio-political and institutional effects have not been fully appreciated.'[9] Some businesses have moved on from step one – reducing carbon emissions – to thinking in these structural political terms. Others have yet to get there.

The US intelligence community understands these threats perfectly. The 2019 Worldwide Threat Assessment report makes clear that these changes are 'likely to fuel competition for resources, economic distress, and social discontent.'[10] The socio-political landscape – and therefore the business landscape – will be very different as a result of our continued destruction of our own environment.

As a friend put it to me, if you think that current political pressures to reduce carbon emissions and environmental degradation are onerous and disruptive, you ain't seen nothing yet.

BEYOND SELF-INTEREST

When President Trump slapped tariffs on imported steel, Harley-Davidson, an icon of American manufacturing, decided to shift some of its production out of the US – a business decision. US workers were going to lose their jobs. We will cover later the broad political impact of such business decisions – one of them being to entrench further the 'anti-globalization' sentiment. Here, I want to focus on values.

One worker interviewed during this process understood that he might lose his job and was asked whether he thought Trump had made the wrong decision in imposing tariffs (the business view). His response surprised the TV interviewer: '*Yes, I know I might lose my job. But it was still the right decision. We must stop others exploiting America through unfair competition.*' His ire, in as much as there was any, was reserved for management. At the time, *The Financial Times* also interviewed a number of Harley employees and reported, '*Many of Harley's own employees, interviewed this week in the* Financial Times, *said they supported Mr. Trump's policies.*'[11]

Why?

Getting back to our previous quote about politics: '*tapping deep-rooted values and beliefs, rather than invoking objective self-interest*', President Trump tapped those values whereas management might have imagined that the workforce would blame the President for a bad decision while considering their own decisions perfectly 'rational'. A perfect example of the difference between thinking in business terms and thinking politically. What seems right from one perspective seems utterly mistaken from another.

One former Harley director described the company culture: '*It's a very blue-collar, very American culture.*' It could maybe have been clear to management that Trump's 'America First' rhetoric would have greater appeal to that identity than greater business efficiency and profit protection – even at the cost of workers' own financial self-interest. Trump the politician was better able to tap into Harley employees' values and identity than their own management. He understood that values and culture beat narrow financial self-interest every time – a frame of mind that is challenging for business leaders who are largely judged on financial performance metrics and, maybe more importantly, whose own sense of identity and self-image is inextricable from the financial performance of the companies they lead.

And, of course, the impact of such a business decision does not fall exclusively on those workers who lose their jobs. It also affects the morale and respect for management of those workers, customers and suppliers who remain and need to continue to support the business if it is to be successful.

Matt Levatich, Harley's CEO at the time, is himself a biker. '*The dealers like him because he's a biker,*' said one former director. In this,

Levatich embodied Harley's culture. What would dealers make of a CEO who could have been accused of 'betraying American values' – if not betraying America itself? Someone who runs one of the most iconic US brands and yet does not put America first and, through some lenses, is not making his contribution to Making America Great Again! What could be the impact on future business dealings?

Levatich may well have considered all these issues and decided that business imperatives outweighed other considerations. Or he might not. I have no inside knowledge. The episode raises the question of whether management had developed the skills to look at their business through a political/cultural lens and made a balanced decision. Or whether the issue was looked at through a purely financial lens. What impact would a different, more politically oriented approach have had on the business over the longer term?

A similar disconnect plagued the Remain campaign in the run-up to the 2016 Brexit referendum in the UK. The Remain campaign had politicians as well as accomplished business people at its helm. The Bank of England and other technocratic institutions also became involved. The campaign was largely focused on the adverse economic impact of leaving the European Union. At its core, it was an appeal to economic self-interest – what came to be labelled by opponents as 'Project Fear'.

The Leave campaign was on a totally different planet. It was about sovereignty, the fuzzy concept of 'taking back control', and the preservation of the British way of life in the face of that being under assault from various directions – from 'excessive' immigration to laws made in Brussels rather than in London.

It's not my intention here to judge the merits or demerits of the different campaigns, rather to point out that the political and cultural abstractions of the Leave campaign managed to turn a deficit in the polls to a win in the referendum. The instrumental, practically focused, utilitarian alternative provided by Remain largely fell flat – despite the mountain of numbers coming out of economic models. Leave appealed to the heart and gut, Remain appealed to what we mistakenly call 'reason'. In politics, the former always – yes, *always* – wins.

The same dynamic will play out in the movement towards Scottish independence from the rest of the United Kingdom. Very few, if any, truly believe that such a move would be economically beneficial for Scotland and the Scottish people. And the Scottish government led by the Scottish National Party has not had a stellar record of performance.

Yet the movement seems to have become unstoppable. Issues of identity and centuries-old resentment of English rule are becoming more effective at mobilizing support than questions around economic self-interest. The UK can only be preserved if the case for the Union can be made in visceral and emotional political terms. Economics alone won't work.

We would all do well to understand that our focus on one particular type of 'rationality' as our guiding light will lead us astray. As Albert Einstein put it: '*The intuitive mind is a sacred gift, and the rational mind is a faithful servant. We have created a society that honors the servant and has forgotten the gift.*' The most successful politicians, on the other hand, are those who have good intuitive instincts and who will not allow them to be derailed by pseudo-rationality. Those who are able to feel the mood in their bones rather than being exclusively led by the nose by focus groups and public polling.

YOU MAY BE SURPRISED JUST HOW MUCH IS POLITICAL

In 2019, the multinational pharmaceutical company Novartis launched a new drug – Zolgensma – a treatment for a genetic disease called spinal muscular atrophy (SMA). Children with SMA suffer degeneration of parts of their nervous system and rarely live beyond the age of two. Zolgensma was launched as a one-time treatment which, if given early enough, could have a big impact on the progression of the disease and, potentially, might even be curative.

The therapy was launched at a price of \$2.1 million for the one-time treatment.

I would now like to ask you to reflect on your initial, visceral reaction to the price of \$2.1 million for a single treatment. Before you've had time to shift into so-called 'rational' mode and think about it. What did you *feel* the instant you saw that price?

Most people experience sticker shock when faced with such a price. It's out of their normal experience and expectations. When I present it to them in person, there is an inevitable widening of the eyes, a sharp intake of breath.

There are various explanations to support such a price. Yes, it's a one-time treatment but it lasts a lifetime. A total cost of \$2.1 million could be seen differently if it were a treatment given daily for the average life expectancy of around 80 years or so. It is a high-value treatment that saves infants' lives and potentially allows them to have a fully productive life – the price reflects its value. The number of patients with SMA is, thankfully, small, so companies have to charge a price that allows a return on the substantial (and highly risky) investment if we are to incentivize research into so far untreatable diseases. And so on.

All these are reasonable arguments. But they are, and are presented as, technical arguments, not political ones. They operate within business rationality, not political rationality.

But the pricing of medicines is a highly political issue. Political because there is no such thing as an objectively 'fair' and socially reasonable price for a pharmaceutical product. Political because it relates to the political choices around how we choose to fund and provide healthcare. At the end of the day, it has an impact on who has access to which healthcare interventions and who does not. Political because responding to the backlash from drugs perceived as being 'too expensive' is about managing public opinion in an area of policy that is highly charged emotionally.

Politics has to contend with all of these complex and inter-related issues. And it has to deal with the public's reaction – a public that will react primarily viscerally and not through careful consideration of the various technical arguments put forward. Such situations – of which there are many in various different businesses – require highly developed political skills to manage. And how these fundamental business questions are managed politically changes over time as the political and social environment changes. What does not work is an attitude that focuses on the technical arguments while dismissing the political ones as somehow irrelevant and illegitimate. 'Damn the politics,' some might be tempted to say.

Staying with the example of the price of medicines for a moment, the playbook used to be clear. Various technical studies targeted at regulators would show that new medicines are 'cost-effective' as measured by standard economic techniques. Patient groups concerned about specific diseases would mobilize to create pressure on politicians, policymakers and healthcare funders to fund these new medicines. This push-pull approach has previously largely been effective in the short run – in other words, effective at pushing through access and funding of individual medicines.

Over time, the environment has changed. The population as a whole – particularly in those countries with government-funded universal healthcare – has internalized the fact that it is impossible for health systems to afford broad uptake of every technological innovation. As a result, patient groups have become more cautious and their effectiveness as activists for their own cause has decreased. In parallel, industry relations and funding of such groups has come under increasing scrutiny, further eating into their political capital.

In spite of continued repeated individual successes at launching new 'high-priced' products, the broader issues around the rising cost of healthcare and, in particular, the price of medicines have risen to the top of the political agenda – even, perhaps particularly, in the 'free market', 'free enterprise' United States. The political position of 'rich, eye-wateringly profitable, pharmaceutical companies price gouging and putting profits before the needs of the sick' has always been an attractive platform for certain political groups. It is time to '*move beyond having to tolerate an industry that subordinates public health to shareholder greed*' according to Dana Brown and Isiah Poole from the Democracy Collaborative.[12]

These are far from nuanced or even well-informed positions. They are ideologically driven but politically appealing in their simplicity and intuitive appeal. Counterarguments, valid as they might be, are complex to explain and don't easily lend themselves to catchy sound bites. In the US, even the GOP has now started to feel the political challenges associated with its traditional pro-pharma industry stance. All this makes it challenging for the industry to develop an effective and long-term viable political platform around the cost of medicines. A situation made worse by the natural tension between the interests of individual companies pushing for their own products to be funded so they can make their quarterly earnings and what may be in the long-term political interests of the sector as a whole.

In 2011, Martin Shkreli founded Retrophin, a portfolio company under the umbrella of MSMB Capital Management, a hedge fund he owned. After obtaining financing, in 2014 Shkreli was able to acquire rights to market Thiola and Chenodal, drugs used to treat rare diseases. Exploiting the monopoly position these drugs had in the market, Retrophin raised the price of each drug substantially. Thiola being marked up about 20-fold, Chenodal about five-fold.

Shkreli left the company in September 2014 and set up Turing Pharmaceuticals with an explicit strategy of acquiring out-of-patent medicines that had a monopoly market position and to make profits by increasing prices without the need to develop its own medicines. Turing acquired the rights to Daraprim and hiked its price 56-fold overnight – from $13.50 to $750 per pill. All of which made sense from a purely profit-seeking perspective. But the political impact was substantial – as many business leaders in the same industry recognized. Much of the political capital that the research-based pharmaceutical industry had built over many decades took a blow.

Which brings us to another point: corporate behaviours have an impact on how the political climate develops.

IT'S A TWO-WAY STREET

At 6 a.m. on 29 October 2018, Michelle Vergina Bongkal, 21, boarded a flight from Jakarta, Indonesia, to Pangkal Pinang to attend her grandmother's funeral. She was travelling with her brother, Mathew, 13, and father, Adonia, 52.

The flight took off as scheduled at 6.20 a.m. Thirty-five kilometres in, the captain requested clearance to return to Jakarta. At 6.33 a.m., communication with the aircraft was suddenly lost. At 7.30 a.m., the Indonesian National Search and Rescue Agency received reports that the flight had crashed into the Java Sea, close to an oil platform. Michelle and her family were among the 189 passengers and crew who lost their lives.

Suspicion immediately fell on human error or poor maintenance schedules by Lion Air. After all, Lion Air was a 'local' company, not a highly regarded Western multinational. The Indonesian Transport Ministry ordered emergency inspections on all Boeing 737 Max aircraft and declared them airworthy just two days later. An audit of Lion Air's internal procedures was initiated. The Australian Department of Foreign Affairs and Trade announced that its staff would be banned from flying on Lion Air or its subsidiary airlines until the cause of the accident was known – a rash assumption as to where the fault lay.

Boeing issued a statement that opened as follows:

> The Boeing Company is deeply saddened by the loss of Lion Air Flight 610. We extend our heartfelt condolences and sympathies to the families and loved ones of those onboard.
>
> Safety is a core value for everyone at Boeing and the safety of our airplanes, our customers' passengers and their crews is always our top priority. As our customers and their passengers continue to fly the

737 MAX to hundreds of destinations around the world every day, they have our assurance that the 737 MAX is as safe as any airplane that has ever flown the skies.[13]

On 10 March 2019, Antonis Mavropoulos, a Greek chemical engineer, was rushing through Addis Ababa Bole International Airport in Ethiopia to catch his Ethiopian Airways ET302 flight to Nairobi. Much to his annoyance, he got to the gate two minutes after the gate closed and watched the flight taking off at 8.38 a.m. Six minutes later, it crashed, killing the 157 people on board.

The similarity between these two crashes finally focused attention on the aircraft itself, eventually leading to its worldwide grounding on safety concerns. Subsequent investigations included a review of internal emails among Boeing staff. Below is a selection.

It seems that Lion Air had requested additional pilot training for the 737 Max – something the manufacturer was avoiding since the lack of need for additional pilot training was one of the aircraft's selling points:

> *Now friggin Lion Air might need a sim to fly the MAX, and maybe because of their own stupidity. I'm scrambling trying to figure out how to unscrew this now! Idiots.*
>
> Boeing internal email, June 2017[14]

Other emails put into question Boeing's declaration that '*safety is a core value for everyone at Boeing*'. *The Financial Times* reported[15] as follows:

Messages released on Thursday show Boeing employees discussing the 737 Max aircraft and its flight simulators:

'I still haven't been forgiven by God for the covering up I did last year.'

'Would you put your family on a Max simulator trained aircraft? I wouldn't.'

Response: 'No.'

'Am not lying to the FAA. Will leave that to people who have no integrity.'

Response: 'I'm sorry, that is not acceptable. Your integrity is priority 4.'

'I just jedi mind tricked these fools. I should be given $1,000 every time I take one of these calls. I save this company a sick amount of $$$$.'

'I'll be shocked if the FAA passes this turd.'

'This airplane is designed by clowns who in turn are supervised by monkeys.'

The impact of these wretched episodes on Boeing, its business, its reputation and its financial performance are well known – not to mention the impact of these tragedies on families. What I want to focus on here are the political consequences – both of the crashes themselves and the dreadful loss of life, and on the industry in general. Consequences that are the result both of the now well-known faults with the aircraft and the development and commercialization process, and of how Boeing management and board behaved following the crashes.

I examine this episode and its political consequences because the underlying reasons are not unique to Boeing. We have all experienced commercial and timeline pressures in our work that consciously or unconsciously led us to cut corners – and to justify it to ourselves. We have all experienced situations where major projects on which a company's future earnings depend become enveloped in a protective cocoon where any criticism that might delay or derail the project becomes impossible to express. We may get away with it because, in most cases, what we do does not have the same life-and-death consequences – fortunately. But the principle remains – culture and peer pressure create the pull of the crowd that eventually overwhelms individuals' own sense of integrity. Bad stuff becomes justified as 'industry standard practice'.

Let's start with the Boeing response.

Following release of the above and many other emails, Boeing management declared them outliers – a few rogue employees unrepresentative of the culture of the company as a whole. I'll leave it to you to judge the credibility of that position.

Politically, Boeing is in an unusual position. The company accounts for around 1 per cent of US GDP and nearly 2 per cent of the country's exports. A vital supplier of US military equipment, it is unusual in that almost all of its some 160,000 employees are domestic. Its supply chains account for up to 1.2 million US jobs (according to the company). With Airbus, it dominates the commercial aircraft industry – for now.

In other words, Boeing is a politically protected company. It is far too important to the US economy and US politics to be allowed to disappear or even to be damaged excessively. Not many companies are in that position – though, unfortunately, the number of 'systemically important' companies seems to be growing as consolidation in various sectors creates behemoths that are too big to fail. An issue that has significance for the future viability of market economies and functioning democracies, as I will explore later. That said, Boeing's actions are not without political and cultural consequences.

In October 2019, a full seven months after the second crash, Dennis Muilenburg, the company's Chairman and CEO, was stripped of the Chairman position but retained his CEO role. Congressional hearings questioned the credibility of him retaining his position and his pay (Muilenburg's total compensation for 2018 when he oversaw the 737 Max programme was $23.4 million).

Pointing to relatives of the crash victims, Representative Steve Cohen (D. Tennessee) asked:

> These people's relatives are not coming back. They're gone. Your salary is still on... You're continuing to work and make $30 million a year after two accidents that caused all these people's relatives to die.[16]

Muilenburg's response was as typically corporate as it was politically insensitive: '*My board will conduct a comprehensive review.*' The lawyers surely drafted that one. (Also, note the 'my' board language, which gives one some sense of just how independent of CEO influence is the board that is supposed to adjudicate on the CEO's behaviour.)

Muilenburg eventually gave up his bonus and stock awards. Dave Calhoun, who took over the chairmanship, stated in November 2019 that the Boeing Board believed Muilenburg had done everything right during the crisis, that the CEO still had the Board's confidence and thus was the right person to continue to lead. Most people reacted to that statement with wide-eyed incredulity. Many, rightly or wrongly, interpreted what was emerging as clear evidence that Muilenburg had presided over the development of a corporate culture that was rotten to the core. Still has the Board's confidence?

Eventually, a situation that was clearly untenable came to a head. In December 2019, over two years after the first incident, nine months after the second and merely a month after the Board had declared its full confidence, Muilenburg was fired. Boeing said the Board had 'decided that a change in leadership was necessary to restore confidence in the company moving forward as it works to repair relationships with regulators, customers, and all other stakeholders.'

The sting in the tail? On leaving, Muilenburg received $62 million worth of long-term incentive payments, stock and pension awards 'he was contractually entitled to' – with no severance payment and having foregone $14.5 million in other awards.

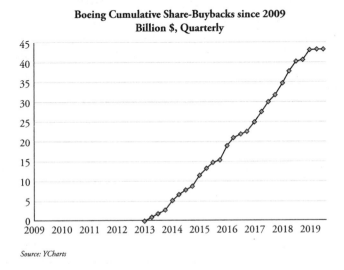

Boeing Cumulative Share-Buybacks since 2009
Billion $, Quarterly

Source: YCharts

Finally, as Boeing was put under the microscope, it became clear that the company had loaded itself up with debt in order to engage in financial engineering to push up its stock price through massive share-buybacks (*see* figure above). This landed the company with total liabilities of $136 billion against total assets of $132 billion. By 2021, the net debt on its balance sheet exceeded $40 billion. As a result, it had to embark on a scramble for cash following the grounding of the 737 Max.

If Boeing had focused on its business – such as designing a new plane instead of doctoring an ancient design to save money and time – and if it hadn't blown $43 billion on share-buybacks but had invested this money in a new design, those two crashes wouldn't have occurred, and it wouldn't have to beg for cash now.[17]

The author suggests that Boeing became a master at financial engineering instead of aircraft engineering. Hence management had blown $43 billion on buybacks – a practice that *The Economist* once labelled as 'corporate cocaine'. In other words, Boeing had become a creature of the current era of financialized capitalism. Internal cultural and peer pressures had overwhelmed the integrity of the individuals concerned. A March 2020 congressional investigation concluded that Boeing had developed a 'culture of concealment'.

There are a number of crucial elements that emerge from this tale. As the Boeing Board rightly said, eventually, the removal of the CEO was essential to repair relations with regulators and other stakeholders – including the public. But the effect of that 'repair' was severely blunted by the time it took to get there and the repeated declarations of confidence by the Board in the CEO on whose watch it had all happened.

In November 2020, the 737 Max was cleared to fly again in the US. In January 2021, Boeing reached an agreement with the Justice Department, in which the company would pay $2.5 billion to resolve a criminal investigation against them and admitted that employees had misled the regulator. Prosecutors said they failed to find pervasive misconduct involving higher-level officials.

But the investigation was not all smooth going. Documents in the case showed that, for the first six months of the investigation, Boeing did not co-operate with the investigation probe and frustrated the work of the investigating prosecutors.[18] More civil suits against Boeing were in progress at the time of writing.

Politically, the settlement did not sit well in all quarters. House Transportation Committee Chairman Peter DeFazio said: '*Senior management and the Boeing board were not held to account.*' Sen. Richard Blumenthal, a Connecticut Democrat, said the settlement '*does nothing to change the rotten corporate culture that allowed Boeing to mislead and deceive regulators.*'[19]

Following the 2008 financial crash, the general feeling was that the bankers who had caused the crashing bubble through irresponsible business practices not only got away with it, they quickly returned to making significant sums of money while everyone else, and especially those whose lives were the most financially precarious, suffered significant hardship for years. Banks, and therefore the bankers they employ, were systemically important to a functioning economy and could not be allowed to go bust. Fines paid out of corporate funds were the only consequence. Nobody, except for one lower-level employee who became the fall guy, went to jail. Senior management who oversaw the whole episode continued to rake in large compensation packages. Just as Muilenburg walked away with a $60 million-plus package.

Politically, all of this is a gift for insurgent political parties everywhere. In Europe and the US, politicians who adopted an outraged insurgent position promising to tear down a rigged system flourished. Some of them gained electoral success, leading governments that created confusion and, in some cases, undermined democratic principles. Anti-business sentiment soared.

Consider whether the Bernie Sanders' bandwagon would have had any chance of becoming what it became had there not been a financial crash and had the financial services sector not continued to reap financial rewards for the havoc it caused. Had the social hardships caused by the financial crash not further highlighted the plight of millions of Americans without healthcare coverage, no access to paid sick leave, or having any other form of state support.

True, Sanders was not elected, but the impact of his movement has changed American politics – possibly forever. At the time of writing, acolytes like Alexandria Ocasio-Cortez are in Congress and pushing a more socialist governance model. They will not be silenced.

These are some of the long-term political effects of business behaviours, but what of shorter-term political impacts?

Returning briefly to Boeing, the Federal Aviation Administration (FAA) – the US regulatory body responsible for, among other things, certification of aircraft safety – was one of the most highly regarded regulators internationally. Most other regulators accepted FAA certifications and felt that they did not have to replicate the work done by a respected regulator in certifying new aircraft.

Since the 1940s, the FAA had been working towards a system where they effectively delegated a significant part of their regulatory function to aircraft manufacturers – a kind of self-regulatory approach. This went as far as having a large number of individuals whose role was a regulatory one (i.e. an FAA responsibility) actually being employees of aircraft manufacturers. They worked within those companies, were paid by them, and were supposed to act as the FAA's eyes and ears. A deep welding together of government and business functions.

In 2017, the FAA produced a blueprint outlining its plans for even more 'collaborative relationships' with industry and less 'direct' involvement by regulators 'in individual projects'.[20] One can understand some of the logic underlying these initiatives. Having 'regulatory' personnel working within the aircraft manufacturers is more efficient, cuts down on the regulator's costs and is more agile, giving people direct access to the development and manufacturing processes. Doubtless, the industry itself pushed for such moves as being better for more rapid and efficient development.

Yet it stretches credibility beyond breaking point to claim that this does not create impossible conflicts of interest. These employees are supposed to live within a company, be part of that company's culture, have colleagues all around them subject to commercial pressures, have salary structures that are, in some way, related to a company's commercial success, yet maintain an objective stance and behave just like independent regulators. It would take someone beyond human to manage that – especially when working in a culture where colleagues are comfortable sending emails like the ones quoted above: 'your integrity is priority 4'. It all shows how, as we shall see repeatedly throughout this book, the relentless pursuit of financial efficiency to the exclusion of all else ends up being highly destructive. ✓

Some senior business leaders I have spoken to also suggested that the FAA let itself become dragged into, and became a part of, the fierce competition between Boeing and Airbus. Given Boeing's political and economic importance to the US, it is not difficult to imagine how pressure could be exerted – directly, indirectly, politically, or even subliminally – for the FAA to play its part in ensuring Boeing's competitiveness is not harmed through certification delays, what might be characterized as an excessive regulatory burden, and so forth.

Following the 737 Max disasters, the credibility of the FAA as a regulator collapsed. What long-term changes will follow remains to be seen. But, short-term, regulators worldwide would no longer accept FAA certification as sufficient. They insisted on doing their own with significantly increased cost, time and complexity implications for the whole sector. It is likely that regulation and regulatory oversight will increase significantly – again with damaging business effects. For Boeing itself, some believe that increased FAA oversight is a factor in delayed deliveries of its 787 Dreamliners.

THE FEEDBACK LOOP

Those in business readily understand that political and regulatory action directly affects their business – and regularly complain about it. What seems to be less readily accepted, or at least less talked about, is that, as this Boeing episode illustrates, the actions of businesses also have an effect on the political and regulatory climate. Most political intervention is a result of businesses' behaviour being out of sync with the political and cultural climate of the time, thereby stoking anti-business sentiment and making political and regulatory intervention not only possible but politically essential.

To a significant extent, much political action that is considered by some to be 'anti-business' is the result of a feedback loop. Business has most often brought such action upon itself.

So, why does this happen? Why does business end up damaging its own self politically?

There are many reasons. One is the issue of misaligned time frames. Business leaders are incentivized to deliver regular short-term earnings performance – and most often judge and incentivize their staff on that basis.[‡] CEOs are incentivized to deliver financial performance throughout their tenure. Political action, on the other hand, is slow-moving. It may take years, sometimes decades, for political culture to change and political will to develop into action – though time frames

---

[‡] I suggest that a five-year time horizon is still short-term when viewed through the lens of evolving political and social culture.

are shrinking. As with all long feedback loops, they have a tendency to obscure the causal link between action and reaction. One forgets or blanks out the fact that something that happens today is the result of what happened five or ten years previously.

Politics also changes over time. Today's government may well be replaced by a more 'business-friendly' one. Combined with heavy lobbying, campaign contributions and the usual 'that was then but now we've changed' arguments, some assume that this may well eventually blunt or even extinguish any political reaction to business behaviour – as happened, for instance, following the 2008 crash, where financial regulation was watered down significantly under lobbying pressure, with some of it being eventually repealed following the election of President Trump.

Such attitudes resemble gambling more than leadership. Over time they change public opinion about the role and trustworthiness of business – particularly big, powerful business – in our society, making it politically easier for those who take an anti-business stance to build a following and get elected. Because, as the quote that started this chapter stated, politics is the people's business.

A MARRIAGE MADE IN HELL

Throughout this chapter, I have argued that business and politics are separate but inextricably interlinked. Here, I'd like to get back to Ludwig von Mises's position as quoted in Chapter 1 (*see also* pp. 23–4). What happens when business and politics, while interconnected, stop being separate?

The Volkswagen (VW) diesel emissions scandal started in 2014 when the California Air Resources Board (CARB) commissioned studies that showed that real world emissions from VW cars labelled with its much-vaunted Turbocharged Diesel Injection 'clean' technology (TDI) were significantly higher than emissions measured during controlled testing of the vehicles. The US Environmental Protection Agency issued a notice of violation of the Clean Air Act to the Volkswagen Group.

The details of the whole sorry tale are well known. VW had, for years, embarked on a process of dishonesty and cheating by installing 'defeat devices' – pieces of software that could detect testing conditions and would reduce emissions during these tests while allowing emissions to soar to multiples of what was allowed once the cars hit the road. It was one of the most egregious examples of corporate dishonesty and fraud to emerge in recent years. According to *Der Spiegel*, a German magazine, at least 30 people at management level in VW knew about the deceit for years.[21] VW management denied the charge and, like Boeing, blamed the whole episode on a few rogue engineers. As one commentator put it, it beggars belief that a few engineers could develop and install such software in millions of cars without management knowing about it in a corporation where it needs at least three signatures before anyone can order a pen.

Further investigation found that VW was not alone. All the major German car manufacturers had bet on diesel engines as the future of cars relying on the lower levels of CO_2 emissions from diesel engines to market them as 'clean'.

Interested readers can find plenty of material about the scandal online, including an episode of the Netflix series, *Dirty Money*. Here, I would like to focus on the dangers of politics losing its way by forgetting what it is supposed to be about – looking after the broad public interest.

The northwestern state of Lower Saxony in Germany owns an 11.8 per cent stake in VW and controls 20 per cent of the voting rights. It receives hundreds of millions of euros in dividend payments and business taxes from VW. The state government has representation on the company's supervisory board. VW's factory and headquarters in Wolfsburg, Lower Saxony, employ some 60,000 people. Thanks to VW, Wolfsburg was ranked as Germany's wealthiest city in 2013.

In Germany, the car industry is important beyond Wolfsburg and Lower Saxony. The whole industry is critical to the country's economy. It employs more than 800,000 people domestically and contributes around 5 per cent to German GDP. More than two-thirds of the cars produced in Germany are exported. This creates a dilemma for politics. To what extent should politics be in the business of protecting the industry's success, jobs, tax revenues and, in Lower Saxony, the huge sums the state government draws in annual dividends? And to what extent is its duty to hold the industry to account?

Over the years, government at both local and national level seems to have prioritized the financial health of the industry over the general health of its population and the populations in the countries to which it exports its cars. The Lower Saxony government representatives on the VW supervisory board pleaded ignorance of the defeat devices in VW cars. Given that defeat devices have been known to the car industry for decades and that, before owning up to the cheating and dishonesty, VW gave the US authorities the runaround for years while the scandal was being investigated, this smells of either direct complicity, wilful ignorance and plausible (or maybe not) deniability, or utter incompetence.

European regulations regarding car emissions are almost identical to those in the US. Yet it took the US authorities to start and complete an investigation. The German government gave its auto industry a pass based on a clause in the regulations that allows the use of defeat devices if they are shown to be essential to protect car engines. The German government accepted without question the industry's assertions that they were essential for this reason – a claim now shown to be utterly false as, following the VW scandal, they are being removed from all cars without them falling apart.

Here we see the dangers of politics and industry becoming buddies. Governments find themselves facing conflicts of interest that pull them in opposite directions. In 2017, the government in Lower Saxony (led by the left-leaning Social Democrats) asserted its determination to hang onto its stake in VW. *'This state holding is of the highest importance for the economic development of Lower Saxony,'* said state premier Stephan Weil.[22] That may not be an unreasonable position. After all, it does give the state a strong position to protect and enhance jobs in the area when it can. But it also raises the question as to what extent the state's role is to act like any other shareholder interested primarily in financial performance and dividend flow, or to act in the wider interest of the population as a whole.

This raises difficult political trade-offs. But it is hard to escape the conclusion that, when it comes to car emissions, Germany's polity failed. Its economic dependence on the car industry led it, at best, to close its eyes to dishonesty, people's health and that of the environment. At worst, it was so captured by one of its most important industries that, knowingly or unknowingly, it became enveloped in a process of fraud and dissimulation that had a significant cost in human health, premature deaths and environmental pollution – besides the damaging reputational costs.

Things have changed.

In 2019, German prosecutors filed criminal charges for fraud against Martin Winterkorn, VW's former CEO, and four other executives. In

September that year, Winterkorn, CEO Herbert Diess and Chairman Hans Dieter Pötsch were charged with market manipulation. In January 2020, six other VW executives were charged with fraud. The judicial process was still ongoing at the time of writing.

Then came the COVID-19 pandemic and its impact on economic activity and car sales. The German government then proved reluctant to be seen to be cosseting the car industry and, at the time of writing, had not agreed to repeat the *Abwrackprämie* – the scrapping bonus scheme implemented following the 2008 financial crisis to stimulate car sales. Instead, it only offered financial help for those buying electric vehicles.

Public opinion had turned against the car industry and the government was reluctant to be seen, once more, as the industry's patsy. '*After years of building the wrong [polluting] models, tax money must not simply be thrown at companies so that they can put cars on the road at a lower price,*' said Olaf Bandt, chairman of environmental group Bund.[23] It is politically difficult to argue against such a position when the German car industry had itself destroyed a significant amount of its political capital.

All too used to being in a position of almost unchallengeable political power, the industry itself seemed surprised. Jürgen Karpinski, President of the German Federation for Motor Trades, which represents almost 40,000 auto-sector companies, said the stimulus package '*did a disservice to the crisis-ridden automobile industry with its 1.3m employees*'. And the industry was still lobbying Brussels to provide exemptions and leniency in the interpretation of emissions rules. While continuing to lament lack of subsidy for new diesel and petrol car purchases and putting 200,000 workers on a state-sponsored furlough scheme, the industry still planned to hand out over €5 billion in dividends to shareholders.

In 2021, the European Court of Justice ruled that between 2010 and 2016 Germany had 'systematically and persistently' exceeded annual limits for nitrogen dioxide produced by diesel engines in 26 of the 89 areas assessed. In bowing to pressure from its car industry, Germany broke European law.

Yes, industry and politics are intertwined but they should never be wedded. For that would be a marriage made in hell. If politics is to discharge its function properly, it cannot afford to put itself in a position of dependence on specific industrial sectors or individual companies. It should not let its broad duties to the whole of society become conflicted by the financial benefits that come from being a corporate shareholder. Nor should politics ever allow any company or sector to become politically untouchable.

Yes, as we have seen in the financial crisis and the COVID-19 pandemic, governments may need to inject capital by taking equity stakes in systemically important corporations to save them from going under. But in doing so, it is vital to keep in mind that such action is being done, and should only be done, to achieve broader societal goals and not as a financial investment with the same goals and objectives as private investors.

STAKEHOLDER CAPITALISM OR CORPORATISM?

In 2008, the head of a German shareholder association published an attack on Wirecard, a German electronic payments company, alleging balance sheet irregularities.

In 2015, *The Financial Times* began publishing a series called 'House of Wirecard', raising questions about the company's financial affairs.

In 2016, the Zatarra report, co-authored by two professional investors and short sellers, Matt Earl and Fraser Perring, and published anonymously, raised serious questions about deficiencies in money laundering controls and oversight at Wirecard. The company's stock price fell by a fifth.

Rather than investigate the claims thoroughly, BaFin, Germany's financial regulator, embarked on an investigation of the journalists and authors involved. In 2018, Munich prosecutors issued a penalty order seeking to fine Fraser Perring for suspected market manipulation. None of the German press sought to investigate Wirecard any further. Instead, they printed unsourced allegations leaked by regulators naming one of the journalists under investigation and making unsubstantiated claims that British reporters had been offered bribes to publish negative reports about Wirecard.[24]

Also in 2018, an internal whistleblower alleged fraudulent activities and Wirecard's legal team in its Singapore headquarters mounted a legal investigation. In October that year, that internal investigation was quashed. A *Financial Times'* article[25] about the investigation was published in January 2019. Wirecard immediately declared it 'false' and BaFin initiated an investigation of the *FT* for possible market manipulation.

In 2019, we have the following list of events: Singapore authorities raid Wirecard HQ; BaFin announces a two-month ban on short selling of the company's stock, citing the importance of the company to the economy; the *FT* tries to visit some of Wirecard's 'partners' in the Philippines supposedly responsible for its outsourced payments but instead found a family surprised that their home was supposed to be an international payments business; EY, Wirecard's auditors, give its accounts a clean bill of health with minor qualifications about its Singapore business; Softbank makes a $900 million cash injection into Wirecard; the company issues $500 million worth of bonds classified as investment grade by Moody's; Wirecard sues the *FT* and the Singapore authorities; the *FT* continues to publish articles alleging fraud and false accounting at the company.

In June 2020, Wirecard collapsed. A whopping €1.9 billion on its balance sheet could not be traced and likely never existed. EY, the auditors, had failed to look at original bank records to verify the existence of that cash. On 22 June, Wirecard admitted the potential scale of a multi-year accounting fraud – for the first time. Even as the company was collapsing, Felix Hufeld, President of BaFin, reportedly raised the possibility that the disappearance of €1.9 billion in cash was faked in an elaborate plot by short sellers.[26] This is a normal human reaction. When people have been conned, the natural tendency is to resist accepting it and to continue to look for evidence that they might have been right all along.

The point of including the Wirecard story here is not as yet another tale of corporate fraud, though it is. Rather more important are the multiple institutional failures in the German political, regulatory and legal system. Despite multiple warnings and many investigations by the *FT*, investors and foreign governments, the German establishment closed ranks – and closed its eyes – to a multi-year fraud. Why?

Wirecard was supposed to be the one 'modern economy' success story in Germany – a country slow to supplement its traditional, twentieth-century manufacturing prowess with twenty-first-century information-driven industry. Wirecard moved rapidly into the DAX 30 index, making it an essential investment for institutional investors. It was hailed as Europe's greatest fintech. As a result, it was seen as a national champion seemingly to be defended at all costs.

Questioned about the regulatory failures, BaFin argued that the company was classified as a technology company not a financial company and that its own regulatory responsibilities were limited to overseeing the company's small banking subsidiary rather than the parent company. This is reminiscent of bureaucrats' standard defence, as famously satirized by Tom Lehrer: *'Once the rockets are up, who cares where they come down? That's not my department says Wernher von Braun.'*

It also emerged that Wirecard had close ties with the Federal Criminal Police Office (BKA). The company seemingly issued some credit cards under fake identities and the cards were then used by police officers to pay bills during criminal investigations. The special investigator suggested that the BKA should have scrutinized its partners more critically.[27]

The Wirecard fiasco has been a slap in the face for a proud German establishment. *'The last place we expected something like this to happen was Germany,'* said Peter Altmaier, the German economy minister. Germany has been proud of its multi-stakeholder focused economy and collaborative atmosphere between business, government, trade-unions and workers. It has, with some justification, been suspicious of the more rough-and-tumble, confrontational Anglo-American approach with its focus on maximizing profits and shareholder returns even at potentially not insignificant social cost. Viewed through this lens, Wirecard became a symbol of national pride. Criticism was interpreted as the undermining of a German icon by foreign journalists and Anglo-Saxon financial speculators only intent on making a fast buck through short selling. That such a framing became the prevalent groupthink is not surprising, that it went on for so long in the face of mounting revelations is.

What this and the VW scandals demonstrate is that stakeholder capitalism, which is to be encouraged, can all too easily slip into corporatism – a relationship between all parties that becomes rather too cosy and blind to obvious deceit. Where the essential checks and balances disappear because 'we're all in it together'.

Drawing the line is never easy. The rot percolates into the system over a period of many decades. As they attend the same conferences and the same dinner parties as top businesspeople; as they engage in a revolving door of private-public job appointments, politicians and their appointed regulators risk sliding unconsciously into a situation where they stop doing their job. Where a healthy culture of collaboration slides unnoticed into a shady culture of collusion that may well become subconscious.

It is futile to point the finger at individuals. They are mere puppets of the prevailing institutional culture in which they work and the expectations of all around them. But it all points to how delicate, and difficult, is the endless dance between business and politics.

In January 2021, the head of BaFin, Felix Hufeld, and his deputy, Elizabeth Roegele, left their positions.

WHY NATIONALIZATION RARELY WORKS

These sorry tales provide another perspective on why nationalization of commercial enterprises should be approached with caution. Those on the Left of the political spectrum often argue for nationalization as 'the answer' to corporate misbehaviour, real or perceived. Those on the Right argue that nationalization is a recipe for inefficiency. We've heard both these arguments trotted out endlessly for decades. Both have merit as well as valid counterarguments.

But maybe the most important reason to approach nationalization with caution is that it represents a marriage between commerce and politics, what I have described above as a marriage made in hell. It destroys the important separation of roles – governments' and societies' role to set the rules of the game and hold business to account, and the role of business to play the game within the rules and within societal norms and expectations, and to engage in the delicate dance between competition and collaboration – concepts I explore further in the next chapter.

Nationalization is the extreme form of what we saw in the large shareholding of the Lower Saxony government in Volkswagen. It gives nationalized enterprises too much political power and creates the inevitable conflicts of interest that undermine the state's ability to hold them to account. It makes it more rather than less difficult to ensure that commercial interests are balanced against the public interest. An outcome that can only be achieved if there is a healthy tension between business and politics underpinned by institutional structures that can focus on their own proper role without being dragged into impossible conflicts of interest.

While some argue that nationalized enterprises can, and should, be managed exclusively for the public interest, experience has shown that it rarely turns out that way. Organizations, whether private or public, tend to end up acting in their own interest. All too often the removal of the essential institutional separation between enterprises and those responsible for holding them to account results in enterprises too close to, or owned by, the state becoming vehicles for political clientelism or, at worst, endemic corruption.

Of course, some will argue that some sectors are important enough that they should not be subject to any commercial interests. But sectors are not homogeneous blobs. They are made up of a number of different actors. Short of nationalizing everything (tried, but comprehensively failed), there will always be commercial interests somewhere. Politics will serve us all better if it maintains the separation necessary to hold these interests to account – and actually does hold them to account rather than being captured by those interests. In the words of President Herbert Hoover in his 1929 inaugural address: '*Regulation of private enterprise and not Government ownership or operation is the course rightly to be pursued in our relation to business.*'

Nothing is absolute. The best way to manage companies that are public utilities, those activities that form part of what has been called the 'foundational economy', how to deal with companies that are too big to fail, how to avoid incestuous relationships between politically powerful private corporations and the state. All these difficult issues require carefully constructed governance structures that are transparent and effective. We should not assume that holding interests to account is automatic just because there is institutional separation, we have to work at it constantly. But it would also be naïve to assume that all is resolved simply through the act of nationalization, or that nationalization automatically increases rather than undermines appropriate governance – difficult as the latter is.

The limits of 'the entrepreneurial state'

'The Entrepreneurial State' is a concept popularized by Mariana Mazzucato, a professor at University College London, in a book by the same name.[28] Mazzucato rightly argues, as I have earlier, that state activity often underpins private sector opportunity. That, in most sectors, the private sector often only finds the courage to invest after the state has made the initial, high-risk bets. She shows that more or less every technology that makes the iPhone so 'smart' was government-funded: the internet, GPS, its touchscreen display and the voice-activated Siri.

Mazzucato goes on to argue that the state should directly reap the financial rewards of such innovation rather than, as she sees it, socializing the risks and privatizing the rewards. This idea is potentially problematic.

As we saw in the Volkswagen case, when the state has a direct financial interest in commercial performance, we see difficult conflicts of interest that can undermine the ability to hold companies to account. This blurring of responsibilities is undesirable and can have significant adverse consequences.

Mazzucato is right that state-funded research and development forms a vital part of the whole ecosystem of our economy – and should be recognized as such. But I suggest that such investment should be considered part of the myriad public services that the state may or may not choose to provide. Starting to look at state-sponsored investments as no different from commercial investments, with the state looking for commercial returns, compromises the state's role and its duty to hold commercial interests to account in the public interest. It also embeds the idea that everything can be resolved by all actors, including the state, seeing themselves as part of 'the market'.

The state is not a business and should not try to become one. Its ability to be appropriately 'entrepreneurial' is precisely because it does not have to look for commercial returns, enabling it to go where private investment dare not go at the time.

Besides compromising the state's proper functions, adopting a financial returns mentality risks limiting the amount of risk the state is prepared to take in funding blue sky research that may or may not have commercial potential many years or decades in the future. It would undermine the very benefits that state financing brings. Mazzucato argues that this need not be the case. But one only has to look at how finance ministries everywhere are now obsessed with cost-benefit analyses and the endless political criticism associated with 'failed investments' made by the state (as though private investors are infallible and never make failed investments in spite of taking less risk) to see that it is pie in the sky to believe that narrow and short-term thinking would not infect government bureaucracies if they had to start reporting what returns were to be made on such funding. Not to mention the Byzantine complexity of the contractual arrangements required to make it work. It would introduce political complications that are best avoided and risks drawing the state into the very fabric of the financialized form of capitalism that is obsolescent.

Besides, governments in most developed countries that would be making such investments don't need the money. Financing is not an issue for any respectable government that controls its own currency. Looking for returns from such activities is an ideological stance more than anything else. It will do more harm than good.

Separate and inseparable

I hope that, here, I have been able to outline that 'politics' is not about electioneering. It is about the values, identities and the broad needs of the population – things that vary widely across countries and within their populations. Politics is both a driver and a reflection of contemporary social norms. Business leaders have the opportunity to learn how such public mores are evolving, and how they can drive sustainable business advantage, by observing with curiosity and in the spirit of learning rather than dismissive critiquing, what is happening in the political world. As Gillian Tett puts it in Anthro-Vision, *'listening to someone else's view, however "strange," does not just teach empathy for others, which is badly needed today; it also makes it easier to see yourself.'*[29]

Today, business may still have sufficient political clout to impact political decision making in the short term. But in societies that are ever more widely connected, and where the ability to influence public and political opinion is now open to many, business's share of voice in directly influencing both policymakers and the general public is decreasing dramatically. As these developments continue, political thinking skills become an ever more important component of business success. Business leaders will do better by building political capital rather than frittering it away. That requires a deep understanding of political culture in the same way that building financial capital requires an understanding of finance.

Politics and business are intimately intertwined. In a functioning democracy, they have different and complementary roles that should not evolve into a conjugal relationship that compromises both.

Now let's move on from politics to markets.

3

Markets are Political Constructs

'I like free markets, but I do like fair markets.'
Rick Santelli
Journalist
Editor CNBC News Network

It was one of those evenings. A drinks party organized by a libertarian think tank. The wine was drinkable, the snacks not so edible. I ended up in a corner in conversation with John, a businessman who ran a large, listed company. Eventually, I asked him what was taking up his time at the moment. He responded that a lot of it was spent in litigation with another large corporation who, he claimed, had broken the terms of their contractual agreement.

Having just stood smilingly through a long exaltation of free, unregulated markets at the start of the conversation, I was left wondering. Given my new friend's belief in unfettered, unregulated markets, why was he suing his partner/competitor company? Surely if left alone, 'the market' would eventually sort it all out? If the other corporation had sharp business practices, they would be found out and eventually go out of business, replaced, through the process of creative destruction, by more trustworthy organizations with which he could comfortably do business. Why did he feel the need to call on the legal apparatus of the state to sue them and push his business forward rather than leaving it to market forces? Did he have so little faith in 'the invisible hand' that he wanted the very visible iron fist of the state-constructed legal system to help him out?

When I brought this up, John was somewhat surprised. He had taken the legal system for granted, seeing it as part of the furniture rather than an institution of the state – that which he had spent the whole evening castigating for interfering with the operation of the free market. It immediately brought to mind the words of Dave Brat, American economist and Republican politician: *'Everyone's for free markets except when it affects your own business.'*

So, let's talk about markets, regulation and the role of the state.

I'd like to start with football (soccer) – or you can pick any other sport. The so-called Beautiful Game is one where teams have a simple objective – to score more goals than the opposition. This they can do while playing within a long and complex set of rules. Those rules are set and clear to all who choose to play the game. A referee is there to ensure the rules are followed. He or she penalizes those who do not follow the rules. Some egregious behaviours are adjudicated off the field by the sport's relevant governing body. Penalties are sometimes imposed on players, teams and clubs – fines, suspension from participation, whatever.

Besides the formal rules, there are conventions – social norms if you like. If a player seems injured and the ball is in the opponents' possession, the opponents normally stop playing and kick the ball out of bounds to allow the player to receive medical attention. Once play resumes, the opposing team returns the ball to the team that had possession when play was stopped. Nothing in the rules requires any of this. It is common courtesy between human beings.

The game, *any game*, is a perfect illustration of how markets work. Players in the game (the marketplace) can use their skills to win. But without clarity of what constitutes winning the game; without a clear set of rules that someone compiled and that, with experience, evolve with time; and without effective ways of enforcing those rules, the game would not exist at all. Just imagine sending a bunch of players on to the field, telling them that this is a free-for-all with no rules and no objectives and asking them to go ahead and play a game. *What* game? It's the same with markets. They are social, and therefore political, constructions. Markets would not work – or even exist in any way we recognize – without a set of rules that reflect social values and evolve over time (laws, regulations and social expectations or social mores) – and ways to enforce those rules so that markets are seen to operate both predictably and fairly. Those who break the rules are penalized.

We should therefore think of markets as we think of football. The state plays the role of the sport's governing body – setting the rules, policing and enforcing them. Players on the field represent 'the free market' – able to collaborate, compete, innovate and use their skills to play the game. But all within a pre-agreed construct.

So, here's the thing: there is no such thing as a 'free market', only constructed markets. Markets that can only exist and function because of a set of rules of the game that are politically designed and enforced by a set of institutions of the state. Given that markets themselves are political constructs, how can anyone operating a business claim that business is apolitical?

Of course, the idea of 'free markets' is relative. In lawless states, there is no effective governance apparatus to set and enforce any kind of rules. It's a wild free-for-all. But even that does not mean no rules. In such situations, the rules are set by the most powerful warlords depending on their current whims and in whichever part of the country they happen to dominate. It's not clear how many businesspeople would prefer to operate in this closer approximation to a 'free market' rather than in well-governed, regulated states.

It brings to mind the dream of a former chairman of Dow Chemicals of establishing the company's headquarters on an island (owned by no nation), beholden to no nation or society.[1] This is not an 'apolitical' stance, it is a purely political statement that asserts that business is somehow totally dissociated from society. Neither is it new nor original. Diogenes (aka Diogenes the Cynic, 412–323 BC) declared himself a 'citizen of the world', who should therefore not be subject to paying local taxes or abiding by local norms.

DO 'FREE MARKETS' EXIST AT ALL?

Some persist in the belief that real free markets do exist and that government intervention is something that does nothing more than distort such markets. The favourite example is stock markets – what some like to believe to be as close to a representation of a 'perfect market' as there is.

My friend and colleague, Nick Silver, in his must-read book *Finance, Society and Sustainability*, puts it like this:

> A stock or a share is not a physical product like an apple or a car, but one that is defined legally. The structure of a company share or bond

was defined by governments and perpetuated and supported by the law
and regulations. The legal structure of companies and what companies
can and cannot do is also defined by legislation and regulation.[2]

He might have added that the financial markets cannot function
unless there were established rules of the game that ensure as much
transparency and fairness as is possible. Contracts between buyers and
sellers are legal undertakings enforced by the mechanism of governance.
Rules ban insider trading that gives some an unfair advantage over
others. Companies are legally required to publish accounts audited to
set standards and to give out reliable and true information that may be
material to buyers of their stock. And on, and on, and on it goes.

No market can exist, let alone operate sustainably, without structures
built by our political system to define such markets and construct and
sustain what is essential to make them function. This realization should
give us a different perspective on the role of politics and regulation in
market economies. But more of that later.

WHY THE RULES OF THE GAME MATTER

In 1904, an American woman named Elizabeth Magie invented a board
game with a political message – The Landlord's Game. She laid out a
board in a circuit marked with place names, each one for sale. Players
would move their pieces around the board and buy the places where
they happened to land by chance.

Magie provided two alternative sets of rules under which the game
would be played. Under the 'Prosperity' rules, every player gained
money every time someone bought a new land block or property. The
equivalent of redistribution through, say, a land value tax – something
Magie's father had championed for a while. The game was won *by all
players* when the player who started out with the least money managed
to double it. A set of rules that encouraged collaboration and the sharing
of wealth to get to a collective win.

Using the alternative set of 'Monopolist' rules, players were successful
by acquiring properties and collecting rent from everyone who
happened to land on their property block. The winner was the single
player who managed to accumulate most money while bankrupting the
other players.

Clearly, the two sets of rules led to fundamentally different player behaviours and outcomes. The first encouraged co-operation and prosperity for all. Everyone got 'richer' and winning – for everyone – was dependent on lifting the person with the least money out of relative poverty. The second set of rules encouraged selfish behaviour and the financial destruction of your opponents as the winning strategy.

As is obvious, the same game structure – or let's call it the politics underpinning market structure and consequent behaviour – yields fundamentally different social outcomes depending on the rules under which it is played. As in real life, the rules end up defining the kind of society we live in, people's attitudes to themselves and to others, and the incentives that drive behaviour. That is why defining such rules is properly a political task. In a democracy, only elected politicians have the mandate and the legitimacy to set the rules of the 'market' or 'economic' game, thereby essentially defining what sort of society we wish to live in. Nobody else has any democratic legitimacy to define such rules – not business, not scholars, not trade unions, not economists, not scientists, nor anyone else – only the elected political class and those to whom they explicitly delegate power on their behalf.

Magie's game was eventually bought by Parker Brothers through an unemployed man called Charles Darrow. Darrow and Parker Brothers ditched the Prosperity set of rules and marketed the game as 'Monopoly', even wiping out Magie's name as the inventor. For a game that was, by then, only about the individual accumulation of wealth, a rags-to-riches story focused on Darrow made a better marketing backdrop than a social activist agitating for a fairer, collaborative society.

Parker Brothers, with what is one of the most successful board games of all time, inculcated a culture of self-focus, greed and the personal accumulation of wealth into the minds of several generations. Testament to the political power of business. Who knows where we would all be today, had Parker Brothers marketed 'Prosperity' instead of 'Monopoly'?

Marketing the game as 'Monopoly' also swept aside one of the fundamental underpinnings of humanity's success. Many have argued that the development of language was the most important human development that distinguished humans from other creatures. Language allowed highly effective communication that raised to a new level humans' ability to leverage their status as a social animal and embark on the previously unseen levels of collaboration that drove human progress. Everything we have achieved as humans compared to other creatures has been driven by our ability to collaborate – mediated by language and its ability to let us communicate at incredible levels of complexity. 'Monopoly' totally ignores this fundamental human gift of collaborative success, replacing it with a culture of individualism and the idea that success is the triumph of one individual over everyone else. The game is a perversion of the world we live in and of what constitutes success and progress in human societies.

Kate Raworth, the economist who wrote the article[3] from which I learned this story, titled it 'Monopoly was invented to demonstrate the evils of capitalism'. While that headline may be satisfying to a left-leaning economist, the title is fundamentally incorrect. The 'Prosperity' set of rules is also capitalist in nature in that individuals bought, owned and sold private property. It was still a market system. What Magie's invention did show is that the outcomes of capitalism are not fixed. They are determined by the set of rules under which the capitalist system operates. And those rules are for societies through, in a democracy, their elected representatives to determine. Different rules for a capitalist system yield societal outcomes as different as what we see in Denmark, compared to the US, compared to, say, Russia with its oligarchic system of crony capitalism, or Libya, which, at the time of writing, is an essentially lawless state.

One more thing … The game also demonstrates that success is not just a matter of skill. It is also, maybe substantially, down to luck – where your piece happens to fall after the next throw of the dice. Something we should all remember as we convince ourselves that all our achievements are a visible demonstration of our own personal skills and capabilities. That was also the power of John Rawls' 'veil of ignorance' that asked the uncomfortable question: what sort of world would you like to see if you had no idea what part of it you were going to be born into and what skills, capabilities, level of health, etc. you were going to be born with? All matters of pure, unadulterated luck.

WHO SETS THE RULES?

So far, I have argued that it is for society as a whole, through the political system, to set the rules of the game. That, while true in principle, is, of course, an oversimplification. Politics does not operate in a vacuum, it is subject to pressure from many, often diverging influences. In 2016, I worked with a few colleagues to set up a policy think tank called RADIX, hoping we might exert some influence on the system. Voters exert significant influence through the ballot box. But others exert influence too. A vibrant civil society exerts influence through campaigns focused on the issues that are important to all the different NGOs and civil society organizations. Others influence largely through money. Whether it is through heavy and expensive lobbying efforts or financial contributions to political campaigns, money influences politics – whether that money comes from corporations, wealthy individuals, trade unions, crowdfunding or wherever else. Let's see where that takes us.

Getting back to our previous football analogy, let us imagine a situation where a particular club, let's call it the Me Football Club (MFC) develops a consistently winning approach to the game. But with one problem – the new approach is outside the established rules. The MFC therefore mounts a massive lobbying effort on the relevant football association to get the rules changed so that their innovation becomes 'legal'. MFC is a wealthy, well-known and well-connected club, the pride of the nation. They wine and dine people, they mount advertising and influencing campaigns, they get the great and the good, including politicians, to be on their side and push for the new rules – rules that would give them what may be a transient but significant advantage over all other clubs.

How would you feel about that if you were a lifelong and avid supporter of an alternative club? It is clear that the campaign has not been embarked upon to improve the quality of the game. Rather, it is driven by pure self-interest.

Let us imagine MFC is successful in its lobbying efforts. They immediately start winning every championship and therefore end up with significantly enhanced revenues from endorsements, TV contracts, etc. They can now afford to buy better players, further entrenching their advantage.

A few other clubs learn quickly and start to adapt. They get better, but for a few years, they cannot really compete with MFC. Many fall to the bottom of the table. Their revenues shrink and their ability to compete goes into a downward spiral. The whole league becomes reduced to an effective monopoly by MFC or, at best, an oligopoly with a few other agile and adaptive clubs. A previously vibrant league of multiple competitors, that which gives markets life, has effectively been destroyed through a rule change pushed through by a single operator focused on its own self-interest.

If you work for a corporation, next time you see your company lobbying for particular changes in regulation or legislation, ask yourself some questions. Is this being done to improve the market structure and make it more vibrant and more competitive? Is it being done to create a better society for us to live in? Or is it to give our company, and maybe our sector, a narrow advantage? Will our society as a whole be better or worse off under the new rules? Whatever the answer, that's not the issue. But if it is all driven by narrow self-interest, then you should be clear that, in spite of any grand pronouncements by senior management of the value of 'free markets' and the evils of government regulation, your company and its leaders do not believe in a thriving market economy that benefits our societies.

Our imaginary MFC described above is not so far-fetched. In 2021 a number of elite European football clubs attempted to form a new European Super League which would guarantee them a permanent position in such a league irrespective of performance on the field. Essentially an oligopoly that would allow them to bank vast sums of money from media and sponsorship deals. The project was stillborn having generated a violent reaction from fans, the sport's governing bodies and governments everywhere. Once again what made sense from a purely financial perspective was a product of extreme political and social blindness – not to mention arrogance among the club owners involved.

At the end of the day, it is the job of politics, in its broadest sense, to make these judgements. Politics has to balance multiple interests and decide which set of rules provide the greatest benefit to societies – while also protecting those whom the rules may disadvantage. More than that, politics has to decide what sort of society we want to live in and which are the best (as far as we can reasonably predict) policies to get there. And it has to do this under pressure from every vested interest there is and, in many countries, with one eye on how they are going to raise the funds to get elected next time around.

Stripping the financial element from what influences politics would doubtless improve our governance structures but I am not deluded enough to believe that it will happen any time soon. We're going to have to live with that and many other rather messy imperfections.

From a business perspective, we are long past the age where anyone still believes that 'What is good for General Motors is good for America' – even if we replace GM with any other corporation whose name is, today, hipper and more fashionable.

Getting past too narrow a perspective on the relationship between business and politics is important if business is to be taken seriously and continue to have a political voice. During a trip to Brussels, I was speaking to a public affairs professional. He had just received a communication from a senior European Commissioner saying that the Commissioner would no longer take meetings with representatives of industry associations – for two reasons. The first was that such associations were so transparently self-interested that he knew what they would be saying before they walked through the door. Why waste time? Second, industry associations are usually membership associations that have to cater to all their members. They were therefore rarely able to come up with usefully innovative approaches as they were held back by the lowest common denominator among their membership. In short, in his eyes industry associations had lost credibility and therefore ability to influence.

Self-interest is transparent to everyone. Businesses that want to be influential will not achieve it through transparent self-interest – nor should they be allowed to. Rather, they can only achieve it by having a full understanding of political imperatives and constraints and presenting a case that will help society and policymakers achieve their objectives, not those of businesses' own narrow interests.

Business is, rightly, a part of our panoply of political institutions – a group that has significant political influence and a significant degree of power in determining the political weather. Business is also political in that it employs people, determines wages, has control over investment, production and distribution, etc. In such a structure, business leaders have a clear choice as to how they use their political status and power. Do they use that power to create a better society, or do they choose to use it for narrow self-interest? Different leaders will make different choices. Let us ask ourselves: have Boeing and Volkswagen, for example, created a better society with their behaviours? There are plenty of examples where businesses have had a strong positive impact on our societies and I will address those later.

Political scientists have for years debated whether the political impact of business is structural or rather an exchange and influence relationship. That debate is beyond the scope of this book (though I tend towards the structural view) and interested readers will find plenty of academic literature to peruse. Rather, I am hoping that some readers will now start to agree that business is anything but apolitical.

Business is political. Markets are political constructs. Maintaining thriving, fair markets is one of the jobs of politics – at least for those political groups that believe in market/mixed economies, as I do. Businesses can, and many do, have a tremendous positive impact on our politics and our societies. Some corporate activities, on the other hand, damage the market economy – and people's faith in it – to the detriment of all, further stimulating political activity that may be damaging to business itself.

A DIFFERENT LOOK AT 'REGULATION'

It was an interesting discussion on corporate governance. A breakfast meeting with about 20 or so chairs and non-executive board directors of major, UK-listed companies. Towards the end, I was asked by one of the participants, Ian: 'If there were one thing you could do to improve things, what would it be?' I responded by saying that I would revise the UK Companies Act so that directors had equal responsibilities towards all stakeholders rather than giving shareholders a privileged position.

Ian flew into a rage: 'So, you're immediately reaching for a regulatory solution. That's unacceptable!'

Let us put aside for the moment whether my suggestion had any merit or not, I'll address that later. Here, I want to focus on the immediate visceral rejection of anything that can be described as 'regulation'. Many equate regulation with 'red tape'. They have mounted a war on regulation and turned de-regulation into a religion. This attitude leads to the reluctance to implement any statutory measures – or in fact for government to do anything much at all except deregulate. For many, this has become a knee-jerk response to the very mention of 'regulation' – as shown by Ian's response. Yet, how many of us would happily fly with an airline that, if that were possible, decided to opt out of all airline safety regulations? How many of us would put our money or investments with a totally unregulated bank of investment house? Or give our children unregulated and untested pharmaceutical products?

Here, the premise is that, as I have outlined earlier, a regulatory framework is essential for markets both to exist and to function. It establishes the rules of the game. Further, regulation is a public good. It is intended to protect citizens from the worst excesses of human behaviour that are intended to favour the few at the expense of the many. True, regulation, like almost everything, is difficult to get right. Like all human actions, it has unintended consequences. That is a spur towards constant improvement, not a reason not to have any.

One of the issues is that regulation is all too often backward-looking. It is frequently a reaction to things that have gone wrong and results in shutting the door after the horse has bolted. I examined earlier how business behaviour has political and regulatory consequences. People and companies that go around existing rules end up distorting markets and generating an unfair advantage for themselves at the cost of properly functioning markets. Sometimes, as we saw with the financial crash, this has significant adverse consequences, forcing regulators to intervene. This makes regulation appear like a policing function – and very few of us like intrusive policing, especially if we are innocent, law-abiding citizens ourselves. Yet, if there were no crime, there would be little need for policing. Similarly, the more people try to do an end run around proper, ethical market behaviours, the more regulators have to spend their time on such a policing function.

But laws and regulations are not, by their nature, policing functions. Rather, they are the processes that define markets and set the rules of the game. Without them, as in football, there would be no game.

And regulations grant privileges as well as limiting freedom of action.

In the late 1500s and early 1600s, the Dutch were looking for ways to finance a merchant navy for global trading. Much of the Dutch economy at the time was agricultural – and not just tulips. Investors and owners of land could make a steady 3 per cent return on agricultural activity with manageable risks. International trading expeditions were seen as far too risky. Ships could sink, be robbed by pirates and the results of long-range seafaring expeditions were highly uncertain. As a result, nobody wanted to finance such activity – they could not be guaranteed the same sort of reliable returns they had become used to.

Enter the joint stock corporation – something that had had its tentative start in China in the Tang Dynasty, in France in the 1200s and in England in the 1500s. In 1602, the United East India Company was established, through the amalgamation of various Dutch interests, as the first recorded joint stock company with fixed capital stock. The company had two important characteristics. The first was the ability to issue stock to multiple investors, thereby spreading risk – not a new concept at the time. The second was the important innovation – that investors' liability was limited to the amount of their investment. Individual investors could now participate in naval expeditions not just by putting up limited amounts of money, but, more importantly, their potential losses were capped through the limited liability structure – something that was not the case with partnership structures.

The limited liability privilege afforded to those investors persists today in all limited liability companies. A privilege that is the direct result of the regulatory framework invented by the Dutch in 1602. Today, the legal framework gives companies a legal personality. Companies are, in law, considered as a fictional person – legally and, importantly, morally. They are empowered, through the regulatory and legal structures, to enter into contracts, buy property, pay taxes and so forth – all separately from their shareholders. As the regulatory structure changed, and as an inducement to investors, shares morphed into tradeable financial instruments rather than a reflection of part ownership. Progressive financialization created increasing separation between the market in stocks and the economic activity of the corporations that had issued those stocks. All these various, complex regulatory and legal structures were set up to encourage business and investment through awarding privileges and protections to those involved. They represent the interaction between business and politics.

Of course, privileges come with duties and responsibilities – something that too many seem conveniently to forget. If you want the privileges afforded you by laws and regulations, you need to behave within not just the letter but also the spirit of the legal framework and the prevailing societal norms. Most do, too many do not.

So, let us ask the question to all those who, like Ian, rail against laws and regulations and constantly hammer the mantra of deregulation: what would you think if the first 'deregulation' initiative were to be the removal of the laws that provide limited liability?

During the Brexit debate in the UK, a group of 'free-market' minded people set up a project that they called 'The Red Tape Initiative' (RTI). The idea was to consult with businesses across multiple sectors as to which mountains of regulation should be immediately blown up once the UK had left the European Union and was free to transmogrify into their imagined buccaneering country that could go forth and conquer markets as a result of what was, after all, a decision as purely political as they come – Brexit.

Two years of work involved consultations with multiple businesses, trade associations and civil society across multiple sectors. When the complete work was reported, it turned out that nobody wanted massive deregulation. They were perfectly happy with stuff as it was. Deregulation would be disruptive to the businesses they had built around the current system. When the final report was presented to the funders of the project, they looked at each other in dismay: 'Is that all we got?'

The reality is that businesses are not really interested in either regulation or de-regulation, they prefer stability. For things to stay exactly as they are is what makes their life easiest. But that is all a chimera. The world is constantly changing. Political and social perspectives change too. And businesses are, or should be, constantly changing. Regulation and market structures must therefore also be constantly changing to keep up with the changing technologies, changing market behaviours, changing world views and social mores of the time.

The benefits of regulation

The Dutch invention of the joint stock corporation with limited liability was a political regulatory initiative that unleashed a torrent of economic activity. The commercial world as we know it today would not exist without it. It created a new market structure that drew in investment and consequent business activity on an unprecedented scale. The Industrial Revolution, based as it was on high levels of capital investment, could never have happened without it – *'Tax and regulation can push market forces to [create a better world], not forever tell everyone how to live'*.[4]

And that is the promise of forward-looking political activity. Regulation has the potential to create the conditions for new business activity and desired behaviours to emerge spontaneously. It can achieve systemic change through emergent effects and has the potential to drive innovation, to make industry more competitive and forward-looking. Above all, the legal and regulatory framework is the mechanism through which societies can answer some fundamental questions such as 'What is business for?'

When my friend and colleague David Boyle and I published a book on globalization, I was interviewed by Daan Ballegeer for a piece in *Het Financieele Dagblad,* the Dutch financial newspaper of record.[5] Ballegeer asked: '*You expect a lot from companies when you say that they should be concerned with cultural, social and moral issues. What is wrong with the pursuit of profit within current laws and regulations?* My response was that there is no divine edict as to what companies are for. That is a social choice that is mediated through the political system. But his question was revealing in that he had made an assumption both about the role of business and the role of regulation. That corporations' role is primarily to pursue and maximize profits was the view. And that laws and regulations are there to set limits as to what they could do to get there.

Neither of these assumptions is correct. The correct formulation would be the other way around: what does our society want business to be for and how does politics set a regulatory framework to drive business, and markets, in that direction?

The answers to these questions change over time and in different cultures and countries. I will address this more in Chapter 5, but to take some examples, in the Soviet Union and some other countries, what we call business activity was seen as a cog in the wheel of a state-planned and state-directed economy. Companies were mere organs of the state. When I led a consulting project to privatize a Hungarian company following the break-up of the Soviet Union, management did not understand the very concept of profit.

That system failed. But now we have China – seen by many as an economic miracle. There, the boundaries between the priorities of the state and the priorities of business are fuzzy to say the least. It is a hybrid system of what some call a state-directed market economy (more later). Businesses are expected to act in the national interest. When necessary, they are mobilized to do so by the regime.

In the West, our capitalist system has also changed over time. We have had feudal capitalism, industrial capitalism, the era of financialized capitalism that we are in now, and what I believe to be the emergent era of the new political capitalism. In all these iterations, the perceived role of commercial activity was different. It has always been defined by the prevalent political ideology, remains so today, and will remain so forever.

All this to say that the very role of business in our society is a political choice. A choice that is politically defined and then implemented through the enactment of laws and regulations. The very meaning and purpose of 'business' is inherently political. And, in a democracy, it is, and should be, continually contested and in constant flux. Those who believe that the answer is both obvious and fixed are either mistaken or have not thought about it enough.

We would all be better served if we looked at regulation in this light. If policymakers themselves would spend more of their time on stimulating and addressing these sorts of big systemic and ideological questions rather than implementing policing-type regulations to plug loopholes and control the rogue players.

Sadly, human nature generates too many rogue players who take up far too much political and regulatory energy, leaving less time and resources available for more imaginative, more visionary and more productive activity. And, as the various stories outlined above and the financial crash showed, rogue players are not just a few shady characters operating on the margins and who can reasonably safely be ignored. They include large, systemically important participants.

How frustrating it must be for the many, many businesses and business leaders who are doing great work, running great businesses within a clear moral and political framework, pushing progress forward, and who, through no fault of their own, get caught in the crossfire when things blow up. They should be speaking up; they should be shunning those businesses and their leaders who mess everything up for everyone. Sadly, we see too little of that. The tribal instinct to defend one's own social group for fear of exclusion is strong even though rogue players have no business belonging to the same tribe as those who behave responsibly.

Maintaining competitive markets

I would now like to look at one particular aspect of policy that crystallizes many aspects of the relationship between business, politics and democracy – competition policy. For many, competition policy is something best left to nerdish competition lawyers. Yet it is fundamental to the survival of our whole way of life; to the survival of democratic capitalism and a thriving market economy.

82 THE NEW POLITICAL CAPITALISM

In 2019 we published a paper titled 'Freedom to Choose: Why competition policy affects us all', written by Tim Cowen, a friend, colleague and highly regarded competition lawyer.[6] In the paper, Tim argues that the traditional political formulation of competition policy, that it should be judged primarily on the basis of consumer welfare (which, in practice, boils down to nothing more than lower prices), was mistaken and outdated. He proposes that the central idea of competition policy should be to stimulate freedom to choose through plurality of supply. In other words, politics and regulation should not only adopt a defensive mindset – intervening to stop or correct consolidation, oligopoly or monopoly on the basis of traditional tests of consumer welfare. Rather, politics should take a more proactive and normative approach that creates and actively stimulates competition and pluralist markets. This idea represents a fundamental shift in political attitude and the role of political and regulatory activity in markets.

Cowen puts it like this:

- Freedom to Choose is the basic idea driving markets to produce ranges of goods and services that people want. It is why we have a rich and colorful range of goods on our shop shelves.
- Freedom to Choose creates incentives on firms to create and innovate. That continuous creativity needs to be stimulated and protected.
- Freedom to Choose has a political dimension. If people feel they have no choice, and nowhere to turn; if our horizons are crowded and our world is one of coercion and constraint; it easily becomes one of resentment.

In the paper, Cowen tracks how political philosophy changed, starting in the 1980s Reagan/Thatcher era towards reducing state intervention, 'supposedly to give people liberty.' The effect, in competition terms, was exactly the opposite. Laxer regulatory standards allowed consolidation in various sectors, decreasing competition and reducing people's freedom of choice. Rather than giving liberty, it made them captives of an ever-shrinking number of corporations, including, eventually, in the tech sector with the likes of Google, Facebook and others. Captives in terms of the variety (or lack thereof) of goods and services available to them and captives in terms of their ability to choose between a plurality of employers in the same market space. And all for what?

Cowen also talks about the impact of these changes on the credibility of democracy and market economics. For markets to work, they have to be competitive. Just as for democracy to work, there has to be effective competition between ideas and different options for voters. A market-based democracy has to have both: it must maintain freedom of choice, both in the commercial and political realm. Monopoly in either undermines values like personal opportunity, self-sufficiency, responsibility and the feeling that one can succeed on one's own merits and have a say in what direction our societies take – '*Absent meaningful competition, the political drive for progress can wither away. Effective competition is just as important in politics as it is in business.*'[7]

This all shows the importance of political philosophy and effective regulatory intervention in maintaining people's faith in, and support for, market-based democracies. Without it, markets become monopolized, thereby undermining faith in the system. It fuels the rise of political forces that can ride on the idea that 'the market system isn't working'.

'But, but, but ...' I hear some saying at this point. 'First, you were talking about the need for a collaborative outlook, now you're telling us that competition is what's important. Can you make up your darned mind!'

Here, we need to take our cue from nature. If we observe it closely, we see that nature works through an endless and delicate dance between competition and co-operation. Both are important and it is this to-and-fro that makes natural systems so successful and so resilient. In our societies it is the job of politics to ensure the same delicate dance happens. Markets, and societies, are eventually destroyed if they are approached with an aggressively competitive mindset with no room for collaboration – as the Monopoly game shows. Neither do they work if the concept of competition is utterly eliminated. We need to sustain the dance – and politics plays the tune.

Should governments play the game?

Here, the rubber hits the road. Getting back to our football analogy, when is it justifiable for governments not only to set the rules of the game and act as referee, but actually to participate in playing the game? The traditional answer has been that governments should intervene only when the market fails.

Let's imagine that, for some reason, nobody wanted any longer to be a goalkeeper in the game of football: 'the market' for goalkeepers has failed. The options are to change the game so that goalkeepers are no longer required, or to keep playing without them – which would make a mockery of the game. Or for football's governing body to provide goalkeepers, seeing as 'the market' cannot.

One small example of such market failure can be seen in the provision of hurricane insurance in Florida. The associated risks in a hurricane-prone state are perceived too high for commercial operators. If we are not to be in a position where nobody can access such insurance, the government must step in. It does so largely through underwriting some of the risks. 'The market' has failed and the state has to step in to ensure that an essential service is available.

What constitutes market failure and therefore justifies government intervention is a subject of constant debate, discussion and conflict. And it is a political debate above all else – in spite of some economists' attempts to reduce it to a purely technical discussion (no discussion of economics can be apolitical, as we shall see later).

Those who tend towards the left of the political spectrum see more market failures and more reasons for state intervention than those who tend towards the right. Here, it is not my intention to enter that particular debate as it is largely insoluble on any logical grounds. It is a debate grounded in ideology and moral frameworks, where perfectly reasonable people with different societal perspectives can reasonably disagree. What is, however, worth bearing in mind is that if we accept the idea that all markets are constructed markets, then the first question that should be explored when markets fail is whether this can be remedied through reconstructing the market in a different way. Only if that proves impossible given the political and societal objectives, should we move towards actual state participation in the market itself.

The financing of healthcare is maybe one of the most prominent areas of debate. In the US, the bias is towards a market system where insurance companies compete to provide healthcare financing. While market failure is recognized through programmes such as Medicare and Medicaid, the prevalent philosophy has been that market-based competition is the best overall approach.

In Europe and many other countries, healthcare is considered an essential service where it is unacceptable to have anyone fall through the cracks – as still happens in the US in spite of the safety nets. The view is that healthcare financing has to be somehow underwritten by the state and, in some countries, there is also the belief that healthcare delivery should also be primarily the role of the state as it is unreasonable to divert scant resources away from healthcare provision towards shareholder returns.

There is also an economic argument for state financing, if not necessarily delivery, of healthcare. If we see healthcare financing as an insurance product – we pay in to insure ourselves when we get ill – then we know that insurance works best when the risks can be spread across the widest possible group of insured persons. The whole national population is the largest practicable pool of insured people, making a national health service as exists, for instance, in the UK, the most economically efficient insurance model. Except, of course, for the absence of competition.

There is nothing to stop or discourage smaller insurance pools to exist alongside the national pool for those who would like to buy additional insurance. In some respects, it is to be welcomed as it decreases the burden on the national scheme. Others, however, worry about the privileges this confers on those who can afford to take out supplementary insurance. These are ideological, and therefore political, questions, not economic or business ones.

What balance is to be found, and how, between public sector provision and the workings of private markets is a societal and therefore a political choice. There is no single 'right answer'. Those who lean left would extend state involvement to many areas from the provision of clean water to retail banking, to public transport, to funding blue-sky innovation, to areas of market failure that they might define more broadly than others. Others with different political beliefs argue that private sector, market-based competition is the best route to progress, that market failures requiring government intervention are few and far between, and that overweening state involvement results in stagnation, removal of incentives to innovation and, eventually, a corrupt system based on political favouritism – as we have seen above. Political capitalism argues that we have to move away from this sterile either/or debate and accept that both have legitimate roles to play.

Another area where this debate comes to life is in how to tackle unemployment. Those who remain wedded to the Phillips curve – the supposed inverse relationship between unemployment and the inflation rate – believe that there is some kind of natural rate of unemployment that is necessary to maintain price stability, i.e. prevent inflation. Modern Monetary Theorists, on the other hand, believe that government should act as an employer of last resort, offering employment to anyone who wants it and that this can be done without stoking inflation or crowding out the private sector. The argument is that unemployment is both socially corrosive and economically inefficient.

Yet, befuddled thinking has led us to a position where governments would rather spend money on welfare payments to keep people unemployed than to employ them, release their productive capacity, give them the dignity and self-respect that comes with meaningful work, and keep them employable by the private sector when such opportunities arise. It's a tussle between those who see any level of unemployment as a sign of market failure and those who see a degree of unemployment as a necessary part of a functioning labour market. And between those who see state employment for the otherwise unemployed as a societal good and those who see it as competition that crowds out business opportunity and, maybe, pushes up wages.

This was the position of J.M. Keynes: '*The belief that there is some law of nature which prevents men from being employed is the sort of thing which no man could believe who had not had his head fuddled with nonsense for years and years.*'[8]

While an effective mixed economy clearly needs both private and public sectors, the preferred arrangement is a subject of constant tension in market-based democracies – and so it should be. Perspectives change, experience teaches us new things every day, societal priorities and political views change over time. The objective should never be to find 'the answer' but rather to make sure that there is constant, open-minded discussion and contestation. A market in opinion and ideas, if you like.

But we should at least try to be honest with ourselves.

My wife, Astrid, is a conservation biologist. While running a programme in the American West that required her to approach ranchers for collaboration, she was told that she had to remove all federal government markings from her vehicle before going on to private land. Otherwise she risked being shot at by the cowboys (literally, not figuratively) who owned the land and hated anything to do with the federal government. Yet these same ranchers happily cash their monthly cheques for government subsidies.

If ever we wanted illustrations of such dual standards writ large, we only have to look back as far as the 2008 financial crash. Extreme mismanagement, widespread unethical practices and deeply embedded conflicts of interest within a financial services industry that purportedly believes in free and fair markets brought the financial system to its knees. The government had to intervene to stop the system from crashing. Yet few of the free-market ideologues among the companies at risk balked at taking government money.

Just like the cowboys.

Such government intervention was unavoidable, but not without its risks. For some, the message was clear – take your risks and enjoy the upside safe in the knowledge that when things go wrong, governments will bail you out. Such moral hazard undermines markets and, if a market system was to be preserved, it was imperative that new regulations be introduced to minimize the chances of it happening again. The rules of the game needed to be changed, the market needed to be restructured because we had tangible evidence of market failure.

Some would have gone much further, arguing the crash was all the proof needed that the market could never work, thereby justifying a much deeper, more systemic, permanent role for government in the game itself rather than just in changing the rules.

My intention here is not to argue for one or the other perspective but simply to point out that such decisions are purely political in nature. Not only are markets politically constructed, as we have seen. The extent to which they exist, the relative balance between public initiatives and private enterprises, where and how risk is managed – all these and many other aspects of market economies are based on values, beliefs and decisions that are purely political.

IS IT ALL ABOUT POWER?

This chapter has, I hope, convinced some that the very idea of a market-based economy is a political notion. Some believe in it, others do not.

For anyone, it should be obvious that the shape, nature and limits of markets are themselves political constructs. Constructs that, in vibrant democracies, are rightly subject to constant change and endless contestation. No stable equilibrium is possible. As academic and private equity executive Bill Janeway put it to me,[9] it's like the three-body problem in physics – a constantly dynamic situation for which no closed-form solution exists, resulting in a state of constant flux. In that context, the relationship between commercial activity and politics can also be understood as a constantly dynamic situation.

In feudal times, power lay in the hands of the aristocracy and the landed gentry. Before that, in the divine rights of kings and religious leaders. During the Dutch Golden Age, power in Amsterdam, then the centre of global commerce, lay largely in the hands of a relatively small number of highly socially conscious wealthy traders guided by the Dutch Polder Model.[§] During the Industrial Revolution, power lay with industrialists, many of whom felt that they were discharging their civic duties through paternalism and philanthropy. Authoritarian regimes believe in their right to absolute power. Plutocracies are founded on the belief that power derives exclusively from wealth. Oligarchies concentrate power in few hands – whether those few are defined by wealth, military power, closeness to the leadership, or whatever.

Democracy, a relatively new concept, is founded on the principle that power must ultimately rest with the people as a whole and be exercised through their elected representatives. That is democratic politics. Of course, democracy is neither a pure nor a perfect concept. It is a practice rather than a system subject to detailed codification. The wealthy still exercise more power than the poor. Business, civil society groups, trade unions, public intellectuals, etc. all exercise power and influence. The essence of a functioning democracy is not stable perfection but rather the ability to maintain perpetual flux through constant contestation and a fluid, self-correcting balance of power. When one group gets too powerful – whether through market monopoly or disproportionate political influence – there need to be mechanisms to curtail its power – like the breakup of Standard Oil in 1911. If such flux were to stop, democracy would wither away.

Democracy is not all about power, it's also about building appropriate governance structures to translate electoral politics into what happens

---

§The name derives from the polder – the tract of land enclosed by dykes – which required management through shared responsibility and broad consensus if flooding that would end up damaging everyone was to be avoided.

on the ground. Electoral politics is highly imperfect in dealing with a plethora of specific market arrangements and policy questions. It often works better when elected politicians define clear principles (giving them less incentives to act corruptly) and other actors – regulatory agencies, civil society groups, consultations between labour and capital – define specific compromises and solutions. This is complex and cumbersome, which explains to a significant extent why the transition to a functioning democracy has proved so difficult in so many countries. It's not enough to have elections and give power to elected representatives. A whole panoply of institutions with clear responsibilities and effective checks and balances has to be built for democracy to function. It's a mammoth task. And those of us, including business leaders, who are fortunate enough to live in democracies should always keep in mind its fragile nature, avoid complacency, and be wary of doing stuff that undermines that delicate edifice.

It is through these complex and delicate mechanisms and institutions that society defines what business should be for. That politics defines markets and how they operate. That government uses its democratically legitimated powers to define, construct, regulate and otherwise intervene in markets – directly or through democratically legitimized institutions. That it provides public goods that commercial markets cannot properly provide. All done (hopefully) in a healthy atmosphere of endless and unresolvable political debate, deliberation and dispute. There is no statement more destructive of democracy than the idea that 'there is no alternative'.

Politics and business are joined at the hip. In later chapters, I will explore how incorporating these political perspectives can help businesses thrive and be successful.

4

The Politics of Globalization

'The foundations of the globalised business world are political.'[1]
Gideon Rachman
Chief foreign affairs commentator
Financial Times

Some time ago I watched the Netflix series *Marco Polo*. It's worth watching. In one episode, Marco Polo's father and his business partner, both traders, were caught trying to smuggle silkworms out of the East, hiding them in hollow walking sticks. Export of silkworms was forbidden at the time. The Kublai Khan punished the two traders with a whipping and by banishing them from doing further trade in his kingdom. Only through the intervention of Marco Polo were their lives spared.

This episode illustrates a number of the characteristics of international trade that have always been there and persist to this day. The first is that international trade is nothing new. It's been around forever – as we shall see later. Second, the structure and limits of trade are politically determined. Third, countries have always done their best to protect their 'intellectual property' – whichever form that came in. And finally, there are always those who push what they do in international trade to the limits – and well beyond – with inevitable political consequences.

But first, we need to clarify something.

WHAT IS GLOBALIZATION?

Talk about globalization has been hijacked by economists and international trade lawyers. Their focus is on international trade and its economic consequences making discussion about globalization far too blinkered in its outlook. Globalization is primarily a socio-cultural, not an economic phenomenon. Increased communication and ease of international travel have exposed us all to cultures that once seemed remote. What was once exotic is now accessible, commonplace even. It is visible daily on the TVs in our living rooms, on YouTube and other social media, in magazines and newspapers, in advertising. In effect, it's all around us in our everyday life: the extraordinary has become ordinary.

Science has become a globalized endeavour with scientists sharing their work in person, in academic journals and building on each other's work wherever it comes from. A reality that has been brought to the fore by the globalized approach to the development of a COVID-19 vaccine – even though global agreement for its distribution was challenging. Top athletes and sports clubs have a global fan base. Roger Federer, Real Madrid, the New York Yankees – all have name recognition among hundreds of millions of people around the world. They are global brands as much as Coca-Cola, McDonald's and BMW.

> Globalization does not necessarily equate with free trade. Odysseus, the Roman Empire generals, the Portuguese and Spanish conquistadors, the British scientific explorers, the Italian renaissance painters, the Swedish female tourists who in the 60s introduced bikinis in Franco's Spain, the Beatles ... were not traders, but they were all agents of globalization. They built on the inner wish of most individuals to expand beyond their immediate neighbourhood, to emulate what others in other parts of the world do, to rise above their cultural horizons and live in a world without constraints. Even countries whose trade is closed to the outside world cannot isolate their populations from the cultural influences of people elsewhere: nowhere is this more apparent than in Iran, where, due to sanctions, trade with the rest of the world has been virtually impossible during the last 15 years. And yet a large part of its population lives in permanent awe of the 'American way of life'.[2]

As a result, we crave that which other cultures that we admire can offer us. Much trade is a consequence of the soft power exercised by different countries. People around the world flock to McDonald's restaurants and

Starbucks outlets not because of any outstanding functional qualities of their product. They are, in effect, buying a slice of 'the American way of life'.

This distinction is perhaps best encapsulated in Apple's products. With parts sourced from far and wide and final product assembled in China, Apple continues to label every product with 'Designed by Apple in California' – a cultural statement that is crucial to its outstanding brand appeal. What would happen to the Apple brand if it became associated primarily with 'Made in China' rather than 'Designed in California'?

And herein lies what is maybe China's potential miscalculation. In prematurely relying on its sharp and hard powers, China may be putting itself in a poor position. While it maintains its authoritarian regime, continues its widespread surveillance and human rights abuses, and pushes forth with its hard-nosed expansionism in violation of international law, how many people across the world are soon to be aspiring to 'the Chinese way of life' in the same way as they aspire to the American or French or British way of life? And the accumulation of soft power is political as well as cultural. It is built on, or undermined by, political choices.

Despite the challenges it has faced, America continues to be the land of opportunity – a free, open, democratic society, where the belief in success linked to one's own endeavours remains strong – irrespective of whether it is real. America still today projects the dream of living in a world without constraints. An image that will doubtlessly outlast the severe dent delivered to it by President Trump.

Similarly, we associate certain cultural beliefs, lifestyles and a certain cachet with a Made in Italy brand, or with a French luxury brand, or German engineering. Which is why in 2020, Porsche (which accounts for 40 per cent of profits of the VW group) ruled out shifting production to China: '*It's a quality and premium argument still to produce from Europe for China*', according to chief executive Oliver Blume.[3]

Politics, and political choices, affect soft power – which in turn affects the nature and shape of globalization and the appeal or otherwise of Made in X.

The increasing visibility of our interconnectedness and interdependence is another aspect of globalization. People the world over now feel they have a stake in what happens to the Brazilian

Amazon. We are all concerned about carbon emissions put out by countries other than our own. We all feel touched when species go extinct in some corner of the globe that we have never visited. We care when others' human rights are infringed somewhere on the other side of the world. And it's the same for achievements. The first landing on the moon was 'a giant leap for mankind' not just for Neil Armstrong, NASA and fellow Americans. The rapid development of COVID-19 vaccines was a triumph for all of humanity.

What went wrong?
Politically and ideologically, the big mistake made by globalists was to mistake people's natural desire to enrich their lives by looking beyond their own cultures with the belief that they were aspiring to replace their local culture with a globalist culture. This was largely driven by an internationalist elite who, like Diogenes (*see* p. 69), considered themselves citizens of the world. In this globalist culture, the nation state, and local cultures, were impediments to progress; to be looked down upon and eroded. 'Progress' was to turn us all into rational global citizens, looking beyond the parochial to the global. In other words, the richness of culture, history and specific identities were all to be subordinated to the common, plain vanilla, emotionless global culture. We were all to change from citizens with complex, deeply-rooted local identities to citizens of the world in order to benefit from globalization. And, as if by magic, all would then be well. We would all, together, be global brothers and sisters. Imagine.

This is reminiscent of aspects of colonialism. When Europeans colonized the Americas, they brought with them their mainly Christian religion. Explaining their religion to the 'natives', the latter found it interesting and showed initial willingness to adopt elements of it alongside their own indigenous religions. This puzzled the colonialists. Their view was that Christianity was 'the right religion' and that it should therefore replace local religions. Sitting alongside these pagan practices would simply not do.

This replacement was eventually largely achieved – mainly through force and the shedding of much blood. However, syncretic religious practices like Haitian Voodoo also emerged through the blending of the traditional religions brought to the island of Hispaniola by enslaved West Africans and the Roman Catholic teachings of the French colonialists, who then controlled the island. Eventually the French colonial government was overthrown through revolution and modern Haiti was formed.

The same is happening with cultural globalism. As globalization transmogrified from allowing people to adopt and benefit from other cultures alongside their own to attempting to become a singular, dominant culture that undermined the nation state, people rebelled. They were unwilling to sacrifice their own cultures, traditions and units of political cohesion to the new, uniform monoculture of a plain vanilla globalism that had no cultural roots in local tradition. A cultural backlash against globalization ensued. The nation state re-emerged as the largest valid unit of political governance, as we shall see below, and we are now seeing more forceful assertions of non-globalist cultures – some of them turning violent.

Yes, everyone wants to benefit from cultural globalization. But we have forgotten that the when, the how and the how much should be matters of voluntary choice by individuals and groups, not things that are thrust down people's throats with their own cultures belittled and demeaned. That is not globalization, it is cultural colonialism. Not only does it have no future, but the many conflicts it is now causing should have been predictable had a small group of people with power not been so thoroughly convinced of the righteousness of their own ideology – much like the crusaders and religious missionaries before them.

A more realistic model comes from the supposed 'Westernization' of Japan. Fukuzawa Yukichi, a young Japanese student, was a key figure at the time: *'He exhibited a pragmatic curiosity about things and notions from the West. They might work for Japan, or they might not; they could be used or tossed away.'*[4] Like Haitian Voodoo, modern Japan is a blend of local history, culture and tradition with some ideas willingly imported from the West. The author concludes *'the idea of westernisation is a fiction produced by groups of westerners at times in the service of western domination.'* Westernization is not a truth, it is a fiction arising from Western arrogance. Much as some notions of what 'globalization' means and its true extent are today.

Syncretism can also be seen in some former Muslim Soviet states such as Tajikistan. Wedding ceremonies merged cultures. *'Although Soviet rituals had been adopted, these did not exist as alternatives to "traditional" rituals, but as extensions.'*[5]

96   THE NEW POLITICAL CAPITALISM

Further overreach arises from the fact that the exotic has seemingly become familiar. Such familiarity may be illusory. As we are increasingly exposed to previously unfamiliar cultures, we forget that what we are seeing is mediated through, and skewed by, our own cultural perspective and the editorial lens of the various media that bring these cultures to our living rooms and electronic devices. We start to believe that we truly understand such cultures when in fact we do not. As soon becomes clear to anyone who has witnessed the frustration and exasperation on both sides when executives from corporate headquarters sit in meetings with their colleagues from far flung subsidiaries. Globalization is not what we have come to believe it is.

ABOUT INTERNATIONAL TRADE

As we saw with Marco Polo, there is nothing new about international trade. In 3000 BC the people of Mesopotamia were trading with the people of the Indus Valley in what is today Pakistan. Soon thereafter the idea of self-sufficiency, that you had to produce yourself everything that you needed or wanted, started to fade. Trade networks spread across Eurasia. Cultures and economies became linked for the first time. The domestication of camels in 1000 BC made land-based trade a viable alternative to more expensive sea routes. India became linked to the Mediterranean. New towns and cities sprang up along trading routes – land routes, seaports and rivers.

Trade was the route to prosperity for many. China prospered by selling its jade, spices and silks; Phoenicia its cedar woods and linen dyes; Britain its tin. Just like today, middlemen prospered most of all.

As economies became more complex and trading increased, so trading also became more complex and multifaceted. From the fifteenth to the eighteenth centuries, international trade morphed into mercantilism – the belief that a country could only prosper if it had a positive trade balance with other countries and thereby accumulate monetary reserves. Tariffs and other anti-trade measures grew as countries sought to maintain the upper hand as trade morphed from a general convenience to competition between nations.

Further liberalization came in the eighteenth and nineteenth centuries following the ideas of economists Adam Smith and David Ricardo. The idea of comparative advantage suggested that countries should only focus on doing that which they are good at – that which they can produce at lower opportunity cost – and trade with others for the remaining goods. This was the start of what today we might call de-industrialization.

Countries would start to shed skills and production and give up markets to those that were considered to have a comparative advantage. For many countries, the net result was a loss of skills built up over centuries and which could not easily be rebuilt as the nature of supposed comparative advantage between nations changed over time. For many, the long-term effect was hugely damaging.

Apart from de-industrialization, a gap in the theory of comparative advantage lay in its sectoral focus. Ricardo famously used cloth and wine to describe the comparative advantages of England and Portugal. But what was lacking was what today we would describe as the systems approach or complexity science. A country shedding one industrial sector would lose skills, capabilities and connections that also fed other industrial sectors. It was a siloed mindset for what are complex systems – a mistake we keep making to this day. But not every country followed this route. Germany, for instance, industrialized while Great Britain de-industrialized. Why?

While the UK was a trailblazer in following Smith and Ricardo and the belief in open markets and international trade, Germany came late to the party. This gave Germany some advantages. It learned from the English experience and could observe the advantages as well as the perils. Alexander Gerschenkron's 'backwardness' model of economic development suggests that not being the first mover (i.e. being 'backwards') results in the emergence of certain characteristics, including the establishment of institutions focused on mobilizing financial and human capital, a focus on manufacturing producer goods rather than consumer goods, a capital-intensive rather than a labour-intensive economy, a reliance on productivity growth rather than innovation. In addition, there is the opportunity to ride on the intellectual property developed by others – what the US and Germany did with British intellectual property in the eighteenth and nineteenth centuries and what China is doing now with Western intellectual property. According to Thorstein Veblen, '*The German people have been enabled to take up the technological heritage of the English without having paid for it in the habits of thought, the use and wont, induced in the English community by the experience involved in achieving it.*'[6]

The nineteenth century (some would say much earlier than that) also saw what has become known as the Great Divergence – large increases in prosperity in the Western world with other parts of the world such as Asia and Latin America falling far behind. This was driven by many factors, including the fact that most trade happened between Western nations.

Nevertheless, over time the development of international trade and the concept of comparative advantage led to a degree of hyper-specialization. Many developed countries focused on knowledge industries; the Middle East became the land of oil-driven economies; Asia for manufacturing; Africa for natural resource extraction. Politically, this became problematic as trade soon enough transmogrified into entrenched dependence on others and, therefore, an erosion of sovereignty combined with a political imperative not to lose access to that which only others could provide. Instead of the imagined peace that was supposed to flow from economic interdependence, we got conflict due to over-dependence. Would we have had so many wars in the Middle East had it not become the world's primary source of energy? Would we today be suffering from our collective paranoia, had China not been allowed to accumulate control over most of the rare earths used in every one of our electronic devices? Would some African states be in seemingly endless conflict and endemic corruption had they not become the source of natural resources that everyone is fighting over?

Soon enough the fundamental problem was no longer the ability to trade. A new monster had been born: monopoly power. Once again, international trade provided one part of the solution. In the UK, in 1846, Sir Robert Peel, following Richard Cobden, joined the Whigs and the Radicals to repeal the Corn Laws in an assault on the monopoly power of the land-owning aristocracy who wanted to keep food prices high and supply limited even in the face of people dying of famine. It was a vindication of Adam Smith's original warning that collusion between entrenched interests ends in 'a conspiracy against the public'.

The new free trade was designed as a means of liberation from the Frankenstein born to the free trade system that had gone before – monopoly power. The clear objective of the new trade liberalization was to make sure that the small could challenge the big, the poor could challenge the rich with the power of the new approach, the alternative provider, the imaginative, liberating shift. It was a liberal project in the true sense of nineteenth-century classical English liberalism.

Trade has since oscillated constantly between openness and withdrawal, with nobody being comfortable for long with either. The early twentieth century showed further moves towards liberalization. The First World War changed that course with countries building barriers to trade. But post-war liberalization was short-lived. The Great Depression of the 1920s saw a return to tariffs and other barriers.

The complexity of modern economies also meant that trade agreements became increasingly convoluted. There was also a desire to create a framework through which the larger and more powerful nations would not always be in a position to subjugate the weaker ones – the nation-level equivalent of monopoly power.

Multilateral Trade Agreements were born. The General Agreement on Tariffs and Trade in 1947 laid the ground for the trade system that we have today and the evolution from nation-level agreements to multilateral agreements within and between trading blocks. Of course, the post-war trade and investment agreements remained highly political in nature. Those with more power were able to craft them to their own advantage, creating increasing tensions as the locus of power shifted with time and newly emerging economic powers felt disadvantaged.

Now, yet again, international trade risks becoming an incubator of monopoly power particularly, though not exclusively, in the tech-enabled world. Many complain that trade agreements have morphed into arrangements favouring producer interests rather than the interests of citizens. A new reckoning is likely to be in store.

There are important lessons to be learnt from even such a cursory glance at the history of international trade. Lessons we would do well to take to heart today.

The first is that international trade is, and always has been, a dance between competition and co-operation – much as we see in complex adaptive natural systems. It's a delicate dance and the steps change as the music changes over time. Trade has never been an end in itself. It should be considered a tool of foreign and domestic policy. In other words, trade is primarily political. The over-riding questions for any government should be: how does international trade affect the social, political and economic structures of our country, and how does trade, and the shape of our trade agreements, fit with our foreign policy goals?

The second is that trade has always been shaped by the nature of political power. Through colonialism and military force, through US hegemony for much of the twentieth century, through the internal politics of individual countries where business influenced politics to entrench their interests – opening up when it suited them, building protectionist barriers when it safeguarded their interests.

Third, the structure and approach to trade has never been stable. It has always oscillated and changed depending on the political and economic conditions of the day. Countries grew *'familiar to the fact that the old schools of thought were no longer going to be practical and that they had to keep reviewing their international trade policies on continuous basis.'* At the time of writing, we are in the midst of another of these great changes.

Finally, trade has always brought both benefits and disadvantages. Over time, trade structures resulted in prosperity for some, suffering for others. Those who accumulated advantages became ever wealthier and more powerful. Eventually their power had to be broken by firm and decisive political intervention.

THE WORLD OF GEO-ECONOMICS

Business talk has a particular penchant for hyping win-win-win solutions. By and large, this is self-delusion. Globalization and international trade, like all political actions, creates winners and losers. While complicated economic models tout the macroeconomic benefits of international trade, they tend to ignore the fact that such benefits are very unevenly distributed at the micro level. Some people gain, others lose out – as I shall explore later.

Even the macroeconomic benefits are subject to debate. A friend relates the story of an economist working for the Canadian government who resigned his post because he was tired of being asked to do and re-do his models so that he could squeeze an economic benefit out of the latest proposed trade agreement. As is so often the case even in business, decisions are made on political grounds and economic models are then constructed to support these decisions.

For those who might find this disturbing, it is merely a reflection of real life – whether at individual or institutional level. We mostly make decisions intuitively based on many factors, conscious and subconscious. We then rationalize those decisions and justify them to others, using what are inevitably reductionist numerate analyses – because no amount of modelling, however sophisticated, can possibly reflect the complexity of the real world or how it will change in the future.

It is no different in politics. As outlined earlier, decisions to strike international trade agreements are political ones that need to balance a number of factors. The justification is then reduced to simple (and often simplistic) economics. And companies cannot avoid but to get caught up in what Professor Edward Luttwak in a 1990 article labelled 'geo-economics' – the interplay of international economics, geopolitics and strategy.[7] Or, in Luttwak's words, *'the admixture of the logic of conflict with the methods of commerce – or, as Clausewitz would have put it, the logic of war in the grammar of commerce.'*

Relations with China are, of course, today's poster child of the world of geo-economics. China attempts to use its newly gained commercial heft to advance its geo-political objectives and, as is only to be expected from any authoritarian regime, to attempt to silence its critics. China and the West are engaged in a geo-political conflict fought, so far, through commercial means. While business may bristle at this conflict, I would argue that long may it last. The struggle for supremacy (or at least for defining respective spheres of influence) between two fundamentally different political systems always had a whiff of inevitability about it. Long may it simply be fought through commercial means rather than escalating into military confrontation.

Once again, we see the divide between political and commercial logic. Lord Hague, former British Foreign Secretary, relates:

Last autumn I listened to a group of CEOs of top US firms explaining their plans to keep expanding in China – 'you can't have global growth without a big presence in China, even if they copy our technology'. Then I had political briefings from Washington where everyone, Republican and Democrat, said: 'We can't have that any more: China is now a strategic adversary'... Major corporations are proceeding as if the world of the last 30 years is carrying on: global competition, supply chains criss-crossing China and America, new technology welcomed everywhere. It has been a world where growth, margins and interdependence had taken over from political conflict. Business executives are now confronted with the inconvenient fact that a global struggle of political ideas is back, and that it will increasingly take priority over those margins and growth.[8]

Companies cannot avoid being caught in this world of geo-economics. Those that understand and accept the *realpolitik* and plan accordingly will prosper. Those that remain trapped in their unreal world of a purely commercial logic will lag.

In 2020, China passed a security law that curtailed freedoms in the Hong Kong Special Administrative Region (SAR) in contravention of the Sino-British Declaration signed in 1984 that defined the 'one country, two systems' arrangement that was to prevail for 50 years following the handover of Hong Kong in 1997. HSBC and Standard Chartered, two UK registered international banks with a substantial business in China, were caught in a bind. They could either support the new security law putting them at odds with the UK and other Western nations, or they could come out against it and upset the Beijing regime. Political neutrality was not an option – much as though they would doubtless have liked it to be.

Both banks chose the former option.

The long-term outcome of this political choice is not yet clear. The US imposed sanctions in response to the new security law. As no international bank can possibly survive if locked out of US dollar transactions, it remains to be seen what the future holds for these banks. Neither is HSBC in Beijing's good books. Chinese state-backed media have accused the bank of 'framing' Huawei with respect to the arrest of Meng Wanzhou, the firm's chief of finance, in her arrest at Vancouver airport in 2018 – a charge the bank has denied.

And then it got worse. In June 2021 China secretly rushed through a law allowing Beijing to impose countermeasures including asset seizures on organizations and individuals that implement foreign sanctions. Corporations would, in future, find it difficult if not impossible to comply with both Chinese and Western policies. Though it is believed that these measures are intended to act as a deterrent for US government action rather than to penalize foreign investment in China, they put corporations in the eye of a political storm, and nobody knows how it will develop.

These developments highlight the very real difficulties that commercial organizations face as they navigate the world of geo-politics. Standing back and hoping it will all pass is one approach – though not a particularly reassuring or effective one. Neither is maintaining a pretend 'apolitical' stance. In giving evidence to the UK's House of

Commons Foreign Affairs Select Committee, HSBC CEO Noel Quinn stated '*It's not my position to make moral or political judgements on these matters.*' For a CEO to claim that he is not only apolitical but also amoral is quite remarkable.

When asked how his response fitted with the decision of Peter Wong, HSBC's top executive in Asia – and a member of an advisory body to the Chinese Communist Party, to sign a petition in 2020 supporting China's new powers for Hong Kong, Quinn argued that Wong was merely signing as a citizen of Hong Kong and, remarkably, claimed that signing the petition was not a political act. Absurd. A CEO caught in one of the defining geo-political issues of our time still claiming that it has nothing at all to do with him or his business.

'*Quinn can opine unconvincingly about staying out of politics, but it's really not that simple.*'[9]

To the extent that there is, at the time of writing, pressure for HSBC to split, separating its Chinese operations from its other activities since their China engagement is seen as damaging the rest of its global business. The bank is accelerating its pivot to Asia. More senior executives have been moved to Hong Kong. It has sold its 150 branch US operation and also sold its French retail business for a token €1 while taking a $3 billion hit. Contrary to Quinn's statements, one HSBC executive was quoted as saying, '*The job for [HSBC chairman] Mark Tucker is 80 per cent politics and 20 per cent business at the moment. The Chinese have the potential to destroy them.*'[10]

For corporations like HSBC and Standard Chartered, the choices faced were impossibly difficult, given that much of their profit then depended on the Chinese market. These choices are not, and can never be, independent of politics. They are the result of previous management choices to increase dependence on the China market. Both, like many other corporations, seem to have become caught up in the rush to China – the widespread misconception that China would become an integral part of a harmonious world of ever-growing, peaceful global trade and would, as a consequence, eventually democratize. It would become just like us. We all wanted to believe it so, by and large, we did. Yet, a clear and realistic understanding of geo-political dynamics would have suggested a degree of caution. Even without the benefit of hindsight, it was always clear that the China rush was surrounded by significant political uncertainty. The question is the extent to which that political uncertainty was obscured and largely ignored by managements worldwide in their pursuit of a billion new consumers, or whether it was well recognized when crucial decisions were taken.

The same dynamic played out in Myanmar. A much smaller home market but a country that attracted foreign direct investment based on low-cost production and on the hope of a transfer to democracy and increased political stability. In the year to September 2020, Japanese investment alone in Myanmar was about $768 million, ranking third after Singapore and Hong Kong.

In January 2021, a military coup overthrew the administration of Aung San Suu Kyi with an uncertain outcome. As a result: '*Foreign companies that have invested in Myanmar, hoping that the end of military rule would open up business opportunities, may be forced to reconsider their strategies in the country.*'[11]

GLOBALIZATION TWENTY-FIRST-CENTURY STYLE

There is, maybe, no greater icon of a globalized world than the Boeing 747 Jumbo Jet. In most people's imagination, *the* symbol of unfettered international travel and commerce.

In 2020, all remaining 747s were retired and Boeing announced the end of the aircraft's production. The COVID-19 pandemic was the final nail in the coffin of an energy inefficient icon that had been heading towards extinction for many years.

The 747 is a symbol of the transformation, and the retreat, of the late twentieth-century concept of a globalization without limits. A world order where 'global governance' around a set of clear international rules would supersede the Westphalian politics of nation states. International institutions – the League of Nations (later, the UN), the International Monetary Fund, the World Bank, NATO, Bretton Woods, the European Economic Community (later, the EU) – were the poster children of this new world order.

In this new world, globalization and ever-growing international trade would be an absolute positive. It would interlink economies, diminish the chances of conflict and spread prosperity around the globe. The highly educated cosmopolitan elite who benefited most from this arrangement were convinced of its unalloyed benefits. They looked down on those who resisted, seeing them as closed-minded, uneducated, parochial nationalists – part of the tribe that Hillary Clinton in the 2016 election described as 'deplorables'. But never mind. They reckoned the deplorables did not have the power to derail the project and, with the international elite thankfully in charge, the whole globe would be skilfully steered to endless peace and prosperity.

The system worked well for decades. Multinationals prospered. 'Think global, act local' became corporate speak as standardized as the Big Mac – parroted everywhere, from business schools to boardrooms. I remember it well. It was thrust down our throats at every corporate meeting – albeit without much clarity as to what it meant in practice.

As with the 747, the signs of the inevitable decline of this belief system have been evident for decades. Ignored by many, actively rejected by others for whom globalization and international trade had become a quasi-religious belief system, the political swing away from the international world order had been gathering steam well before Donald Trump, Brexit, the US-China trade conflict and the COVID-19 pandemic – all of which should be seen as having accelerated previously existing trends rather than heralding a fundamental change in direction.

After all, the Bretton Woods system collapsed, for political reasons, as long ago as 1971. Set up in 1944, it took close to 15 years to become operational only to fall apart as we hit the 1970s. Political constraints led to flaws in the original design (all human-designed systems inevitably based on political compromises are flawed – cf. the Euro) and its death knell came when key sovereign states showed themselves unwilling to follow its rules – even though the system was intended to shore up state sovereignty when the flaws of late nineteenth-century liberalization became apparent. It fell apart for exactly the same reasons that are undermining the broader globalized structures of the late twentieth century – and maybe the same reasons that risk, eventually, also corroding the European Union if it tries to move too far, too fast.

Given that the late twentieth-century model of globalization is no longer viable, what, therefore, are the political foundations that will shape what globalization will look like in the twenty-first century?

Let us start with the perspective provided by liberal economist John Maynard Keynes in his 1933 Finlay Lecture delivered in Dublin:

I sympathize, therefore, with those who would minimize, rather than with those who would maximize, economic entanglement among nations. Ideas, knowledge, science, hospitality, travel – these are the things which should of their nature be international. But let goods be homespun whenever it is reasonably and conveniently possible, and, above all, let finance be primarily national. Yet, at the same time, those who seek to disembarrass a country of its entanglements should be very slow and wary. It should not be a matter of tearing up roots but of slowly training a plant to grow in a different direction.

This goes against much of what were to become embedded beliefs by the late twentieth century. The belief that goods should be manufactured in the lowest-cost geography. The boom in international financial flows. The blatantly misguided idea that 'economic entanglement among nations' is a sure route to everlasting peace. After all, Keynes was writing this in the aftermath of the First World War – a horrendous event that was not prevented by what was, at that time, the greatest period of inter-country economic integration ever seen.

The table below puts forward some suggested comparisons between the characteristics of the late twentieth-century, post-war global order and the emergent twenty-first-century one. I then address some of these key changes in some more detail.

Late Twentieth-century Global Order	*Early Twenty-first-century Emergent Features*
1. Political	
Global free trade overseen by global governance structures. Individual countries sacrificing sovereignty for economic growth opportunities	Rise of forces that re-assert the nation state as the primary locus of democratic legitimacy. Politics' primary responsibility is to its own citizens
Politics of prosperity through the free flow of finance, goods and services	Reaction against the threat to democratic legitimacy by trans-national economic forces at the expense of citizens and their governments through arbitrage between countries in investment, jobs and taxes

Western political hegemony with liberal democracy as aspirational goal for all countries	Multiple centres of power. Liberal democracy only one of many alternative political structures. Multiple failures to replace autocratic regimes with democratic structures
Trade between large number of smaller economic players (plus a single hegemon – the US) supported a rules-based, co-operative multilateral system under US leadership	Trade agenda dominated by three major trading blocs more likely to lead to competitive rather than co-operative behaviour
National security seen as largely separate from trade	National security issues become enmeshed with trade practices

2. Cultural

Free movement of people and 'multi-culturalism'	Social cohesion fundamental to sustaining functioning societies and social solidarity
Cultural and religious co-existence	Culture wars and identity politics
Increase in global communication opens up global markets and mutual exchange	Concern over concentrated control of communications platforms, potential abuse of personal data, fake news, and cultural, political and national security impact of uncontrolled social media platforms
Consumption is king and perpetual growth the aim	Concerns on the sustainability of consumption-driven growth in a world of finite resources

3. Economic

Comparative advantage underpins global trade	Comparative advantage no longer sustainable
'Mercantilism' a dirty word	Increased concern about the impact of perpetual trade deficits
Global value chains bring down costs and increase prosperity	Local production increasingly valued. Closed Loop value chains emerging
Externalities largely ignored	Environmental and social costs of globalization becoming more difficult to ignore

The above table highlights the direction in which attitudes are changing. As always, there will be steps back and forth over time. But it is undeniable that perspectives have changed dramatically – politically, culturally and economically. Much of what is being said today would have been inconceivable 20 years ago. What has driven these changes and how will they affect the politics of globalization as we move forward?

GLOBALIZATION AND GEOPOLITICS

The structure of free trade deals is driven by the relative power of the players involved. Each party will fight for a structure that suits its own national interest. Relative power is largely a function of the size of the respective economies and their growth prospects underpinned by the ability and willingness of different nations to use their other powers.

The late twentieth century was characterized by US hegemony and multiple smaller players whose self-interest lay in co-operation and multilateralism – albeit all steered by the US and its dominant framing and support of the post-war world order. The twenty-first century, on the other hand, is characterized by the dominance of three trading blocs: the US, the EU and China, each with their spheres of influence.

It is not yet clear where Russia will end up in this new alignment. Whether its desire to be respected as a world power will lead it to strike out on its own and create yet another bloc of influence, or whether it will slowly align with one of the existing blocs.

The potential impact of the three-bloc world has long been clear. In a 1989 paper, Paul Krugman constructed a model that concluded:

> Consolidation of the world into a smaller number of trading blocs may indeed reduce welfare, even when each bloc acts to maximize the welfare of its members. Indeed, for all plausible parameter values world welfare is minimized when there are three trading blocs.[12]

This is exactly what is emerging. Global trade today is framed by competition between large trading blocs with the attendant risk that multilateralism will collapse and countries outside of these trading blocs

THE POLITICS OF GLOBALIZATION

will find themselves at permanent disadvantage. Whether this shift actually amounts to decreased 'welfare', and for whom, is debatable but let's park that discussion for the moment.

The rise of China has served to highlight these issues for Western powers. According to *The Economist*:

> [The West] bet that China would head towards democracy and the market economy. The gamble has failed.[13]

That gamble has failed politically but it has also failed in terms of the hopes for integrating China into a Western-led international trading system. It can reasonably be argued that China has proceeded down what we might call 'Free trade with Chinese characteristics': *'China is not a market economy and, on its present course, never will be. Instead, it increasingly controls business as an arm of state power.'*

China initially gained its power by being seen as providing the best source of future growth for Western businesses – businesses that ended up aiding and abetting the rise of an authoritarian geo-strategic rival power. Now China forms one of the three trading blocs and is able to gain advantageous terms of trade. It showed itself able to work the system to its advantage. China uses its leverage to force foreign companies to transfer skills and technology to local companies as the price for access to the Chinese market.

> In industries from power generation to high-speed rail and computer chips to electric cars, China has forced US, European and other foreign companies to form joint ventures or share research with local counterparts. Access to China's booming marketplace is often linked explicitly or implicitly to the foreign company's progress in transferring technology.[14]

This approach has been described as 'unfair and sometimes cynical' but it has worked – because China learned to use its powers to extract concessions from its trading partners and to coerce Western businesses to bow to its demands if they were to gain limited access to its emerging market – a compromise most businesses were willing to make, possibly without being overly concerned about the long-term geopolitical consequences of their decisions.

Since its accession to the World Trade Organization, China has, if anything, doubled down on its approach. Its 'Made in China 2025' plan unveiled in 2015 calls for widespread import substitution by domestic products and the favouring of national companies at the expense of multinationals.

No wonder the greatest beneficiaries of globalization were nations like China that eschewed the official rules and danced to the beat of their own drum. It and other Asian countries engaged the world economy but did so on their own terms: they employed trade and industrial policies prohibited by the World Trade Organization, managed their currencies, and kept tight controls on international capital flows.[15]

China's approach has generated suspicion, defensiveness and, eventually, hostility. Dr Kai-Fu Lee, Chairman and CEO of Sinovation Ventures, put it like this during a visit to the UK:

If the UK is to keep its position as a leading research hub for AI it will need increasingly to build bridges with counterparts in China. The number of hyper-engaged users and vast oceans of data mean that the market is ripe to harness the cutting-edge research happening in the UK.[16]

Today, many people reading these words are, rightly or wrongly, tempted to interpret 'building bridges' as code for the transfer of technology, know-how and intellectual property in return for limited market access that will only be allowed in close collaboration with local partners and with the ever-present long arm of the state. Western countries are now shifting their political stance with the creeping ban on Huawei 5G equipment and increasing concerns about data security being some of the more obvious examples.

Neither, argue some, is protectionism an issue limited to China. Many have accused the EU of protectionist tendencies through its inward-looking stance (you can't have full access to the single market unless you are part of the single market) and the erection of regulatory barriers.

China can, of course, argue that its approach is perfectly reasonable. It cannot maintain an economy that is successful in the long term by permanently remaining the low-cost workshop of the world. Therefore, it has to manage its trade policies to make sure that it grows skills, capabilities and industries that are internationally competitive in the future. Who can argue against that? After all, as we have seen, in earlier times America and Germany both prospered on the back of British technological know-how. Maybe what distinguishes China above all else is that it has refused to swallow, hook, line and sinker, the fable spun by neoliberal economics.

The open free trade system we know today was initially driven by the West (particularly the UK at the height of its imperial and industrial power and subsequently by the US). It is largely a Western construct. At its peak, and driven by its colonial success, the West was dominant and more technologically advanced than other countries. An open trading system therefore served it well. It was able to dominate markets. It could reasonably be argued that the system was not 'fair', it simply favoured those in charge. Yet the West either failed to recognize or simply failed to accept the finite nature of geo-political dominance. There was no adequate preparation for a changing world. The West is now reaping the consequences. The reality is that while an open trading system that it largely controlled served Western interests in the past, it may no longer do so to the same extent today. The same can be said of all other countries as the nature of comparative advantage changes.

In challenging the established order of international trade, Donald Trump may well have intuited something that seems to have passed his predecessors and his opponents by – in the new multi-polar world, the old system may no longer be serving America well. A perception that will outlast Trump's term of office.

China's approach seems to be more forward-looking. It is using the position it finds itself in today to build for a future it knows will be different. Its Belt and Road Initiative (BRI) creates a large sphere of influence funded by Chinese debt that, crucially, asks countries to sign up to dispute resolution mechanisms that are under Chinese control. Some have started to see this as debt bondage or colonization through financial rather than military means.

The West is, belatedly, scrambling to find an appropriate, co-ordinated political response to the new world. While the US has enough power and heft to take China on directly, and has done so, others remain cautious. The European Union struggles to find a consensus position.

Some of its members, like Germany, are torn between seeing China as a strategic adversary and protecting it as an export market on which it has allowed itself to become dependent – with political consequences. The German presidency of the EU chose to push through an in-principle trade deal with China a mere three weeks before the inauguration of President Biden rather than waiting to co-ordinate with the incoming administration. The European Parliament subsequently failed to ratify the proposed agreement – more evidence of growing political barriers to unfettered international trade.

Other EU member states such as Italy and Greece have signed up to the Belt and Road initiative and have welcomed Chinese investment and financing of infrastructure projects – financing they may have had difficulty obtaining elsewhere.

Germany faces a dilemma with Russia, with which it has built the Nord-Stream 2 oil pipeline, much to the chagrin of the US and some Eastern European countries that argue that it is foolish for Europe to increase its energy dependence on a political rival.

With the US taking the lead and some others like Australia also standing up to Chinese pressure, a loose consensus seems to be emerging in the West, with China's role as a geo-political rival starting to gain a profile as much as China as market. Sanctions, 'entity lists' with restrictions on Chinese investments and cutting off access to Western technologies are all gaining pace – albeit so far mainly US-driven. China has recognized these dangers and is taking steps to mitigate them. At the 2017 World Economic Forum conference, President Xi presented the international trading model from which it benefited as an inevitability: '*The global economy is the big ocean that you cannot escape from.*' By early 2021, the new China buzzword had become 'dual circulation' – a concept that stresses the need for boosting its home-grown capabilities and a thriving economy based on its domestic market concurrently with its international entanglements that are becoming more fraught.

The G7 nations are trying to catch up. At their summit in Cornwall, England, in June 2021, they agreed a 'green belt and road' initiative to counter China's. '*We will develop a new partnership to build back better for the world, through a step change in our approach to investment for infrastructure, including through an initiative for clean and green growth.*'[17] They embarked on their own COVID-19 vaccine diplomacy with promises to finance vaccine distribution to less wealthy countries. It remains to be seen how much of this will materialize and whether the desire for a unified front will be sufficient to overcome divergent interests. Many emerging economies continue to feel disadvantaged as the multilateral system creaks and no longer reflects the realities of today's world. They do not feel they have a sufficient voice in global governance institutions that *'have had trouble adapting to the rise of the emerging economies: the United States and Europe still dominate them, eroding their credibility and influence among developing countries, especially in Asia.'*[18] Western countries, on the other hand, have started to feel that such institutions, besides being neither democratically legitimate nor properly accountable, can no longer serve their interests in a changing world. Yes, the West continues to dominate these institutions, but that is insufficient to stem the tide of power flowing from West to East.

Impact on innovation
A further issue has also been raised. The idea that global trade, while encouraging innovation through the sharing of know-how and ideas, can also in some instances become a substitute for innovation.

If corporations in developed nations can sustain revenue and profit growth by exporting their existing, obsolescent products, it decreases the pressure to seek out innovations for their more mature domestic markets. Maybe one of the better-known examples is the 1970s controversy of Nestlé marketing its infant formula products in developing countries leading to the publication of a 1974 book titled *The Baby Killer.* Nestlé compounded the damage to its reputation by having sales reps dressed as nurses selling a product believed to be harmful. Since then, Nestlé has made much progress as acknowledged by the author of *The Baby Killer*[19] and, responding to evolving social norms, is now pushing to be at the leading edge of producing 'healthier' foods.

Today, car manufacturers faced with curbs on the sale of fossil fuel-powered cars in developed countries, strive to increase their exports to less regulated markets. Tobacco companies long relied on developing markets for growth before they eventually tried to innovate with smoke-free alternatives.

Globalization also provides a shield from necessary innovation in production processes. For instance, companies faced with stricter rules on carbon emissions and other environmental damage have shifted production to jurisdictions where regulations are more forgiving.

Rather than investing to develop less-damaging production processes, we are instead exporting our environmental damage even as we are all affected by its consequences – wherever the damage is done. We might be able to export our damaging processes, but we are not able to avoid re-importing their consequences.

GLOBALIZATION AND DEMOCRACY

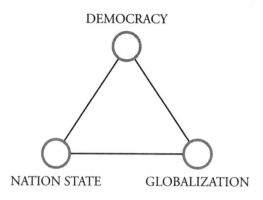

It has finally dawned on many that free trade involves some loss of sovereignty for nation states. Pooling of decision-making across countries is inevitable if trade is to flow. Free trade agreements *'reach well beyond national borders and seek deep integration among nations rather than shallow integration'.*[20]

Harvard professor Dani Rodrik argues that democracy, globalization and the sovereignty of nation states are mutually incompatible.[21] We can imagine them as three rings held together with relatively inelastic string. The more one pulls on one or the other, the more the others have to give. Rodrik argues that globalization may have gone too far at the expense of democratic accountability that rests primarily with the nation state.

This was not an issue in the post-war world. Then the focus was on a US-led economic recovery from the devastation of war and the desire to use trade to bind nations together and, it was thought, prevent further conflict. The failure of the huge rise in international trade at the turn of the previous century in preventing the First World War seems to have been forgotten. Yet, the post-war international trade structure was aligned with the prevailing foreign policy environment where, except for the Soviet Union, by and large, co-operation was preferred to confrontation and all was done under the umbrella of US leadership.

Post-1945, sovereignty and national and cultural identity were not top of people's minds. In a post-war world, national and sub-national identities were considered a hindrance to progress and, more locally, identity was equated with class wars, religious intolerance, ghettoization and all manner of other evils. Scarred by a world war, the powerful nation state was seen by some as the enemy of peace.

Sovereignty would be shared or pooled – even though nobody quite knew how this was to be successfully achieved without destroying social cohesion. Neither did anyone bother to seek popular consent. It was an elite decision believed to be for the greater good.

The end of the Cold War further embedded Western complacency and, some would say, hubris. The much-heralded 'peace dividend' was largely frittered away. The West had won the battle of ideas. It was the end of history. An economically integrated, globalized world based on the inevitable spread of democratic values would seal the dominance of Western ideals and Western hegemony. We could now afford to de-militarize much as we had already de-industrialized. The new cultural colonialism was to be spearheaded by the relentless spread of global brands and high streets and shopping malls that would be identical the world over.

All this has changed. The backlash against the perceived erosion of local culture and identity as a consequence of globalization has been one of the drivers of a re-emergence of the nation state or sub-national political units as the loci of perceived democratic legitimacy. Combined with the increased realization that trade involves, to a greater or lesser degree, a loss of sovereignty and an erosion of democratic accountability, the current pull is back towards a greater prioritization of national (and maybe regional) over supra-national and trans-national interests.

A Europe recovering from the ravages of war pushed post-war thinking further than most: '*The countries of Western Europe must turn their national efforts into a truly European effort. This will be possible only through a federation of the West.*'[22] That was Jean Monnet's thinking at the time.

On that road, the European Coal and Steel Community eventually evolved into today's European Union and the Single European Market – a construct where, today, harmonization has been pushed to levels that are, in some cases, greater than those seen, for instance, between the provinces in Canada or different states in the US. And where, in Europe, the cradle of democracy, the euphemistically named 'democratic deficit' was accepted by the ruling class as the price to be paid for greater integration (despite the rhetoric, few of those who gain power by democratic means continue to believe that they should themselves remain fully democratically accountable).

Monnet was a technocrat and recognized that Europe was unlikely to integrate if the project was to seek popular consent at every step. The erosion of national sovereignty would have to be done by stealth and the European project would be '*forged in crisis*' – each crisis numbing the population sufficiently to provide the opportunity for pushing through further integration technocratically.

Yet, the backlash described above has not passed Europe by. Brexit and the growing rebellions against 'Brussels rule' in a number of other EU countries, including increasingly frequent challenges to European monetary integration in the German constitutional court, risk causing destabilization. A destabilization that will get worse if the EU pushes its project too far too fast and attempts to airbrush away centuries of local culture, customs, belief systems and sense of identity.

What all this shows is that we have belatedly recognized that an excess of globalized thinking has fractured the concept of a political economy. While political legitimacy remains primarily embedded in the nation state or sub-national units, economics and finance have become trans-national, putting them beyond democratic accountability. This has caused tensions that are resulting in cracks and fissures ever more difficult to paper over.

Some have long fantasized about a world that is apolitical; a world governed solely by commercial logic; where a web of economic interrelationships governed the globe; where economic entities would compete and co-operate solely on the basis of commercial logic and without any constraints related to political frontiers.

But …

Things are not quite that simple. The international scene is still primarily occupied by states and blocs of states that extract revenues, regulate economic as well as other activities for various purposes, pay out benefits, offer services, provide infrastructures, and – of increasing importance – finance or otherwise sponsor the development of new technologies and new products. As territorial entities, spatially rather than functionally defined, states cannot follow a commercial logic that would ignore their own boundaries.[23]

The result of the tensions between rising economic interdependence and national political legitimacy has not been, as some imagined, the erosion of the political importance of the nation state in favour of a world that runs on a purely commercial logic. Instead, it has meant the increasing use of economic and commercial tools as weapons in the political relationship between states and blocs.

Transnational industries have, by their behaviours, contributed to this trend. By constantly playing off one state against the other to extract political concessions in return for making investments, they have fuelled and normalized the idea of political conflict by economic means. They should not be surprised when they end up caught in the crossfire.

In 1995, sociologist Ralf Dahrendorf argued that globalization demanded that states ended up having to make 'perverse choices'. He suggested that to remain competitive in international markets, countries had to make policy choices that threatened social cohesion and political freedom.[24] How does this happen?

GLOBALIZATION AND EQUITY

Two things are now widely accepted about the effects of globalized trade as practised with a twentieth-century mentality. The first is that trade has probably increased the size of the economic pie. The second is that those gains have been unevenly spread.

An analysis by Christoph Lakner and Branko Milanovic for the World Bank[25] examined the evolution of global interpersonal income inequality between 1988 and 2008. '*In many respects, this might have been the most globalized period ever in history,*' according to the authors. They conclude that, in terms of reducing inequality, 90 per cent of the gains accrued to Asian economies, with China the biggest beneficiary of free trade. On the other hand, '*almost 90 per cent of the worst performers are from mature economies*'. The other winners have been '*the global one per cent*', i.e. the wealthiest 1 per cent of the global population. The poorest countries fell furthest behind everyone else. In much of Africa, wealth actually fell.

The chart below shows the net effect. Inequality between nations has decreased while inequality within nations has tended to increase. In short, the gains from globalized trade have been asymmetric. The prosperity of the average citizen in the developed world has regressed relative to their counterpart in some of the emerging economies and, particularly, relative to the top 1 per cent of earners in their own country. It is no consolation to the decades-long unemployed in de-industrialized areas that citizens in other areas of the country have seen accruing benefits. It is inevitable that, as such distributional issues continued to grow, they would eventually lead to a political backlash.

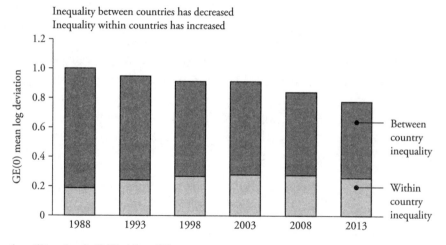

Source: *Taking on Inequality. World Bank Group, 2016.*

Lakner and Milanovic also constructed the now-infamous Elephant Chart (*see* below). It shows that, over the period examined, the poor and the upper middle classes have been the greatest relative losers in terms of income growth.

According to the IMF, World Bank and World Trade Organization:

Adjustment to trade can bring a human and economic downside that is frequently concentrated, sometimes harsh, and has too often become prolonged.[26]

... as so many people who have been displaced and whose employment prospects have disappeared as a direct result of globalization have known for many decades before the global governance institutions finally got around to noticing these people and acknowledging the problem.

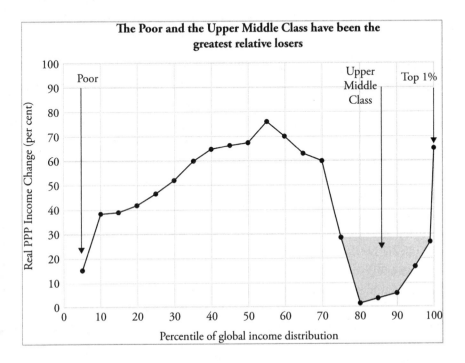

Of course, increased international trade is not the only thing that has been going on during the period examined by Lakner and Milanovic. We have seen the collapse of the Soviet Union, the rise of China (mainly on the back of trade), widely variable domestic policy choices in different countries, the rise of new technologies, and increased financialization of our economies. It is therefore unreasonable to draw a straight-line cause and effect relationship between globalized trade and the evolution of the spread of income and wealth.

A report by Adam Corlett for the Resolution Foundation[27] deconstructs the Elephant Chart and re-analyzes some of the underlying data. Corlett shows that globally aggregated data over long periods inevitably hides wide variations between countries as well as uneven shifts in population and changing country selections over time. The report suggests that:

> While global trends are likely to have played a structural role in driving lower income growth for some groups and higher growth for others, it is clearly only one factor among many, and the distribution of gains is susceptible to domestic policy choices as much as global pressures.

Such distributional asymmetries were, in fact, predicted by the Stolper-Samuelson model as far back as 1941. In the 1990s many economists assessed these impacts using this and other models. The general conclusion was that trade would have a wage-depressing effect on less-educated workers in developed countries. But, at the time, these effects were modest. What economists failed to do was to project the size of that effect as trade increased – as it did in the 1990s and beyond. Because the analyses were based on empirical data, and therefore by necessity backward-looking, they lulled everyone into a false sense of security. The major disruptive effects were yet to materialize and were not visible by looking in the rear-view mirror.

Some highly educated, well-paid workers may be tempted to believe that they are, and will remain, shielded. Not so.

The COVID-19 pandemic has led to an increased prevalence of home working. Some corporations have decided to make this permanent. Many highly skilled people, for instance in the technology industry, have decided to escape the dreadful commutes and eye-watering cost of living in San Francisco and the Bay Area by moving as far as Wisconsin and North Carolina while still keeping their job – albeit at slightly reduced salaries. What these people should be asking themselves is, if I can do the job in California from Wisconsin, why can't someone do it from India? Are highly skilled workers going to become victims of the commercial rather than the political logic of globalization in the same way as blue-collar workers were a few decades ago? And, if so, how do they feel about that? And what will be the political implications?

Which brings us to the question of 'domestic policy choices' and the role of business.

As the IMF, the World Bank and the WTO point out, technology replacement of jobs has been a significant contributor to the dislocations and asymmetric gains that we are seeing. They argue for domestic policies that compensate those considered 'losers' via re-distribution through the social security system as well as better preparation for the dislocations caused by the open trading system. But it's not as though countries have been idle in their domestic policies. The figure below shows the impact of re-distribution policies on the Gini Coefficient (so far considered the best measure of inequality) in a number of countries. We can see that governments have been active and redistributive policies have already had a meaningful impact, but it is not enough.

Inequality of incomes before and after redistribution

Source: OECD. Visualization adapted from ourworldindata.org

Apart from re-distribution, re-training and lifelong training programmes to make workers more flexible and continually employable as the nature of work changes must also be an integral part of any country's system in a fast-moving world of work. This does not come as news to anyone but there is scant evidence that such programmes can, in practice, be effective on any significant scale – especially in larger economies. The rust belts of previously industrialized economies still remain, by and large, economic deserts decades later.

Such programmes are always likely to be too small to have much effect. They are conceptually very difficult to design, let alone implement; and far from contributing to the political acceptance of globalization, they may well simply perpetuate an unduly pessimistic view of its effects.[28]

Which is why Hillary Clinton was met with stares of incredulity when, during her presidential campaign, she promised threatened industrial workers that all would be well because she would implement a massive retraining programme. As one friend put it to me, '*She's trying to make them believe that people who have been mining underground for the last 30 years are all going to be magically converted to Google engineers.*'

And even those Google engineers may soon be in India.

As Sir Paul Collier puts it: '*the cheery [economic] models show only potential. Moving from potential to realization depends upon public policies that the models finesse.*'[29]

It is also somewhat ironic that the institutional bastions of neoliberal economics are now arguing for increased government involvement through re-distribution and other government-financed support programmes. But in the globalized world under the current rules, this risks simply becoming a downward spiral.

As governments increase their intervention through fiscal means, corporations and capital flee to lower tax jurisdictions, tax arbitrage increases, the bond markets demand higher yields on government debt, government coffers are increasingly squeezed and on it goes. Safety nets are necessary, but they may be neither a viable nor a desirable long-term solution. People want the dignity and satisfaction offered by decent and decently paid work. Few relish the prospect of being converted to wards of the state. The proposed combination of unfettered globalization, with its now undoubted distributional consequences and compensatory domestic policies has, so far, proved to be no more than illusory.

We may all point to the few exceptions, such as Denmark, that have, for now, managed to find a better balance than others. But it would be hopeful to say the least, if we all simply pinned our hopes for adjustment on the idea that much of the world can successfully imitate the Danish model – a small, innovative, highly educated, well-organized country with high levels of social cohesion, little or no corruption to speak of and a model of social democracy that has been refined over many decades. Some also believe that even the finely honed Scandinavian social democratic model is starting to look shaky.

What is quite remarkable is that, still today, many still mechanically trot out the same old line that globalized trade produces a net benefit. It's as though in the world of mathematical economics and commercial logic dissociated from the social and political realities of life, as long as the final single number is positive, it doesn't much matter what else is happening around it. Even today, as various bodies calculate the potential impact of increased tariffs, we are regaled with net impact on trade and GDP with the distributional impact only referred to in ideologically laden assertions that anything that interferes with trade must be all bad rather than any serious analysis of alternative options.

Let us accept that the single figure net benefit does matter. After all, geo-political power is, at least in significant part, a function of how many resources you control and the extent to which others depend on you. Which raises the question – is the net benefit positive enough to justify the disruption? In other words, are we paying too high a social and political price for the amount of net increase in economic activity (it is plain wrong to keep calling it 'welfare') that accrues from globalized trade?

Maybe the best answer to that question has been provided in analyses of the impact of the North American Free Trade Agreement (NAFTA) in the United States. A multi-sector, multi-country analysis concludes that NAFTA increased US 'welfare' by 0.08 per cent.[30] But half of this gain did not come from an increase in efficiency but from the US being able to use its muscle to improve its terms of trade (achieved at the expense of other countries, mainly Mexico).

Analysis of the distributional impacts of NAFTA shows very sharp adverse effects for certain groups of workers. For instance, high school dropouts working in industries that were heavily protected by tariffs on Mexican exports prior to NAFTA experienced a fall in wage growth of as much as 17 percentage points relative to wage growth in unaffected industries.[31]

So now it's worth asking some questions. Is a gain of less than a tenth of 1 per cent in economic activity worth the social displacements? Has it been a sufficient gain to make us comfortable with the now-obvious political consequences of these disruptions? If we continue down this path, what further social and political consequences may we fuel?

That globalization has a *structural role in driving lower income growth for some groups and higher growth for others*, to use Corlett's words, is now beyond dispute. If we are to work towards better outcomes, it is time that we moved past the Punch and Judy show, where the opponents of globalization blame trade as the source of all evil and refuse to do the hard work to reform; while proponents sit back and, with an attitude of unchallengeable superiority, try to shift all the burden for adjustment on to domestic policy. International trade policy and domestic policy both need to evolve in tandem, not each one pulling in opposite directions. How they do this is primarily a political question, not a commercial one. Commerce will need to adapt to the political imperatives.

There is a further question to be considered. In mercantilist framing, power accumulated to export oriented economies where a positive trade balance allowed them to accumulate wealth and therefore power. Does that still hold among today's developed and large economies? Are exporters in a position of power, or are they putting themselves in a position of relative weakness where others might use their purchasing power for political ends? For instance, Australia's China policy is made more difficult because of its export dependency on the new Asian power. It is possible that in a twenty-first-century world it is not trade in itself but rather over-dependence on potential geo-political rivals that could become increasingly problematic. Germany, as we have seen, is dependent on the China export market and is making itself dependent on Russia for access to natural gas. Both strategic dependencies that may constrain its foreign policy options – and maybe those of the whole of the EU.

Some recognize this changing world. In 2021, New Zealand's foreign minister Nanaia Mahuta warned exporters that they needed to diversify. Over-dependence on China as an export market was too risky given the chances of increased geopolitical tensions.

Some argue that the period of hyperglobalization is now over. The distributional effects and the consequent social disruption have already played out and cannot be reversed. There is therefore no longer any imperative to act seeing as the horse has bolted.[32] This argument has two major flaws. The first is that it depends on a level of certainty about future developments that cannot possibly exist. What makes us think that economists' predictions of what will happen over the next decades will be any more reliable than their failures to predict the developments of the 1990s?

The second is that it ignores the politics that have arisen around the disruption caused by globalization. Failure to act is not a viable political option. Being seen to act, on the other hand, leads to potential gains over the electoral cycle, irrespective of the largely unknowable longer-term consequences.

Finally, the COVID-19 pandemic has brought us all face to face with both the strengths and the weaknesses that we have built into the system. From the lightning spread of infection across the world driven by mass international travel to the immediate collapse of international co-operation in obtaining and distributing crucial equipment, to the quite understandable national focus on access to vaccines, it gave us a different perspective on globalization. It made us realize that, for all the grandiose talk of global governance over the last 70 years, in the end, politics is primarily local and national – and likely to remain so within any time horizon that it is credible to talk about.

Conversely, the remarkably rapid development of multiple vaccines and the manufacturing of billions of doses for distribution would simply have been impossible in a world where scientific knowledge was not widely shared across borders and where there were not the international supply chains necessary for the various components necessary for vaccine manufacturing.

In spite of initial fears and hiccups, some transnational supply chains held up reasonably well during the pandemic. Food still reached our supermarkets, we could still order much of what we wanted online. But some supply chains were not as resilient. The construction industry had significant problems accessing the materials necessary to meet demand. Customers were being warned of months of delay before construction projects could be completed because of supply chain bottlenecks. Some manufacturers also suffered from supply bottlenecks that made it difficult to sustain a business model that had been built on just-in-time delivery processes that were built for efficiency not resilience. Over the longer term, supply chains also risk being disrupted in some industries for political and national security reasons, as we shall see later. The shape of what new arrangements will emerge is yet to be seen.

CAPITAL FLOWS

Capital account liberalization – the free flow of global capital – has been another, more recent feature of a globalizing world. The benefits in terms of encouraging foreign direct investment are clear, yet we are now also seeing the risks.

Most economists have become more sceptical about the benefits of uncontrolled capital flows. They are seen to contribute to destabilization and financial crises and to limit governments' abilities to deal effectively with such crises. '*There is…no presumption that full liberalisation [of capital flows] is an appropriate goal for all countries at all times,*' according to the IMF.[33]

The 2008 crisis clearly showed that globalized financial markets had become fragile. Access to huge amounts of international financial flows allowed institutions to become highly leveraged through financial engineering mediated by an ever-growing set of algorithms intended to replace human judgement: '*But with leverage at such extreme levels, even a modest decline in asset values proved disastrous: a balance sheet leveraged at 30 to one could be rendered insolvent by an asset-price decline of less than 4 per cent.*'[34] As with the impact of international travel on the spread of a pandemic, free flow of capital across the globe meant that the financial contagion spread far and wide, causing untold misery to many and threatening sovereign states.

Recognizing the potentially destabilizing impact of large capital flows, the IMF view is now that capital controls can serve to protect economies in certain circumstances.[35] It is also worth noting that, in spite of continued pressure from the US and others, China has not fully liberalized its capital account – maybe wisely. Apart from the issues with financial stability, liberalization of capital flows facilitates industrial scale tax arbitrage as well as money laundering activities.

In opposing a UK initiative to tax tech companies on local revenues rather than locally booked profits, Russ Shaw, Founder of Tech London Advocates and Global Tech Advocates, perfectly illustrates the bankruptcy of arguments in support of tax arbitrage. He makes an empty nod to the idea that '*the biggest multinational tech firms have a responsibility to contribute a fair and adequate level of tax*' – without in any way suggesting how that might be achieved. He then goes on to provide the only justification against a crackdown: '*It is therefore imperative that the UK remains an attractive destination for large investment at a time when other European cities are gaining appeal.*'[36] In other words, the only available justification is international tax competition and the threat to disinvest – arguments that continue to fuel economic warfare and to undermine the very foundations of globalization by turning voters and policymakers against it.

In 2021, 130 countries agreed a co-operative approach on taxation requiring the largest multinationals to pay their 'fair share' of taxes in the countries where they generate revenues. A minimum tax rate of 15 per cent was agreed. Overturning a century of taxation convention, convention established when the main concern was the avoidance of double taxation and when a digital world littered with tax havens was not even imagined, the largest global companies with profit margins of at least 10 per cent would have to allocate 20 per cent of their global profits to countries where they make their sales. While more hurdles will need to be overcome for full implementation, one thing is clear: the political winds have turned against the race to the bottom.

NATIONAL SECURITY

National security, including data security, has become the latest issue confronting globalization. Huawei is the poster child of these concerns. Accused of being subject to the Chinese political regime, its equipment has become classified as a national security risk and is being excluded from core 5G networks in an increasing number of countries. A situation made worse by the application of US sanctions that cut it off from sourcing some US-made technologies.

We should not assume that national security concerns around the current model of globalization will remain limited to the digital sector. Or, maybe more properly stated, as digital technology becomes embedded in every nook and cranny of our lives and in every product and service we buy – from phones to refrigerators and toothbrushes – how far will security concerns go in limiting the potential of the globalized model?

Qi Lu, Chief Operating Officer of Chinese internet company Baidu, talks of how autonomous, driverless cars can be hacked and turned into weapons:

> The days of building a vehicle in one place and it runs everywhere are over. Because a vehicle that can move by itself by definition it is a weapon.[37]

The internet itself is part of the new political battlefield: '*The conflicts surrounding internet governance are the new spaces where political and economic power are unfolding in the twenty-first century.*'[38]

Some of these conflicts represent different political imperatives. China, for instance, is pushing New IP – a system that embeds centralized enforcement of rules into the very fabric of the internet, thereby giving significantly more power and control to nation states. Others with less authoritarian tendencies, like the US, UK and Europe, want to adapt the current system to include greater regulatory oversight and strike a balance between data privacy and national security while maintaining an open and adaptable infrastructure. But, politically, few are happy with today's state of affairs where cyberspace has become the new Wild West, beyond any meaningful political oversight, and where power is largely held by a few major corporations. Where cyberspace is also the new locus of warfare between nations. How it will all evolve remains to be seen. The prospect of a Balkanized internet with a patchwork of different systems, each controlled by different nations or blocs, is no longer unimaginable. And the shape of it will be politically determined.

Much will depend on business itself. If the internet giants continue, in their own narrow, short-term self-interest, to resist changes to their business model and the use of reasonable regulatory measures, the eventual political backlash could be substantial and to everyone's detriment.

Cyber-security issues are also affecting corporations' internal working processes. In July 2020, Morgan Stanley blocked interns in China from logging into its virtual network from remote locations. This was due to a combination of factors. The difficulty in ensuring that inexperienced interns working remotely and unsupervised would be unable to comply reliably with increasingly complex Chinese cyber-security laws coupled with the fact that banks have noted that the threat of cyber-attacks was infinitely greater in China than in other countries.

Another threat comes from the fact that the West has sleepwalked into a situation where China now accounts for 80 per cent of the global mined supply of rare earths. It has an even higher share of the manufacturing of powerful rare earth magnets. All these are important components of all our digital toys as well as wind turbines and advanced weaponry. Such dependence is unsustainable and will doubtless be subject to political intervention.

CROSS-CONTAMINATION

Companies are subject to political intervention also because, in international trade relations, the consequences of their actions have implications outside their own company and their own sector, affecting others that may be innocent casualties.

The year 2004 saw the start of a legal battle at the World Trade Organization between Airbus and Boeing. Washington accused France, Spain, Germany and the UK of providing illegal subsidies to Airbus. A year later, the EU alleged $1.9 billion in US government illegal subsidies to Boeing.

The dispute dragged on, as is usually the case, until the WTO ruled in favour of the US in the Airbus case, authorizing the US to impose its biggest-ever penalty – up to 100 per cent in taxes on $7.5 billion of European goods. Washington slapped 25 per cent tariffs on a number of EU goods, including wine, cheese and olives. A 10 per cent tariff on Airbus planes was increased to 15 per cent. A further $3.1 billion of tariffs on EU goods were threatened but not levied.

The WTO has also ruled in favour of Airbus in its own dispute though no retaliatory tariffs had been levied at the time of writing. In trying to de-escalate the dispute the EU and Airbus claimed, vaguely, that it no longer took government handouts. Unimpressed, the US was floating the idea that Airbus would have to pay back a chunk of the money received over the years before a deal could be done.

Trade tensions arising from issues in the airline industry have affected a number of industries that have no stake in the actual dispute. Airbus benefits from illegal state aid, for which it no doubt lobbied for decades, and cheese and wine manufacturers end up carrying the cost. Such disputes can only be resolved at the political level, not by individual corporations or sectors focused on their own interests.

In 2021, the US and the EU agreed to de-escalate the tensions by mutually suspending retaliatory tariffs for a period of five years while the issues were sorted out.

THE MULTINATIONAL CORPORATION

The transnational/multinational corporation[*] stands at the epicentre of the globalization of commerce. For decades, the multinational

---

[*] These two terms are often used interchangeably. Yet they transmit subtly different messages. 'Multinational' acknowledges that corporations are operating within multiple political units as represented by nation states. 'Transnational' implies a commerce that transcends the nation state and its attached political legitimacy.

corporation was hailed as the paragon of economic efficiency. By being able to move sourcing and production to the geographies that provided either the best skills and technology or, more frequently, the lowest costs, multinationals could improve efficiency and productivity, thereby providing better products, lower consumer prices and higher returns to shareholders while also selling largely standardized products the world over. It was the perfect model in '*a world where growth, margins and interdependence had taken over from political conflict*'. Countries and regions the world over competed for foreign direct investment from multinationals to bring skills, technology and employment.

Today, political and public attitudes have changed. Multinationals are now more likely to be seen as engaging in industrial-scale tax arbitrage that allows them to use publicly provided infrastructure without paying their fair share of taxes. Their investment is seen as increasingly unreliable – they move out just as quickly as they move in – and without carrying much responsibility for the unemployed they leave in their wake. They do not fit the growing desire for place-based business activity – businesses that are embedded in their locality and have a long-term stake in the communities in which they operate. And the political tussle between where power should lie – with democratically elected governments or with what some see as unaccountable commercial organizations – is gaining traction.

In her epic battle to break union power, Margaret Thatcher famously rallied the UK around the question: 'Who runs the country – the government or the unions?' Many are now asking the same thing about multinationals. It would be foolish to ignore these rumbling sentiments or to assume that governments would not dare to do to industries what they have done to unions. In the late twentieth century, trade unions pushed their power too far and were met with fierce backlash in many countries. In places like the UK, the resolution was adversarial and violent. In countries like Germany, where there is a greater consensus culture, the Hartz employment reforms enacted under Social Democrat Chancellor Gerhard Schröder were agreed to by all parties.

A similar correction related to the role of the multinational company in our societies is in progress. It might turn out to be adversarial or consensual – or some mix of both. We shall see. Maybe the tech titans will end up being the first targets, maybe not. What is noticeable is that the tone of the political conversation has changed. In the summer of 2020, the leaders of the leading tech companies were submitted to a congressional grilling. '*Our founders would not bow before a king,*' opened David Cicilline, House antitrust subcommittee chair. '*Nor should we bow before the emperors of the online economy.*'

Mere political grandstanding? Empty words that will result in no action? Or, if action is decided upon, will it take years to get through the political system? Maybe. But the change in tone from previous years was remarkable and multinational business would be foolish to ignore the changing political mood.

In June 2021, lawmakers in the US House of Representatives put forward four bills proposing the breakup of the largest tech companies.

Misinterpreting comparative advantage

Much of the groundwork that led to the rise of international trade and, later, the multinational business model came from the nineteenth-century work of David Ricardo. Ricardo's theory of comparative advantage argued that countries should focus their energies on those industrial areas where they had a comparative advantage – in other words, wherever the *opportunity cost* of producing a particular good was high, then that good is better sourced elsewhere where opportunity cost was lower.

This makes sense as a piece of theoretical economics where the sums could be shown to work on a piece of paper (Ricardo's work was theoretical, not based on empirical evidence). But since then, his work has been used to do many things that are not in line with it. Prime among them is the fact that Ricardo only talked about opportunity cost. His theory was that if opportunity costs were high, countries would be better placed importing those goods and re-deploying those resources to higher value-added work. Ricardo also made it clear that it was opportunity cost that mattered, *not* cost of production.

What have we found out since?

The first is that corporations moved assets and investment in search of lower production costs – as specifically excluded from Ricardo's theory. The second, as outlined earlier, is that re-deployment of abandoned resources into higher value-added activities was a theoretical construct, not a practical one. While capital could relatively easily be re-deployed, labour could not. Experience has shown that, by and large, workers in de-industrialized areas cannot easily be re-deployed, leading to long-term regional economic decline, significant human cost and difficult political issues. Companies that move their production elsewhere have relatively little liability for these consequences. Their stake in what the totality of 'comparative advantage' is supposed to mean is only partial.

In other words, the gains from rapid shift in production are privatized to corporations and their shareholders, while the losses are socialized to the socio-political system. All overlain onto a pattern of corporate tax minimization that makes it even more difficult for some national governments to cover the cost of these disruptions. Given that, it is hardly surprising that these questions are becoming increasingly political and that there is increasing discomfort with the multinational model.

Unfair competition and exporting externalities
It's a fine line between comparative advantage and unfair competition. In Ricardo's time, comparative advantage between nations changed only very slowly. The nature of the production of wine and cloth (the examples he used to explain his theory) did not change dramatically in a few short years. The transfer of technology and know-how did not happen in months. There were not as many multiple definitions of 'quality' as there are today. There were none of the highly sophisticated marketing machines of today's corporations that could magic up new definitions of quality and desirability from essentially similar goods.

None of these conditions hold today.

If we look at the drivers of today's world of globalized trade, they can broadly be divided into three categories. The first is the legitimate need to source the best components, wherever they happen to come from. Who has the best and most effective chips to go into a smartphone? Who makes the most reliable micro-dosing valves to go into an asthma inhaler? Where is the best place to grow tropical fruits? And so forth. This can reasonably be considered comparative advantage which, today, can shift relatively quickly from one place to the next. This is desirable global competition that drives innovation and investment – subject to the growing national security concerns covered earlier.

The second component is labour costs. Corporations seek the lowest available labour costs worldwide. Here, the political questions are more difficult. One formulation would be: is it reasonable to ask workers in developed countries to compete with their counterparts in developing countries where wages are naturally lower and often very much lower? Is this reasonable or unfair competition? Is it acceptable even when working conditions in some countries may be below what we would consider acceptable? The answer to these questions may well look very different if viewed from a firm perspective as opposed to a political one.

The third component is regulatory avoidance. Firms faced with, for instance, tough regulation regarding carbon emissions or other environmental harms may well choose to move operations to those countries with lower regulatory standards. This is regulatory avoidance or, another way of putting it, the exporting of externalities from countries that try to limit them to those that don't. And, when it comes to issues such as climate change and environmental harms, these decisions harm us all in the long run.

Multi-national corporations may well seem to behave perfectly reasonably when viewed through the lens of firms' short-term financial performance. But the political lens projects a very different and much fuzzier picture. As we shall see in the next chapter, the political lens will, eventually, prevail – and maybe much sooner than many might think. 'The exploitation of people, nature, and child labour must not become the basis of the global economy and our prosperity,' according to Gerd Müller, Germany's minister of economic co-operation and development,[39] speaking in the context of a proposed new law requiring better due diligence of global supply chains.

For the purely financially focused firms, the boardroom discussion will be around how long that will take, how they can present arguments as to how such a law will damage the German economy, how long they can lobby to delay or kill implementation. Or around trying to shift the regulatory responsibility onto source countries as proposed by Stefan Genth, secretary-general of the German Retail Federation, knowing full well, as does everyone else, that this is simply a device for kicking the idea into the long grass. And around when and how they should adjust their practices so as not to be caught napping while not travelling so quickly as to put themselves at a competitive disadvantage in the interim. All of that is textbook commercial logic.

For the more politically-savvy firms, the political direction of travel is clear and the earlier they find ways of adjusting their business model, the better. Which is why over 60 large companies came out in support of the proposed German law.

WHERE IS IT ALL HEADED?

There seems little doubt that the political runes suggest that globalization twentieth-century style will no longer remain the preferred model going forward. How a relatively new political direction will evolve, at what speed, in which countries and sectors it will drive faster and what model will emerge in its stead are all questions still to be resolved. But the answers will be determined almost exclusively politically. To those who remain locked in a purely commercial logic, some of the political decisions taken may seem irrational. But they are not, they will follow the political logic of the time.

Neither will the progression be neat and linear. It will resemble the course of a sailing boat rather than a power boat. Just like sailors tack and zig zag their way to their destination, trying to capture the power of the prevailing winds, so political action will swerve this way and that, depending on the domestic and geo-political winds. Neither the course nor the precise eventual destination are clear many years out but the general direction of travel is.

Some business leaders have detected the change and are adjusting their businesses accordingly. Inge Thulin, then CEO of 3M:

> Our strategy has changed. If you go back several years, there was a strategy of producing at huge facilities at certain places around the world and shipping it to other countries. But now we have a strategy of localisation and regionalisation. We think you should invest in your domestic market as much as you can.

Or GE-then-CEO Jeff Immelt:

> The days of outsourcing are declining. Chasing the lowest labour costs is yesterday's model.

Both statements were reported in mid-2017[40] – when the great disruption of the COVID-19 pandemic was not even imagined.

Of course, it is the perceived unpredictability of the political process that frustrates so many business leaders. They would rather operate in a safe and predictable environment where long-term investment decisions can be made with some degree of certainty. But the political process is not as unpredictable as it might seem to the business mind. While the details and timing of public policy initiatives will vary, direction of travel, as well as specific political interventions, are quite predictable for those who learn to look at the world through a political lens.

The good news

When I was a junior doctor working in hospitals, I worked, at one time, in a highly specialist, internationally renowned centre for liver diseases. Every patient referred from the world over (another facet of globalization) had liver disease. In my world, liver disease was more prevalent than the common cold. When one patient sadly died, I called her primary care physician to let him know. I was trying to get him to recall the patient. Finally, it clicked: 'Ah! You're talking about Mrs Bailey – my patient with the liver problem.' I was in shock. I finally realized what should have been blindingly obvious – I was living in a bubble. Among his list of over 1,000 patients, this primary care physician had only one with liver disease. Most other primary care physicians had none. It was a salutary lesson.

For those managers who bemoan the passing of the great age of globalization, a similar reality check is in order. Business managers' perceptions of the extent to which globalization dominates the world are well out of kilter with reality, as the figure below shows.

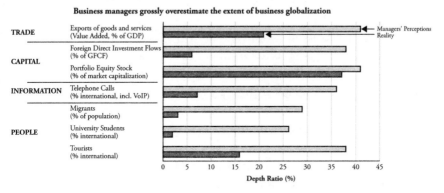

Business managers grossly overestimate the extent of business globalization

Source: DHL Global Connectedness Index, 2019.

Large surveys show that most people do not realize the limited extent of global connectedness. Actually, one commonality between many of globalization's supporters and its critics is that they tend to believe the world is already far more globalized than it really is. And CEOs and other senior executives had even more exaggerated perceptions – perhaps because their own lives tend to be far more global than those of most other people.[41]

Like me in my liver unit, too many business executives are caught in their own bubble. They believe that globalization dominates much more deeply than it does. This reflects the world they live in rather than the real world. Most trade is, and will remain, domestic. The shape and nature of that which isn't will likely change over the coming decades. But the impact of these changes need not be, and will not be, catastrophic. It will only be damaging to those who continue to insist that the world should remain as it was and who doggedly stick to their own logic and worldview in the face of a world where political change is more rapid than it has been for some time.

Trade is politics as much as, if not more than, it is economics. It was always so. Richard Cobden's drive to repeal the corn laws in the UK – in its time one of the most iconic actions to open up trade – was a fundamentally political act. Open trade as a means of achieving political as well as economic ends.

The political constraints around trade are illustrated by the sticking points that arose during the UK–EU negotiations post-Brexit and the UK–Japan trade deal.

For the UK–EU deal, fish quotas for EU fishermen in British waters became one of the most difficult areas of negotiation. Fishing accounts for 0.12 per cent of UK GDP and 0.1 per cent of UK employment. In Spain, fishing accounts for around 1 per cent of GDP – although only a proportion of that is dependent on catches in UK waters. In France, the fishing industry is no more than a rounding error in GDP calculations. Yet fishing is politically important for everyone. Fishing has emotional resonance, concentration in limited coastal communities and, in some countries, a degree of political influence that is out of proportion to its economic importance. Enough that, for some time, it looked like it might derail a deal that would benefit both the UK and all the 27 EU member states.

The other big issue was that of the so-called 'level playing field' provisions. The EU was insistent that the UK should have domestic policies on issues such as environmental and labour standards that were not widely divergent from EU standards. This was presented as essential to ensure 'fair competition' as outlined above. The UK resisted these conditions as an invasion of its own sovereign right to set its own standards. Back to Rodrik's tension between trade, democracy and sovereignty.

In the UK–Japan case, the issue was cheese. The UK pressed for a quota on cheese exports to Japan. While economically unimportant, this was politically important as the UK government, having promised that post-Brexit trade deals would be better than the deal it received while an EU member, did not want to be seen to have foregone cheese quotas that were part of the Japan–EU agreement. Japan, on the other hand, had promised its farmers that it would not open up their market to more foreign competition. Both parties had made political promises that were mutually incompatible.

Eventually, compromise solutions were found for all the issues. But the fact that, in all cases, politically important but economically irrelevant sectors could have derailed major trade agreements highlights the political nature of international trade.

The vital role of business
We all face the risk that the backlash against globalization will go too far. That the rise of the politics of nationalism and competing political blocs will indeed disrupt the positive and essential aspects of globalization in the process of trying to contain the downsides. It is here that business, and particularly large, multinational business, has a crucial role to play.

I have outlined how business practices in terms of arbitrage and playing off jurisdictions against one another have been important drivers of the backlash against globalization. If business decides to continue with or even double down on these practices, then the future of globalization is indeed in danger. The political backlash will continue to grow with unknowable consequences. Business will, in effect, continue to pour fuel on the anti-globalization fire.

However, business could play a very different role. By adopting a more politically sensitive set of practices, business has the potential to guide us all into a more effective and less politically toxic form of globalization. Where the benefits are enhanced and the downsides mitigated. This requires the development of the skills and capabilities that I shall describe in the next chapter – and the will to do so.

To a large extent, the political choices between increasing nationalism and consequent balkanization or the alternative of a better form of global collaboration and commercial flows will depend on business leaders themselves and the choices they make. Business will, to a significant extent, itself determine how much it will be harmed by future developments.

I have argued in this chapter that trade is an instrument of foreign and domestic policy. It is not an end in itself. What we are seeing today is a structure and flow of trade that, while making perfect commercial sense from firms' perspective, is not fully serving domestic and foreign policy objectives for many countries. As a result, there is politically driven change.

As always, change will favour those who, rather than just watching, and reacting to, how it unfolds day by day, understand the underlying drivers and adapt accordingly. Those drivers are to a large extent political.

Ultimately, geopolitics is about relative power. The commercial world focuses heavily on economic growth and consequent economic power. Politics focuses also on other forms of power – military power, soft power and sharp power – the willingness to use the other powers to push one's own interests and agenda. As China does using its increasing economic heft and trade policy as sharp 'wolf-warrior' powers to further its objectives, both domestically and overseas, and as the US does with the extra-territorial reach of the dollar.

All forms of power are interlinked and interdependent. For instance, the development of military power depends on having the economic power to do so. But it does not arise simply from economic success. Governments have to be both able and willing to collect enough revenue and devote it to military capabilities. In other words, all forms of power need to be exercised and built up in concert.

The figure below is a rough visualization of the relative powers of the three largest economic and political blocs. So far, the US remains geo-politically dominant, with China catching up and Europe seemingly falling behind.

The US remains geopolitically dominant

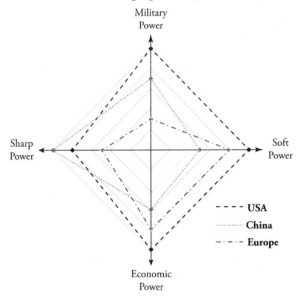

For business, it is worth bearing in mind that the politics of globalization will take all these different forms of power into account. Political action will not be driven exclusively by commercial needs. For instance, it could be argued that Europe's seeming unwillingness, in the interests of short-term commercial gain, to use its sharp powers and its reluctance to take responsibility for its own defence capabilities, will over time undermine its global heft and reduce rather than increase the chances of sustained economic success.

Business has a large role to play in what shape globalization will take going forward. Politically aware and politically sensitive business practices will act to preserve the good of globalized trade and collaboration. Sensitivity to the various aspects of geo-political power that go beyond short-horizon commercial interests will preserve the balance of power necessary for economic stability.

Conversely, politically insensitive behaviours focused exclusively on narrow and short-term financial interests will almost certainly guarantee progressive breakdown of global commerce.

5

Cultural Leadership

*'The dogmas of the quiet past are inadequate to the stormy present.
The occasion is piled high with difficulty and we must rise with the
occasion. As our case is new, we must think anew and act anew.'*
Abraham Lincoln
16th President of the United States

It was a pre-election political dinner. Senior businesspeople had been invited to provide their input on upcoming political platforms. The host declared he was disappointed that none of the political parties had clearly declared their support for business as a force for good in society as part of their electoral platforms. When asked for my view, I asked why the participants thought it was that political parties did not feel moved to declare unconditional support for business. Could it be that some business practices and behaviours did not encourage political support? Surely parties would have explicitly backed business if they felt it would enhance their support among voters.

My question was met with outrage: 'As long as businesses focus on making money while operating within the restrictions laid down in law, then they are doing their job', I was rebuked in no uncertain terms. A response so twentieth century, it reflects the disconnect between entrenched belief systems and the realities of a rapidly changing world.

The first issue to get out of the way is that the law should not be our only guide to thinking about what constitutes acceptable behaviour. Social norms, moral intuitions and moral emotions – our intuitive, affective sense of what should and should not be considered acceptable

– are important components of what makes society function even when they do not have the force of law: '*Moral emotions are evolved mechanisms that function in part to optimize social relationships.*'[1] There are many activities that are perfectly legal but still offend our moral intuitions. Conversely, many laws still on the books are routinely ignored as they no longer represent the prevailing moral standards.

Legislation tends to follow rather than lead evolving social norms and often with some considerable lag. Some consider legislation around corporate behaviour as one area where legislation remains weak, lagging behind current social norms and moral intuitions, and with penalties that, when they kick in at all, do not necessarily serve as a deterrent. We should not therefore allow those who believe that current legal interpretations favour their position to use the law as a tool to cut short reasonable discussion and open exploration. That which is legal is not beyond discussion of whether it is ethical or acceptable in our societies. I can choose to be rude and unpleasant to my neighbours every day. That would be perfectly legal, but it is does not fit within the social norms that make our communities function. The challenge is to understand societal expectations, how they will likely evolve and how they will eventually play into the political and social discourse.

McDonald's is a corporation that elitist snobs love to hate. In the early 1990s, a small volunteer organization produced and distributed approximately 2,000 pamphlets criticizing McDonald's and other fast-food chains for a number of their practices including, among others, destruction of the rainforest and cruelty towards animals. McDonald's investigated the organization then issued writs for defamation against five individuals from the group. Two refused to withdraw the allegations and went to court. The case lasted seven years in the English courts.

The two defendants collectively earned an annual income of about $12,000. McDonald's was capitalized at approximately $30 billion. The defendants represented themselves; McDonald's spent over $16 million on its legal representation. This was as close to a David and Goliath case as one gets – and we all know where public, and therefore political, sympathy ends up in such circumstances.

Unsurprisingly, the whole episode was a PR disaster for McDonald's – described as scoring one of the most extended own-goals in the recent history of public relations. To cap it all, in spite of hiring the best legal minds at huge cost, McDonald's failed to achieve a clear legal victory with the court stating that the defendants were telling the truth about McDonald's on a number of issues. McDonald's won on about half its legal points, the defendants the other half.

How did McDonald's react to this debacle?

We should bear in mind that the modern animal rights movement started in earnest only in the early 1970s. While it grew substantially throughout the 1980s and 90s, it was not clear when the suit was filed whether this would be a sustained movement or another activist flash in the pan that would peter out. By the time the lawsuit was decided, animal rights were only just starting to become more established. In 1992, Switzerland became the first country to include animal protections in its constitution. In 1997, the European Union added an animal protection protocol to its treaties (its effectiveness later somewhat undercut by a 2001 ruling by the Court of Justice of the European Union). It wasn't until the 2000s that animal rights activism started to get more political purchase and, in the eyes of many, protections against animal cruelty remain highly insufficient to this day.

In 1997, it would therefore have been quite reasonable for McDonald's to learn from the mess, lick its wounds, keep quiet and go about its business – somewhat chastened but otherwise a going concern focused on what needs to be done to maximize shareholder value. That is not what happened.

Instead, the company hired Temple Grandin, a renowned animal welfare expert, to tackle animal welfare in slaughterhouses. Over a period of years and using its huge buying power, McDonald's transformed the slaughterhouse industry. It established new animal welfare standards for cattle that had to be met by anyone wanting to sell to the chain (which slaughterhouse could afford not to?). A team of auditors travelled around the US, measuring how loud it was in the cattle pens (mooing is a stress indicator), the percentage of animals killed in one shot, how many times a worker uses an electric cattle prod and much more.

The attention to detail was impressive. '*We did it with maintenance of existing equipment, non-slip flooring, and lots of repairs to facilities. We changed lighting, so cattle wouldn't be afraid of the dark. We taught workers not to leave hoses lying around or jackets hanging from fences. Those are things that scare cattle,*' says Grandin.[2]

The effect was revolutionary for the slaughterhouse industry. To the extent that, today, talk in the industry remains about the pre-McDonald's and post-McDonald's eras. An example of how business can use its power for transformational societal effects – if it is so-minded. It also shows how business can achieve societal change quickly and effectively if it chooses to. Much more quickly than can happen through the political process which inevitably involves the long, difficult and laborious grind of balancing multiple constituencies, all with different views and different levels of political power.

Following the McLibel case, as it became known, McDonald's could have done very little except carry on with its business until all was forgotten. After all, there was little evidence that the episode was having a substantial effect on the company's earnings outlook. It could have filled its website with virtue signalling platitudes of the sort to be found everywhere, handed the problem over to a PR agency charged with improving its image and coming up with useful new marketing slogans rather than doing anything substantive, and instituted some kind of superficial supply chain auditing processes that would be enough to tick the appropriate boxes and no more.

Sure, other episodes would have come up but they could all be swatted aside easily enough with the usual corporate press releases that would go something like this: 'We take our commitment to animal welfare very seriously and all our operations are in full compliance with the relevant local legislation. We have a robust supply chain auditing system that has been in place for a long time and that we continue to improve. We hold ourselves and our suppliers to the highest industry standards and have no tolerance for such practices. We have mounted an internal investigation,' and all the other boilerplate wording we all know so well. Back to business. And no more seven-year court battles that make things worse rather than better.

Why did McDonald's not go down that route and instead did something that was transformative? One explanation is that the shock of its legal defeat and the attendant PR consequences galvanized the company into an understanding that animal welfare issues were not a passing fad. That it represented, in fact, the start of a significant and sustained cultural and political shift that had legs. Something that would eventually result in meaningful political and legislative action. The time period over which that would materialize was unknowable, but materialize it most likely would and it would benefit the corporation if it got ahead of that curve.

But how do such things happen in practice? What goes on inside companies that causes them to make these shifts?

I spoke to Professor Grandin to get some insights as to what happened at McDonald's. Grandin was not approached by senior management but rather by those in charge of supply chain management who asked for advice. The first thing she did was to take these managers on a tour of slaughterhouses: *'It's all very well to sit in the corporate office looking at spreadsheets and PowerPoint charts that are dissociated from reality. But when you go out into the field, you see what's happening in the real world'*, she said.

All Grandin's work was done in collaboration with supply chain management who, having experienced reality for themselves, decided to clean up. They had enough leeway to move forward with change without having to seek permission from senior management at every turn.

Two further factors made the transformation possible.

First, the changes being asked of their suppliers were not particularly costly. With only a couple of exceptions, there was not much need for suppliers to make investments in new equipment or new facilities. Rather, it was a question of improved process, new performance metrics and adjustments to existing facilities.

Second, the programme was focused on the supply chain within the US. Making changes and monitoring those changes effectively was reasonably possible. This contrasts with those companies that choose to have globally distributed supply chains in the endless search for the lowest cost. With the best will in the world, and many corporations do have the will, or at least the intent, it is well-nigh impossible, not to mention highly costly, to audit effectively such widely scattered supply chains of contractors, sub-contractors and sub-sub-contractors peppered across the globe, many of whom operate in cultures fundamentally different from our own.

In other words, when companies choose to build their business around globally scattered supply chains, what they are, in fact, saying is that, for the benefit of lower-cost sourcing, they are willing to tolerate a degree of hidden practices that they find unacceptable. The idea that supply chain monitoring can totally eliminate such practices is just not credible. For most corporations, it is simply an impossible task however hard they try and however genuine their efforts.

In a 2020 report, The Australian Strategic Policy Institute showed that *'Under conditions that strongly suggest forced labour, Uyghurs are working in factories that are in the supply chains of at least 82 well-known global brands in the technology, clothing and automotive sectors, including Apple, BMW, Gap, Huawei, Nike, Samsung, Sony and Volkswagen.'*[3] And the findings of this report are by no means unique. Barely a week goes by when similar abuses involving forced or child labour or inhumane pay and working conditions don't make the front pages of the newspapers.

And it would be beyond cynical to assume that senior management in these companies doesn't care. The issue is not one of not caring, it's of being realistic that widely scattered supply chains will inevitably have dark pools.

This has political consequences. In 2020, the US imposed sanctions on the Xinjiang Production and Construction Corps (XPCC), the dominant business force in the area. Imposing penalties under the Magnitsky Act, the US government warned, *'businesses with potential supply-chain exposure to Xinjiang to consider the reputational, economic and legal risks of involvement with entities that engage in human rights abuses in Xinjiang, such as forced labor.'*[4] I will examine these issues further in the next chapter on the political brand.

At McDonald's it seems that its new practices have become embedded in corporate culture. In 2000, it shook the poultry industry when it ordered its egg suppliers to comply with strict guidelines for humane treatment of hens or be dropped. It established the Chicken Sustainability Advisory Council to set higher standards for chicken health and welfare. McDonald's was, years ago and before it was fashionable, one of the first companies to engage with NGOs and others to deal better with waste from its food packaging. It has worked with the Marine Stewardship Council to ensure that 100 per cent of its fish are sustainably sourced. All signs that the company takes all these political movements seriously and incorporates them meaningfully in its operational practices.

And good practice is contagious. Wendy's and Burger King have followed suit. Grandin is advising them both.

Of course, all these companies have further challenging political issues still to address. In 2021 a group of UK activists blockaded four McDonald's distribution centres demanding that the company become fully plant-based by 2025. There are also questions around what fast food companies' role should be in tackling the obesity pandemic. All new political fronts to be tackled.

THE ROLE OF BUSINESS IN SOCIETY

UK Prime Minister Tony Blair said that it's not the role of business to solve social problems. Business should just get on with making money and leave social issues to others (i.e. him). How things have changed.

The twenty-first-century culture in which business operates is evolving into something fundamentally different from that which Blair expressed in the dying days of the twentieth century. Then business could afford to keep away from messy ethical and social issues, follow the letter, if not the spirit, of the rules and get on with the business of making money. No longer. Most now realize that business is embedded in society. It is not separate from the broad, messy and chaotic social, cultural and political expectations.

Much has been written in the past few years debating the questions: 'what is a business?' and 'what is a business for?' That the debate is happening in earnest is encouraging. It means that the assumptions that seemed to underlie our belief system in the late twentieth century – that business is there primarily if not exclusively to make money for shareholders – is finally being accepted as representing '*the dumbest idea in the world*,' according to former GE CEO Jack Welch.

The discussion about businesses needing a 'licence to operate', the idea that they can only be successful if society approves of what they are doing, is a concept around which there has been a lot of talk. Yet plenty of businesses operate across the world with operational practices that many find unreasonable – and they continue to do so. As David Rouch points out in *The Social Licence for Financial Markets*, '*the social licence is not a set of carefully crafted written rules or standards. Rather it is an observation of practice, and identifies a set of aspirations that are present.*'⁵ In other words, 'social licence' is about tackling the question as to what we, as a society, want business to be for. Will those businesses that operate at the margins of social acceptability be quite as successful and sustainable in the medium- and long-term as those that operate in line with the prevailing and evolving social mores, or even use their deep knowledge of cultural expectations as a source of competitive advantage?

This makes some business leaders uncomfortable. It would be preferable if everything were to be clearly codified in clear rules rather than the fuzziness, fluidity and constant disagreement that is inherent in cultural frameworks. And the idea that business is there primarily to make money further simplifies the issues. It just no longer works.

Does anyone remember Bear Stearns? That bank reputedly had a large sign in its offices that proudly stated: 'We make nothing but money'. The eventual collapse of a company with that philosophy underlines the fact that if one sees one's business as being nothing more than a money-making machine, one can easily end up being unable to make money at all.

Consider these statements:

Statement 1

> While each of our individual companies serves its own corporate purpose, we share a fundamental commitment to all of our stakeholders.
>
> We commit to:
>
> - Delivering value to our customers. We will further the tradition of American companies leading the way in meeting or exceeding customer expectations
> - Investing in our employees. This starts with compensating them fairly and providing important benefits. It also includes supporting them through training and education that help develop new skills for a rapidly changing world. We foster diversity and inclusion, dignity and respect
> - Dealing fairly and ethically with our suppliers. We are dedicated to serving as good partners to the other companies, large and small, that help us meet our missions
> - Supporting the communities in which we work. We respect the people in our communities and protect the environment by embracing sustainable practices across our businesses
> - Generating long-term value for shareholders, who provide the capital that allows companies to invest, grow and innovate. We are committed to transparency and effective engagement with shareholders.
>
> Each of our stakeholders is essential. We commit to deliver value to all of them, for the future success of our companies, our communities and our country.

Statement 2

> After all, only as civic conditions are ideal can business conditions be made ideal. Businessmen have come to see their duty to the general public in an entirely different light.

Statement 3

> The manufacturers of our country can make no investment that brings them greater dividends than that of contributing largely to aid in the formation and sustaining [of local communities].

The sentiments expressed by these statements are similar. What is the difference?

The first statement was released by the US Business Roundtable in 2019 and signed by an impressive roll call of CEOs.[6] The second came from a speech by Harry A. Wheeler, President of the United States Chamber of Commerce – in 1913. The third was a statement issued during a business convention in Detroit and signed by the delegates – in 1868.[7]

The fact that business has been using similar language for one and a half centuries while, many would argue, little has changed, is perfect fodder for the cynics. Indeed, I can easily stand accused of some cynicism myself. Following the World Economic Forum meeting in Davos in 2020, I wrote:

> Last week's Davos carnival was an orgy of virtue signaling. A group of senior executives flew in on private jets to talk about how to tackle climate change. Standing out in the general virtue signaling fest was President Donald Trump. His focus was on economic growth, American superiority, and casual dismissal of the climate change 'prophets of doom'.
>
> We shall see over the coming years whether Trump was simply a reactionary outlier, or the only honest person in the room.[8]

But the overall thrust of this book is that things have, indeed, changed. Why? And why should anyone believe it?

What has changed is that, up until relatively recently, all these statements were made under the overall umbrella that developing some kind of corporate social responsibility was important because it was 'good for business' – in other words, good for making even more money. Fundamentally there was no change in the idea that the primary function of business was to make as much money as possible. Civic responsibility was simply another route to better earnings – 'investment that brings them greater dividends' – as stated above.

What has changed, and what I argue throughout this book, is that our understanding of the very reason why business exists is now changing. Business exists to better people's lives and to be an active and integral player in creating the sort of society in which we want to live. A society where we don't have to put up with effluent discharged into our water supply, pollution of the air we live in, pay structures that drive social inequality and undermine social cohesion, an approach to globalization that leaves places decimated for decades – maybe forever, practices that employ forced labour, that cause collapse of the financial system, thereby heaping hardship on millions, etc., etc.

As Professor Sir John Kay puts it: '*Business has lost political legitimacy and public trust by pandering to an account of itself that is both repulsive and false. The corporation is necessarily a social institution, its success the product of the relationships among its stakeholders and its role in the society within which it operates.*'[9] This is what underlies the story I related at the start of this chapter – why did none of the political parties come out with an explicitly 'pro-business' platform?

In short, what's 'good for business' is in the process of being re-defined from simple financial metrics to a much broader set of evaluations that define the overall contribution of individual businesses to our social and environmental fabric, as we shall see later. Nobody is arguing that business should not have making a profit as one of the essentials for continued existence (though the valuation of some businesses that have no visible route to profitability does make one wonder somewhat). Neither should we go overboard and expect business to solve all of the myriad issues facing our societies. It's just a question of degree, focus and alignment. What society is asking for today from business leaders is a broader focus; one that balances various factors and outcomes, including clear stances on issues that can be defined as being political in nature.

CEOs MUST LEAD
Percent who agree

It is important that **my employer's CEO speak out**
on one or more of these issues

CEOs should take the lead on change rather
than wait for government to impose it

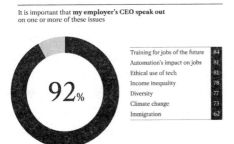

Training for jobs of the future	84
Automation's impact on jobs	81
Ethical use of tech	81
Income inequality	78
Diversity	77
Climate change	73
Immigration	62

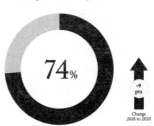

Source: 2020 Edelman Trust Barometer

And this re-definition is not coming solely from the business world itself. If it were, then one might reasonably have some doubts. But this change in perspective is increasingly widespread in the civic and political realms and is now largely unstoppable. The pace of change remains uncertain, but acceleration is evident.

The Edelman 2019 Trust Management Survey found that, among the population, ethical drivers were three times more important as drivers of trust than a company's competence. A full 76 per cent of respondents valued ethical factors over competence among business.

**ETHICAL DRIVERS 3X MORE IMPORTANT TO COMPANY TRUST
THAN COMPETENCE**
Per cent of predictable variance in trust explained by each dimension

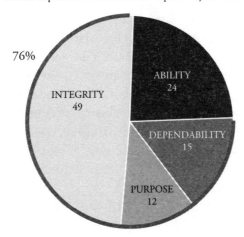

Source: 2019 Edelman Trust Management Tracking Study.

Social and cultural expectations have changed. As we shall see, companies find themselves buffeted by all sorts of politically driven socio-cultural movements to which they are expected to respond. It is increasingly seen as essential that business makes a visible positive contribution to the broader social good – a contribution that goes far beyond employing people and generating economic activity. This is a new world where senior executives brought up in a world where financial performance and their perception on Wall Street was not only their main business goal but tended to define their whole ego and self-image are now faced with a set of expectations that are different, somewhat fluffy and intangible, and ever shifting.

This changing landscape is also reflected in what boards and shareholders expect from senior business leaders. Kearney, a consulting firm, undertook an Australian study comparing reasons for 300 chief executive departures from ASX-listed companies across two periods – April 2011 to March 2016 and April 2016 to March 2021. The number of involuntary exits increased by 27 per cent over the two periods. The number of involuntary exits for non-financial/ Environmental, Social and Governance (ESG) reasons rose almost fourfold. By the end of the period, non-financial reasons accounted for 37 per cent of all involuntary exits.[10] A similar study by PwC found that in 2018 'ethical lapses' for the first time overtook exits for financial performance.[11]

Philanthropy – and its limits
Some companies have for some time responded to wider societal expectations by setting up charitable foundations through which they make philanthropic contributions. It's a concept that dates from the nineteenth century when it was driven by Christian values and was paternalistic in nature. In not so organized a form, philanthropy dates from well before that. The Medicis were patrons of the arts. Long before that, groups of wealthy men in ancient Greece regularly paid for all the equipment necessary to stage the great Greek dramatic festivals. In ancient Rome Cicero and Seneca composed manuals on the arts of proper gift giving and receipt.

In a seminal article titled 'Wealth' and published in the *North American Review* in 1889, Andrew Carnegie claimed that a man of wealth ought:

...to consider all surplus revenues which come to him simply as trust funds, which he is called upon to administer, and strictly bound as a matter of duty to administer in the manner which, in his judgment, is best calculated to produce the most beneficial results for the community—the man of wealth thus becoming the mere trustee and agent for his poorer brethren, bringing to their service his superior wisdom, experience, and ability to administer, doing for them better than they would or could do for themselves....

Such words delivered from a position of superiority of the man of wealth to the ordinary citizen would not be considered acceptable today, yet echoes of the underlying attitude remain. That philanthropy is a conscientious way to use 'surplus'. That the philanthropist knows best how to direct such expenditure.

Philanthropy is to be appreciated and encouraged. Many corporations have done, and continue to do, enormous good through their philanthropic foundations. But, on its own, it is no longer sufficient to absolve companies from tackling the more fundamental questions around how one's business, at its core, is making our societies better.

Make no mistake, this is a seismic change.

One such example is that of Anders Povlsen – a Danish billionaire who runs fashion company Bestseller. Povlsen is also the largest landowner in Scotland, having acquired several estates. His stated aim is to use those estates for environmental conservation and re-wilding purposes. He believes that the future of the Scottish Highlands needs to be reimagined and that conservation should be an integral part of that new vision. For many, this is a laudable aim; maybe one inspired by the impressive work done in Latin America by the late Doug Tompkins and his wife Kris.

In fulfilling his aims, and the benefits it will bring, Povlsen has to deal with two issues. The first is that Carnegie's pretention of '*doing for them better than they would or could do for themselves*' does not fly so easily nowadays. Many in Scotland disapprove of his vision for the land and believe that it could be put to better use to provide greater employment. All of it also wrapped up with the high political sensitivity in Scotland of the increasing foreign ownership of their lands and the concentration of land ownership in few hands (half of all the private land in Scotland is owned by less than 500 people). For

Povlsen, his cause has become wrapped in people's lingering memories and resentments of The Clearances – the period in the eighteenth and nineteenth centuries when landowners caused masses of people to leave in search of better lives.

Others are dubious about his motives. They suspect some ulterior motive rather than a purely philanthropic one. This is all reminiscent of the same issues faced by the Tompkins in Argentina and in Chile, where conspiracy theorists revelled in all sorts of fantasies from the idea that the Tompkins intended to split Chile in two at its narrowest point to the theory that they intended to set up a separatist Zionist state. It seems that people's imagination, abilities to conjure up the most absurd conspiracy theories and the desire to put the most negative interpretation on anyone's actions is endless.

Povlsen says:

> We could probably have communicated our intentions here in Scotland better. The trouble with the attention this attracts is that people assume there is an angle in play. That I am buying all this land for reasons that are not entirely altruistic. I am not going to pretend it was easy when I first started here in Scotland. But today the locals here are less suspicious of our motivation.[12]

While making progress, the question is whether this is simply a matter of better communication or whether there are deeper issues at play. Much of the resistance to such philanthropic efforts arise because people form fundamentally different political views of what such efforts are about. While, for many, Povlsen's and others' efforts are seen as welcome environmental restoration projects, others see them as a form of neo-colonialism – rich people buying up 'their' land to do with as they please whether the locals like it or not. Such different political interpretations can only be reconciled, when they can, through hard slog. It involves making local people part of developing the overall vision rather than it being developed separately and then 'communicated' effectively. Some would argue that, seeing as the uses to which land is put are political questions, to what extent should the wealthy be allowed to exercise explicit political power in this way?

Philanthropic initiatives such as this one and many others need to be approached with a purely political mindset as they are primarily political issues, not technical ones. In politics, one person's virtuous mission is another's vision of hell. In the words of William Blake, '*The tree which moves some to tears of joy is in the eyes of others only a green thing that stands in the way.*' Povlsen might care about the environment and conservation. Others care more about jobs and putting food on their families' table. No philanthropic exercise should start from the belief that everyone will, eventually, see it as a good thing, provided it is communicated well. That will never happen.

As in politics, total consensus will likely never be achieved. What one can hope for is the successful co-design of a narrative that brings together a sufficient coalition of interests in its support. This is pure politics – and should be treated as such. It affects every philanthropic endeavour and it is difficult for many in business to deal with as it is slow, painful, can seem 'irrational', and it's not the environment that businesspeople are used to working in. Some might feel hurt interpreting it as a lack of gratitude for their philanthropic efforts. It is not. It is normal politics.

The second issue for Povlsen is Bestseller – a sprawling fashion business that, like all fashion businesses, can be described in many ways, but sustainable and environmentally friendly are not the first adjectives that spring to mind. Povlsen argues that without the successful business, he would not be able to fund his conservation efforts. But he also knows that such a response is insufficient. It opens him up to what philosopher Slavoj Žižek says about philanthropy – that it can descend into trying to fix in the afternoon what you have messed up in the morning. Povlsen is intent on making his fashion business more sustainable while recognizing the difficulties of doing so convincingly in an industry for which product obsolescence (and therefore waste) lies at the core of what it's all about. He clearly understands all these issues – and that they are not easy to deal with. But he continues to strive to get there and to tackle the difficult issue of a conservationist running a business that is pretty far from being environmentally friendly.

For business, it is likely that philanthropy, through foundations or in any other form, will continue to form part of that now trite and rather tired phrase 'corporate social responsibility'. That is welcome but insufficient. Today's reality is that the social milieu in which we are living requires societal, cultural and political positions to be embedded in what corporations are about – why they even exist. This is what we call Cultural Leadership: a leadership approach that puts at its centre the interdependence between businesses and the social context in which they seek to operate. It implies a substantial shift in awareness that requires leaders to view their role within the much larger political and cultural context.

Businesses have become used to the idea that technological or business model disruptions may upend how they do things. They keep an eye out for such developments and try to anticipate or react as best they can. What has not been such an issue is the idea of cultural disruption. Where socio-cultural-political mores and perspectives change in such a way as to create the same sort of business disruption – or maybe one that is even more foundational – than technological or business model disruptions. It is understandable that business has not been totally adept at cultural leadership since cultural expectations usually only change slowly, maybe generationally or over multiple generations, absent some major catastrophic shock to the system. No longer. Cultural expectations are changing fast. Cultural disruption is now as rapid and as foundational as technological disruption – if not more so.

There is also the question as to how much corporate philanthropy works to improve the image and perception of those businesses that set them up. Its value in this regard is limited if philanthropy is off to one side, doing its thing separately from the core of the business. Better integration provides greater benefit as well as helping to drive the core of the business in new directions.

And, increasingly, issues like those that Povlsen has to face affect business directly – not just their philanthropic efforts.

All this was illustrated in glorious Technicolor some time ago when I was advising a mining company that faced resistance by environmental activists. They did almost everything 'right'. Yet, investigating the political landscape in some more depth, it became clear that environmentalists were the most visible but far from the only political force at work. Other vested interests lined up on either side of the battle – some out in the open, others far in the shadows. The company tried to tackle the issues as best it could. The only thing that, to their credit, they refused to do was to walk into the relevant ministries with suitcases stuffed with cash – something other businesses might not have been quite so shy about.

Mapping all the political forces at play, how they interacted with each other and what each agenda looked like revealed a complex picture where it was impossible to find a way forward that would satisfy all parties. Sensationalist (if untrue) headlines were deftly deployed by opponents. The highly detailed, and expensive, scientific studies commissioned by the company were, by and large, useless; totally ignored in what was a pure political power play. Yet it was hard for company management to come to terms with the fact that they could not address the issues with facts and data. That requests for further data were, in fact, simply instruments of further delay and obfuscation while the political landscape evolved. They were the equivalent of what every salesperson knows as false objections.

In the end, the issues became too complex and difficult for the company to handle effectively. Some of that was because it was practically impossible to do so. Some of it was a reticence on behalf of management to see the problems as exclusively political rather than ones subject to data, numerate analyses and discussions on the technicalities. In the end, the project had to be abandoned after some $500 million in investment.

It's hard to know whether anything could have been done better. Things could certainly have been done differently. But whether that would have produced a different result – who knows? Seeing the issue as a political problem early on might have helped – or, at the very least, reduced the sums spent before the investment had to be abandoned. But it took several years before management switched their thinking from technical/commercial mode to political mode and even then, not completely. Reluctance to approach the issue full on as a cultural and political one, with the implications of what that meant, lingered. Understandably. It was a difficult space for management to feel totally comfortable in. They did not have the level of political skills that their opponents so deftly deployed.

By the time I got involved, much water had flowed under the bridge. Much money had been spent. Political positions had become entrenched. Power plays had solidified. The narrative around the project had changed from an economic and commercial project that would bring much-needed foreign direct investment to poor parts of the country to one that had become culturally and politically demonized. Foreign direct investment had been successfully re-cast by opponents politically as neo-colonialism. It was then impossible to turn around.

I don't know. It could well be that the project was doomed from the get-go. Management felt frustrated and aggrieved at the ineffectiveness of the excellent efforts they put in over many years. But prior political issues – maybe around land ownership, previous longer-term projects that had resulted in environmental pollution, the conflict between mining and logging industries, etc. – simply became embodied in this new project. That the project became a lightning rod for broader political struggles in which the respective groups had been involved for some time. Which raises the question as to whether there had been sufficient social, cultural and political due diligence before committing what was a not insignificant investment.

In circumstances such as I have just described, the traditional approach when everything has fallen apart is to fall back on the last resort – Investor-State Dispute Settlement (ISDS) procedures. These are mechanisms through which investors can sue states if the latter change the rules of the game or do not abide by treaties or agreements made before investments are committed. Yet, I suggest that ISDS procedures are not long for this world. The political backlash against them has been fierce. They are now seen as ways in which powerful corporations can interfere with nation states' sovereign right to regulate their markets as they see fit, when they see fit. None of it helped by the fact that most such dispute settlement procedures have traditionally been shrouded in secrecy. The eventual disappearance of these procedures will fundamentally change the political landscape surrounding foreign investment – and the attractiveness of some locations as sites for future investment.

What we are seeing today is a pace of cultural change and an evolving importance of political perspectives that is rapid, disruptive and, in many ways, utterly chaotic. It can upend businesses and leave them behind, or give others significant advantage, just as quickly as the latest technological advance. Why?

CULTURAL REVOLUTION IN BITS AND BYTES

The rise of social media and increased access to information of all sorts in a digital world was initially seen by many as simply another channel of communication to be mastered if businesses were to reach their customer base. What we have learned since those early days is that digitization has driven nothing less than a cultural revolution. A rapid and fundamental shift in cultural expectations, power structures and political perspectives. Digitization has changed the world. For better or for worse. Or, maybe, for better *and* for worse.

I will address the political position of social media companies and brands in the next chapter. Here, the focus is on the impact of the digital world on the politics of business in general.

I was recently having a conversation with the manager of a hotel where I was staying for a few days. He observed that, in the past, whenever a customer complained about something, they would make nice noises, apologize, maybe give them a cheap gift or upgrade, and then, by and large, just file the complaint away. Today, that simply won't do. He realizes that any complaint can be placed on social media or as an evaluation on the hundreds of available travel sites, thereby reaching thousands of people with consequent negative impact on their business. If the complaint is about something around which there is significant activism, the impact gets multiplied several-fold.

This is a small example of how the digital world is altering power structures. There was a time when corporations wielded an almost unchecked amount of power – market power as well as political power. They had the resources to flood the market with one-way communications that shaped perceptions and how markets function. Through political donations and respect for their leaders' opinion, their direct influence on the political process itself was also significantly greater than many others. All in all, their 'share of voice' was overwhelming.

No longer. People everywhere now have a significant slice of that share of voice. Corporations must compete within a chaotic cacophony of noise generated about their business, their behaviours, their ability to meet expectations, and, maybe, even the personal lives of their executives. They still, individually, have more resources than others in this battle. But their voice is much less credible than it used to be. And, collectively, their voice is now slowly being matched by individuals, NGOs and activists of all sorts. All research shows that, on social media and other outlets, people are more likely to be influenced by the opinion of their friends or of other 'trusted sources' than by the self-promotion pumped out by business. And everyone is now wise to self-promotion that tries to hide behind 'influencers'.

The digital world has also driven a significant cultural shift in self-perception. People now feel empowered in a way that they didn't before. They will no longer be bullied by large corporations, or anyone else for that matter, or feel they have to take sub-standard service or unacceptable behaviour lying down. They fight back; organizing boycotts around companies that have upset them, or BUYcotts intended to back companies they support. And they can be highly effective.

One example among many is Danone's problems in Morocco, where a social media campaign urged shoppers to boycott the company's products in protest at the high prices charged. Within weeks, Danone's Morocco-based subsidiary lost 40 per cent of its sales and suffered a net loss of €13.5 million in the first half of 2018.

Forced to cut milk production by 30 per cent, Danone did not renew work contracts for 880 temporary workers out of its 6,000 Moroccan employees. Affected workers protested in front of the national parliament against the boycott. Emmanuel Faber, then Danone CEO, travelled to Morocco for a listening and consultation exercise and announced a cut in milk prices and new, cheaper lines of milk products.

Such a chain of developments would have been unthinkable before the world went digital. Companies could afford to ignore dissatisfaction because they had enough market power to do so and customers felt, and largely were, powerless. None of that is any longer the case.

Morocco is not one of Danone's biggest markets. That the company handled this issue at the highest level and found a workable solution is testament to its culture and well-developed cultural and political antennae.

Danone has championed a certain idea of what its business is about since 1968. Shareholders voted in favour of its aim to become the first listed company in France to be listed as an *'Entreprise à Mission'* – a mission-driven enterprise fashioned on the B-Corp model. This model promotes a clear purpose to deliver social and environmental benefits and balance the interests of all stakeholders. In developing its strategic goals, Danone sought the input of its 100,000 employees in how to build a company that delivers a better future for the company, its employees, and its communities. The company measures its performance by evaluating social, environmental, health and nutritional issues alongside financial performance.

Danone is on a journey – and its management knows that it is not there yet. Research shows that it is still among the top companies subject to consumer activism, largely on the basis of the Morocco episode. It's hard to know whether even sharper antennae across the whole company could have avoided it, and the consequent reputational damage, altogether. But it's easy to be blindsided as to why and where activist activity will hit next. Or for companies' senior leadership to know, let alone control, what is happening on the ground in every nook and cranny of operations that may span the globe. Gaps, missteps and unexpected events are inevitable. They can be minimized but likely not totally avoided. How businesses react to such episodes (compare Danone with the previously covered reaction of Boeing to a much more serious issue) ends up revealing the true nature of the corporate culture.

Of course, Danone – and Faber in particular – did not find themselves free of challenges. During the COVID-19 pandemic, Danone's financial performance lagged significantly behind that of its peer group. An investor revolt led by Bluebell Capital and Artisan Partners resulted in Faber being forced out. He also seemingly lost the support of honorary chairman and former Danone boss Franck Riboud, who had handpicked Faber for the top job and had remained a loyal supporter. As Danone's stock price dropped 27 per cent in 2020, Riboud was reported as saying that Faber was 'more interested in saving the planet than saving his firm'.[13]

But the two men's positions may not be as far apart as Riboud suggests. It may be simply a matter of operational implementation and different time horizons. Because Riboud, like the rest of us, knows perfectly well that if natural fresh water dries up through over-exploitation, there is no future for Danone brands like Evian, Volvic and Badoit. If there is no livable planet, there is no business at all. While shareholder interests focused on the immediate short term are understandable, it is more surprising that the same attitude seems to have been taken by Riboud, the son of the company's founder and the originator of the stakeholder focus.

The revolting shareholder groups were careful not to condemn the company's broader stakeholder focus, maybe understanding full well just how toxic such a stance would be in the current environment. Instead, they attempted to finesse the issue by arguing that the 'balance' between shareholder and stakeholder influence was wrong under Faber. In due course we shall see what that means in practice.

The emotional fuel
But not all protests and boycotts succeed. To do so, they have to tap into strong feelings of unfairness or abuse. While comments about shoddy products or poor customer service have an impact today far beyond what they used to, it is when activists manage to tap into people's deeper values and moral intuitions (i.e. their political views) that things start to snowball. '*For any protest to succeed, people have to be mobilized, they have to be persuaded of the righteousness of their cause,*' according to John Chalcraft, professor at the London School of Economics.[14]

Chalcraft's 'righteousness of their cause' in effect refers to people's socio-political views. As described earlier, politics is all about tapping into individual's deeper values and it is these deeper values that eventually lead them to mount effective campaigns that can damage or help businesses. We are therefore rapidly approaching a stage where the political perspective (broadly defined) will impact business performance at least as much as the usual things that companies focus on – product quality, customer service and so forth. It's hard to motivate and mobilize a crowd because you've had a terrible and frustrating phone conversation with a customer service representative (who hasn't experienced that constantly?), or because the brand-new product you've just bought broke on the second day of use. Not so hard to motivate people and create the necessary emotional fuel around a campaign targeting child labour in a major corporation's supply chain. The political is more important to people than that which relates to the mundaneness of their everyday consumption.

This turns on its head what businesses need to focus on. Product and service quality become minimum requirements to be in business. Their ability to focus on issues that have a political dimension become important distinguishing factors – positively or negatively, as we shall see.

The age-old question arises: is it more effective for activists to target 'bad' companies or to support 'good' ones (each of us will have our own definition of what constitutes 'good' and 'bad')?

Research in the US and the UK from communications company Weber Shandwick[15] shows that, in people's eyes, BUYcotts are growing in popularity relative to boycotts, *see below*:

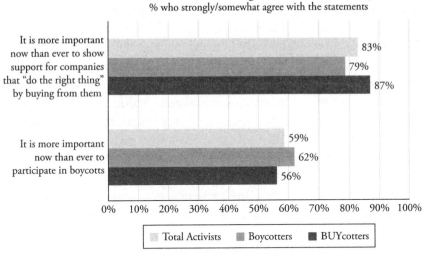

Desire to BUYcott is higher than desire to boycott
% who strongly/somewhat agree with the statements

It is important to treat such findings with caution. Many companies I have spoken to report that although their own research suggests that customers will reward companies who 'do the right thing' with purchasing their products or services, such statements are not fully reflected in actual buying behaviour. That does not mean that there is no advantage to be had by 'doing good'. I will examine this further – and how to do it so it is effective – when talking about political brands in the next chapter.

But it is as well to recognize that it is just human nature that anger is a more powerful motivator of action (boycotts) than are feelings of approval and gratitude (BUYcotts) – '*When the gall rises, it propels the irate toward challenges they otherwise would flee and actions to get others to do what they, the angry, wish*'.[16] Converting approval into action is perfectly achievable but requires much more sophisticated approaches than simple virtue signalling – especially given that the number of people who take seriously such virtue signalling by corporations continues to decline.

THE FRACTURED SOCIETY

The social media world has changed the landscape in other ways. We are all now highly aware of the issues with algorithms creating echo chambers where people are largely fed content that reinforces their opinions while shielding them from alternative perspectives. We all know that the amount of garbage, misinformation, outlandish conspiracy theories, and downright lies circulating on social media dwarfs the 1.6 million square kilometres of the Great Pacific Garbage Patch. All this makes governing at the political level much more challenging as the concept of shared narratives and shared 'truths' that bind people together in common cause is being shattered – with significant negative consequences for the social cohesion without which democracy, and a functioning society, cannot survive.

As a result, we are seeing the rise of a polarized, pressure-cooker society. Those who feel aggrieved by any particular situation or issue are fed an endless stream of content that reinforces their grievances. The pressure continues to build until some form of explosive relief becomes necessary.

'Traditional' media such as TV and newspapers have a vital role to play in our societies – the Fourth Estate that holds the powerful to account. Yet they, too, risk fracturing into different channels catering to specific political orientations and creating further echo chambers. The rise of the 24-hour news channel and de-regulation, such as the Federal Communications Commission scrapping the 'fairness doctrine' that put limits on the editorializing of news, further polluted the information that is broadcast to the public. Watching and reading the same 'news' item on three different channels or in three different newspapers, one often wonders whether it's the same news item at all.

Sometimes, the bias goes so far that it alienates the very people it is supposed to be charming.

During the 2016 US presidential election, I was speaking to a friend about media coverage. She is Californian, about as Democrat as they come, an avid and highly successful environmental activist and a former CEO of a significant corporation. Her words: '*I've stopped reading the* New York Times. *I don't like Trump, but the* Times's *bias for Hillary has become so extreme that I can't bear to read any of what they write.*'

Echo chambers also continue to nourish the 'us against them' mentality. If you're not with us, you're against us. If you're not in my camp, you are the enemy that must be destroyed. The result is an increasingly polarized and hostile public space that risks descending into a Hobbesian war of all against all with social and political consequences that are not pretty.

We should also understand that these changes have significant long-term effects on the commercial world. Commerce and markets operate well when they are oiled by one key social component – trust. It is no coincidence that 'My word is my bond' has been the motto of the London Stock Exchange for centuries. If trust is lost, commerce slows down, becomes unmanageably bureaucratic and expensive – to the delight of the lawyers – and risks stagnation. One only need look at the explosion of banks' compliance departments, systems and procedures to see just how expensive, unmanageable and bureaucratic is the impact of eroding trust. This piling on of unmanageable bureaucracy driven by lack of trust has reached such a degree that my own banker told me that he sees one of his main jobs as being to shield me from having to navigate the snakes and ladders of the multiple procedures involving endless departments now necessary to complete even the most basic banking task. For that service I am eternally grateful.

Polarization undermines social cohesion because it undermines trust. As that spreads to commercial relationships, its effects are reflected in the vibrancy, or lack thereof, of our economies. It is, to me, quite remarkable that when economists talk about the idea that we have reached a state of 'secular stagnation' they all too rarely explore how the changing social and cultural landscape is imposing huge costs on business and strangling our economies.

Professor Sir John Kay in his review of equity markets commissioned by the UK government concludes, *'Trust and confidence, or their absence, are the product of the prevailing culture. Trust and confidence are not generally created by trading between anonymous agents attempting to make short-term gains at each other's expense.'*[17] Yet trading between anonymous agents in this way is the key characteristic of the digital world. If efficiency gains are outweighed by eroding trust, it may not be at all surprising that no studies have yet been able to show an improvement in overall economic productivity from digitization. Professor Diane Coyle also puts it clearly: *'Economic policymakers have also largely ignored social capital – the trust among strangers that is vital to any sustained economic effort.'*[18]

None of this was foreseen or in any way intended when the idea of social networks was launched or when more traditional media outlets did all they could to compete in a changing landscape. In fact, it was just the opposite. Social networks were intended to bring us together by providing a public space where we could all interact even if we happened to be on opposite poles of the planet. And, by and large, that promise has been fulfilled. The unintended consequences described here were not anticipated and they are largely not welcome. It's hard to know how the net effect will play out in the long run.

This fractured, militant, polarized and belligerent social and political climate has implications for business in many ways. A campaign for or against business practices thrown into the right pressure cooker can have a significant impact – one much greater than would be the case when trust, reasonableness and compromise occupied a significant part of the public discourse. Today, such a campaign is much more likely to generate feelings of rage, mobilize a significant number of people into combative mode and affect corporate reputations and performance – positively or negatively – more than used to be the case.

None of this can be countered using the old playbook. No amount of corporate press releases designed by the legal department to separate words from meaning will cut it. It's becoming ever more difficult just to ride it out using Margaret Thatcher's dictum that any scandal only makes the newspapers for about ten days and, if one can keep calm through that period, it will be forgotten. That may have been true in the 1990s. No longer. While mainstream newspapers are largely driven by short-term sales and therefore need to keep refreshing their headlines with ever more sensationalist ones, activists are single-minded and viscerally mission driven. They will continue to hammer their point over and over – however long it takes.

Some campaigns will, indeed, fade – at some point. Others will snowball. It may seem hard to tell which is which. It's easier for those who have developed effective cultural and political antennae. Because simply waiting to see whether it will all fizzle out or not is perilous. And neither can corporations cling any longer to the idea that their role is to be acultural, asocial and amoral – and therefore apolitical. Even in their everyday operations they now face political decisions, some seemingly totally unrelated to their business, that they cannot duck.

My good friend Simon Zadek's outstanding book, *The Civil Corporation*, contains a story about a utility company that was approached by an activist group and asked to stop issuing hunting licences on land that it owned. The response from the company was: '*To be honest, we don't have a view on hunting, and we do not particularly*

want to have one. Where does it all end? If there is a church but no mosque
on our land, will we eventually have to have a view on God?[19]

Yet, in this example, it is simply impossible for the company
concerned not to have a view on hunting (or on religion, if it ever
came to that). Whether it continues to issue hunting licences or stops,
it is taking a view – either in support of or against hunting. The only
available choice is essentially a political one: whether to come down on
the side of the hunters or the animal rights activists. Not having a view
and not upsetting anyone is not an option. And whichever position
the company takes, it risks an onslaught the eventual effect of which
is largely unknowable. The desire not to have a view is understandable
but it is simply impossible. Not of this world – and not in the world we
are now living in.

The trouble is that many businesses have not, so far, had much
exposure to such messy dilemmas – debates that are fundamentally
cultural, social and moral. About purpose, values, beliefs, emotions,
ethics and other soft, intangible, difficult-to-grasp ideas. Concepts
that make many senior managers uncomfortable because they are not
technical or operational. They do not lend themselves to 'rational'
analysis or to putting into neat financial models. Notions the cultural
meaning of which is ever-changing. Competing narratives that will be
constantly contested and for which there is no resolution.

Many feel that they should not have to face such decisions as they are
not directly related to their business. That it's not reasonable that their
businesses are targeted in this way. Too bad. In today's world, getting
down in the mud to wrestle with these political issues is unavoidable for
more or less any business. Even then, there are broadly two alternative
routes any company can take.

The first is to tackle such issues in a purely instrumental fashion. Taking
the above example, one could debate who is likely to be more disruptive
– the hunters or the animal rights activists? Who are we most likely to
be able to contain with minimum hassle and minimum distraction from
the business of business? That then drives the decision – which may turn
out to be right or wrong. This approach probably appeals to many.

The second is actually to take a political position because that's what
the company wishes to communicate that it believes in. That is the
political space it wishes to occupy. This too has implications and I'll
address them in more detail in the next chapter when we talk about

how some brands have responded to political campaigns like Black Lives Matter. And we have seen a significant number of businesses taking action, or, at least, making noise about taking action, following the storming of the US Capitol in January 2021.

Non-engagement is the one option that, in most cases, is not viable.

THE POLITICAL EMPLOYEE

One of the longstanding characteristics of the business world is that when you go to work you are expected to check your humanity at the door. At work, you are expected to be 'professional'. Some would say a cog in the work machine striving for ever greater performance and efficiency. Crying or any other display of emotion is frowned upon. The atmosphere is expected to be 'businesslike'. The expressing of political opinions or anything else that might distract from the desired efficiency is usually not welcome.

Google decided to break from tradition and management stated that they expect people 'to bring their whole self to work'. And the staff did.

In November 2018, Google employees staged a mass walkout in protest at what they perceived was too lenient a treatment of those accused of sexual misconduct – a political issue. Two male executives had left the company with pay packages amounting to some $90 million despite the fact that complaints against them were found to be credible. One employee wrote '*Happy to quit for $90m – no sexual harassment required.*'

Protestors made five demands: an end to forced arbitration in cases of harassment and discrimination; a commitment to end pay and opportunity inequality; a publicly disclosed sexual harassment transparency report; a clear, uniform and globally inclusive process for reporting sexual misconduct safely and anonymously; and for Google's chief diversity officer to report directly to CEO Sundar Pichai and make recommendations directly to the board of directors — which should include an employee representative. All of it a highly political agenda.

A few weeks earlier, Google had taken itself out of the Maven contract with the US Department of Defense after a staff outcry against the company agreeing to let its AI technology be used for military purposes. Yet more politics. Dropping out of the contract put paid to potential future work that could have earned Google some $10 billion over a decade.

Earlier that year, employees at both Microsoft and Salesforce had protested against their companies' work for US Immigration and Customs Enforcement (ICE) in opposition to President Trump's policies that separated children from their parents. CEO Satya Nadella issued a memo to employees with an explicitly political title: 'My views on US immigration policy'. In it, he denies that Microsoft was working on anything that related to the child separation policy. The memo opens with politics: *'Like many of you, I am appalled at the abhorrent policy of separating immigrant children from their families at the southern border of the U.S.'* He went on to describe government policy as 'cruel and abusive'.[20]

In October 2018, an Amazon employee anonymously wrote an article titled: *I'm an Amazon Employee. My Company Shouldn't Sell Facial Recognition Tech to Police.*[21] The article was published after a letter signed by 450 employees had been sent to Jeff Bezos, Amazon founder and then CEO, making the same demand and also seeking to remove from Amazon Web Services the software firm Palantir that powers much of ICE's deportation and tracking programme.

The article referenced above opens with a key statement:

When a company puts new technologies into the world, it has a responsibility to think about the consequences.

Such explicit mass action by employees on political issues may take time to become mainstream. Not many people are in the privileged position of Silicon Valley tech workers, whose skills are in high demand, thereby giving them power. It is, however, possible, maybe probable, that such issues will start to run alongside the usual grievances about pay and conditions that have previously driven worker activism. Even if they do not burst into explicit action, a more politicized workforce will still have views on the stances taken by their employer – as we saw earlier in the Harley-Davidson case (*see also* pp. 41–3). For the most skilled workers who are in the greatest demand, they may become one of the factors determining willingness to work for one corporation rather than the next. And they may have an impact on workplace atmosphere, satisfaction and productivity.

In 2020, award-winning journalist Suzanne Moore was the subject of a complaint in a letter signed by 338 of her colleagues at the *Guardian* newspaper. Her offence was to stand up for a certain type of feminism (called 'second-wave feminism'), stating that gender was a biological fact not a matter of 'feelings' and decrying the fact that Selina Todd, an Oxford professor of modern history who had expressed similar views, had been de-platformed. The 338 argued that such opinions were, in their own view, 'transphobic', and that, *the pattern of publishing transphobic content has interfered with our work and cemented our reputation as a publication hostile to trans rights and trans employees.* Many readers would have difficulty relating that statement to the *Guardian*. Moore eventually resigned her post, feeling that she did not get the expected support of the editorial team in a newspaper that purported to promote liberal views on freedom of speech. She claimed that many other employees had privately expressed their support for her but felt unable to speak out for fear of losing their jobs.

If we take these events and statements at face value (and it's always difficult to know what is going on behind the scenes), they suggest a house divided. A group of employees (338 out of a total of some 1,600 or more) who feel emboldened to express their own political/cultural views and another group who are nervous of doing so for fear of being fired. That is not optimal for a newspaper business that is trying to encourage pluralism in its coverage and, presumably, harmony among its workforce. It feels like a microcosm of the 'cancel culture' that is becoming all too prevalent – a vocal and aggressive minority that will not contemplate the idea that alternative views to their own have any right to exist and are determined to demolish the lives and careers of anyone who dares question their position. We used to call it bigotry.

I have not seen any public statement from the *Guardian* management or editorial leadership on their stance in this matter. Yet it may be particularly important for a newspaper to clarify whether its editorial stance is one that supports a plurality of opinion, or whether it supports certain views on certain subjects and will not give airtime to alternative perspectives. There is no right or wrong answer to this question, it's simply a choice that management has to make.

Neither are these sorts of political actions limited to the middle and lower ranks of management and employees. In 2020, a number of senior executives at Shell left the company. One of the reported reasons was disagreement over the nature and pace of change, moving away from its traditional oil and gas business to a more climate-friendly business based on renewable energy. The weeks leading up to publication of its strategy saw a wave of departures of senior executives who led various parts of the company's renewables businesses.

One insider put it like this: '*People are really questioning if there will be any change at all. Part of the frustration is that you see the potential, but the mindset isn't there among senior leaders for anything radical.*'

Senior managers within Shell clearly felt that the company was not doing what it should to tackle one of the most pressing political issues of our time. The episode illustrates how socio-political issues have started to disrupt businesses from the inside with staff at many levels no longer willing to work for companies that, in their view, are not doing their bit. Such disruptions are based on people's values and worldview, not on inadequate compensation or any of the other issues that have usually driven people's behaviours within corporations.

None of the above incidents are conducive to a positive workplace environment. Businesses leaders have choices. They can make their political positions more explicit and attract a workforce that buys into their stance and feel comfortable and happy working there. Or they may continue to refuse, in so far as is possible, and it's likely to become ever less possible, to take any political stance and maintain the position of being apolitical in order to attract the sort of workforce to whom that appeals. Or they may leave it all rather ambiguous, a stance that may not promote workplace harmony. Every business will make its own choices. It remains to be seen which approach will be the most sustainable in an increasingly polarized, uncompromising political world.

For business leaders, the question is not which is the 'right' stance to take. Rather, as we shall see later, it is whether they can build the culture and capabilities to be able to address these challenging issues meaningfully. Neither need they, nor should they, cave in to every kind of employee pressure. Simon & Schuster, a publishing house, came under employee pressure to refuse to publish a book by former US Vice President Mike Pence. The company published the book anyway believing that it is not its role to censor publication based on one or other ideological viewpoint.

Many businesses will find it all somewhat countercultural. The issues to be addressed cannot be resolved using the same decision-making frameworks and tools that are appropriate for day-to-day business decisions, frameworks that have been honed over time and are now almost automatic in most businesses. We are now wading into issues that have no 'right answer', with consequences that are uncertain and impacts that, by and large, cannot be quantified. Questions that are emotional, cultural and political and cannot be subject to what most people have come to understand as 'rational' analysis (which, by the way, is, itself, nothing of the kind). Where there are obvious winners and losers and where the latter can, and likely will, kick up one heck of a fuss.

THE KNOTTY PROBLEM OF EXECUTIVE COMPENSATION

On 16 December 2020, the *Guardian* website in the UK carried two articles more or less side by side. The first was titled 'Unicef to feed hungry children in UK for first time in 70-year history'. It reported that 2.4 million children in the UK – one of the world's wealthiest countries – lived in food-insecure households. Unicef was to provide funding to a community project providing nutritious breakfasts to schoolchildren. This came piled on top of a surge in the use of food banks in the UK during the COVID-19 pandemic.

The second article, titled 'The Guardian view on shameless CEOs: because they're worth it?', focused on Tim Steiner, CEO of food delivery company Ocado: '*Mr Steiner last year earned £58.7m. This astonishing rate of remuneration is 2,605 times the average wage of one of his employees, which stands at £22,500. Put another way, 24 hours of Mr Steiner's time is allegedly worth a year's toil from an average Ocado worker.*'

It is clear that the juxtaposition of these two articles is politically toxic. '*This gulf between the top and bottom of our society is not inevitable. It is immoral,*' continued the second article.

Some argue that from a purely business/financial viewpoint, it is reasonable to take the view that executive compensation receives much more attention than it deserves. Whatever a few senior executives get paid in large companies has very little direct financial impact on corporate profits or shareholder returns. Which is one reason why investors have, in the past, only made token efforts at reining it all in. The idea that executive compensation is a marginal issue is untrue – as we shall see later.

As regards Steiner himself, he is, of course, quite different from many other executives as he is a co-founder of Ocado, worked from the ground up and took personal risk to get himself and his company to where they are today, maybe against the odds. What is appropriate remuneration is always a matter of judgement and there is no doubt that £59 million is substantial. That said, Mr Steiner was not being rewarded for failure, as in some of the examples cited previously. He had skin in the game rather than climbing through the ranks in a relatively risk-free career.

A Green Paper on corporate governance published by the UK government in 2016 stated: '*Executive pay is an area of significant public concern, with surveys consistently showing it to be a key factor in public dissatisfaction with large businesses*'.[22] The reality is that once an issue like executive pay becomes a political issue, then criticism becomes more or less universal. Everyone ends up getting caught up in the melee however much they might convince themselves that their own executive packages are perfectly justified.

It is also worth bearing in mind that the COVID-19 pandemic played a role in corporate performance. For some, it produced windfall profits. For others it created significant challenges. Wm Morrison, a UK based grocery company, saw its profits fall due to the increased costs associated with the pandemic meaning that directors would have missed out on bonuses. The remuneration committee used its 'discretion' by stripping out the negative impact of the pandemic as something out of management's control and restored the bonuses. Seventy per cent of shareholders voted against the move. Conversely, I could not find any instances where remuneration committees used their 'discretion' to reduce executive compensation in those companies where the pandemic created windfall profits.

Activision Blizzard, a video games company, saw a spike in performance and market capitalization as the pandemic stimulated bored youngsters to play video games endlessly. As a result, the pay package for Bobby Kotick, its chief executive, soared to $115 million for 2020. An investor revolt was envisaged leading the company controversially to adjourn the shareholder vote on pay giving it time to engage further with shareholders while infuriating many shareholder groups. The pay package was eventually supported by 54 per cent of shareholders. Michael Varner, director of executive compensation at CtW Investment Group that led shareholder opposition was quoted as saying '*With only 54% of votes cast in favor, the proposal nearly failed to receive majority support – it appears Activision did just enough arm-twisting for the measure to pass*', while suggesting that the matter was not considered closed.[23]

Outrage at executive pay is fuelled by ever-increasing evidence that, in many cases, there is no correlation between high pay and financial performance – never mind performance on non-financial matters. The financial crash of 2008 brought attention to this issue. Some of the world's most highly paid executives were at the helm of companies that brought much of the global economy to its knees – and were then bailed out using public money – yet more transfers from the poor to the wealthy.

A study of 701 companies from the Vlerick Business School's Executive Remuneration Centre[24] found, among other things, that: '*across Europe, better performing companies do not pay their chief executives more. Pay differences are a function of company size not company performance.*' In a collection of essays for the High Pay Centre, Alexander Pepper from the London School of Economics said that studies since 1990 had either failed to demonstrate a positive link between executive pay and corporate performance or, at best, the link was very weak.[25]

The pairing of ever-increasing levels of executive compensation with relentless downward pressure on wages for other workers also gives the impression that, in spite of the mellifluous words that routinely flow from HR departments, senior executives are seen as a valuable resource while everyone else is regarded as an undesirable cost. A perspective hardly designed to create harmonious relationships or political acceptability.

But there is evidence that this, too, is slowly changing. In 2021 when the Biden administration was starting to propose a gradual increase in the US minimum wage from $7.25 an hour to $15 per hour, CEOs from McDonald's, Best Buy, JP Morgan Chase, Starbucks and others supported it.

The overall political impression created, rightly or wrongly, is that senior executives pay themselves more simply because they can. The larger the company, the more they can pay themselves because their pay becomes less than a rounding error in corporations' overall income statements. And the embedded practice of setting compensation packages in comparison to those in other corporations ensures that executive compensation is subject to a continuous upward ratchet.

The political and the economic
The issue of executive compensation is primarily a political issue. As with the situation outlined previously regarding the pricing of pharmaceutical products (*see also* pp. 44–7), and despite the pseudo-science put forward

by remuneration consultants, there is no objective way of evaluating what any individual CEO is worth. Whether a 5, 10, 20, or 50 million compensation package is justified. Rather the overall impact depends on fuzzy public perceptions of 'fairness' and which political narrative gains traction among the public. There seems little doubt that the narrative that is currently gaining most traction is that executive pay is excessive and possibly out of control. A situation that costs business significant political capital.

Neither is it convincing to argue that this is a functioning market and that pay levels are set by market forces. Functioning markets only work if they have price competition as one of their foundational characteristics. But I don't see many senior executives competing in the marketplace on the basis of offering to work for lower compensation. Nor do I see many corporations handing their CEO's appointment to their purchasing department with instructions to squeeze prices.

High compensation received by some (e.g. in sports) have not raised the same outrage as have executive salaries. Salaries in the UK charities sector have, on the other hand, also come under fire when it was reported that 270 charities were paying executive salaries that were greater than the salary of the UK Prime Minister with the highest earner on £4.7 million a year – money that is coming from donors' funds intended to support good causes.

It is not high salaries per se that are at issue, but the broader political context.

Whilst the *size* of executive compensation packages is primarily a political issue, package *structures* also likely have an economic impact. It is highly doubtful whether the relatively recent fad of tying executive compensation to stock price performance has been a net positive. It tends to drive increased short-termism and increased management focus on stock price movements rather than on long-term value creation through industrial development. This drives ever more precarious forms of employment and has likely been a contributor to economic stagnation. It has given rocket boosters to the age of financialized capitalism that, as we shall see later, is well past its sell-by date.

Can anything be done?
Whether anything can be done effectively about executive compensation is debatable. Even if it could be done, whether anything will actually be

done even more so. While some boards may feel it is in the long-term interests of both business and society that the issue is addressed, many do not. And many will feel that they cannot move unless everyone moves. The standard riposte for those vested in the status quo.

And those who try to do something about it risk getting ostracized by their peers. In 2015 Dan Price, founder of Gravity Payments, set his company's minimum salary at $70,000 and cut his own salary to the same amount from $1.1m, hoping that other companies might feel the need to follow suit. It didn't happen. He relates how a CEO he had looked up to all his life went up to him, said 'F*** you', and walked away. According to Price, such reactions are not unusual.

Can investors be the ones to drive meaningful change? One director of an industry association for pension funds put it to me that the issue is far too complicated, seemingly insoluble, and not high on investors' agenda. Might that be slowly changing? Support for pay packages dropped to 87.6 per cent from 91.8 per cent in 2015. Not much, but maybe the start of a trend. In the first half of 2021 six S&P 500 companies failed to win majority shareholder support for pay packages. From 2017 to 2019 most companies that failed pay votes underperformed the S&P 500 and their sector peers according to analysis by Morgan Stanley. Maybe what will start to emerge is that, in fact, there is an inverse relationship between executive pay and long-term corporate performance. Excessive pay, whatever that may mean, may yet turn out to be a good indicator of poor corporate governance that will affect corporate performance. That would turn the conventional belief system on its head.

Is government intervention a viable route to change? It's not an easy issue to resolve through regulation. Governments do not want to, nor should they want to, get into the business of defining private sector pay packages. And, when they have been attempted, nudges in that direction through public policy initiatives have largely failed. Initiatives to date have focused mainly on increased transparency and strengthening shareholders' say over compensation packages – though largely in a non-binding fashion. The idea of setting maximum pay ratios between executives and staff is also in discussion. In Switzerland, in 2013, popular referendums tightened the conditions attached to approval of executive pay while rejecting a 12:1 maximum pay ratio. The UK Trades Union Congress has suggested a maximum 20:1 pay ratio. France, Germany and the EU are all reviewing the issue as part of corporate governance reform.

Some argue that the problem is best resolved through high levels of taxation of such pay packages. That, too, is not without its own pitfalls. Are we to be trapped in a world where executive compensation will remain one of those things that simply continues to erode people's faith in, and respect for, business? Steadily eating away at business's political capital and giving fuel to political forces that run on a platform of bringing business to heel? It's not good for any of us but we may be stuck with it. Until, that is, the pressure grows to a point where determinedly anti-business political forces start to gain real traction.

INSTITUTIONAL CHANGE

Years ago, I was in a meeting with senior commercial and R&D executives in a major pharmaceutical company. The research people were presenting their ideas for future innovation. Towards the end of their presentation, a senior commercial executive piped up: '*This is all very interesting scientifically, but you guys seem to forget that our job here is to make money.*'

The president of R&D, a wise and experienced Scotsman, looked the objector in the eye: '*Laddie, we're not here to make money.*' Silence around the room. '*We're here to make medicines that improve people's lives and make them better. And if we can do that well, then we'll make money.*'

There was a time when such a statement of the obvious didn't need saying. But, over the last several decades, common sense has been eroded. 'Making money' became the *raison d'être* of many businesses rather than being seen as a consequence of providing, profitably, a product or service that improved people's lives and how our societies function. Senior leaders in many businesses spend more of their time preparing for presentations and meetings with Wall Street and City analysts than meeting with customers or other stakeholders. Quarterly financial performance – and its impact on stock prices – consumes a huge amount of headspace. As outlined above, it is deeply built into internal metrics and incentives – did you make your numbers this month? In some businesses, little else seems to matter.

Of course, companies have to operate profitably. Otherwise they have no future and will be unable to provide the benefits and innovations that help us all. But there is a difference between having the discipline to operate profitably so as to fund future investment, as opposed to making profit, especially short-term, quarter-on-quarter profit numbers, become the be-all-and-end-all of why a business exists.

Or using any extra cash for massive share buyback programmes rather than long-term business investment. The shift in perspective has been a relatively rapid process resulting in a financialized economy.

In a financialized economy most of the value that is exchanged becomes reduced to a financial instrument that can be traded. Or, as Greta Krippner of the University of Michigan puts it, a '*pattern of accumulation in which profit making occurs increasingly through financial channels rather than through trade and commodity production.*'[26] Trading of financial instruments (stocks, bonds and other financial products) then becomes a money-making activity in and of itself, with the underlying value that was created in the real economy largely becoming irrelevant.

Financialization leads to growth of the financial sector in economies relative to industrial sectors. Over time, it inevitably directs companies – and particularly those where senior executive compensation is tied to stock price performance – to prioritize short-term stock price performance over providing real economic value and investment in the patient growth of their business whenever the two objectives are in conflict.

A 2005 US survey of 401 financial executives by Duke University's John Graham and Campbell R. Harvey, and University of Washington's Shivaram Rajgopal, reveals that companies manage earnings with more than just accounting gimmicks. A startling 80 per cent of respondents said they would decrease value-creating spending on research and development, advertising, maintenance and hiring in order to meet short-term earnings benchmarks. More than half the executives would delay a new project even if it entailed sacrificing value.[27]

Financialization has taken over from the previous economic model of industrial capitalism. I will explore this further in the closing chapter, where I contend that political capitalism is the next stage of economic development that will overtake financialization – over time. This is driven by many of the factors already discussed, combined with direct social and political backlash against financialization and an increasing realization of its corrosive impact on sustainable and broad-based prosperity. All of which was accelerated by the Great Financial Crash of 2008 when people were brought face to face with the human, social, political and economic risks associated with highly financialized economic systems.

As we have seen above, individuals, whether employees, customers, or senior executives, are making their voice heard. Insisting that we need to pull back from the financialized economic model to one that takes a broader view of the role of business in our society. While individual pressure does have an impact, change accelerates when the push for reform reaches powerful institutions – whether private or public. Institutions are slow to change, yet the pace of change that we are seeing in institutional approaches would have seemed inconceivable only a few short years ago.

The idea that profit is merely a consequence of adding value to society is back – this time re-wrapped in the concept of corporate purpose.

As I have written in past letters, a company cannot achieve long-term profits without embracing purpose and considering the needs of a broad range of stakeholders.

This statement appeared in a letter headed 'A fundamental reshaping of finance' from Larry Fink, Chairman and CEO of BlackRock – the world's largest asset management firm – to his client base. '*Ultimately, purpose is the engine of long-term profitability,*' Fink goes on to say. A statement that is, at its core, no different to that by the previously mentioned president of R&D – just decades later. Decades where common sense seems to have gone out the window.

This evolution is politically driven. Issues like climate change, continued destruction of natural capital, rising wealth inequality, stagnating economies, increasing levels of poverty even in the wealthiest countries have combined with public outrage to lift these issues to the top of the political agenda – at government, institutional and individual levels. As the regulatory framework increasingly targets such social concerns, we are seeing a massive re-allocation of capital to what have become known as ESG investments – investments that focus on the Environmental, Social and Governance standards of corporations.

There is also an increasing realization that, as Umair Haque puts it in *The New Capitalist Manifesto*, '*shareholder value isn't a reliable measure of whether authentic economic value has been created. It is value that can be transferred from other stakeholders rather than created anew.*'[28] In other words, what economists label as 'externalities' are forms of capital that corporations access and utilize but do not pay for. Such capital is extracted from our environment, from the depletion of natural capital, from our health and security through pollution and climate change, from social cohesion through tax arbitrage and consistent downward pressure on wages leading to increasing inequality with its social and political consequences. Politically, these actions are increasingly seen as extracting value out of 'the commons' – that from which every citizen benefits (clean air, ecosystem services, water availability, social capital, etc.) and transferring the wealth to shareholders. The amount of value truly 'created' is lower than that stated in standard financial accounting.

And different companies have different levels of impact – even when they operate in the same industrial sector.

Harvard Business School is running a major project looking at impact-weighted accounting. This project is intended to measure and account for the externalities imposed by different corporations. The hope is that, eventually, this sort of accounting will become standard.

For the moment, effort has gone into measuring environmental impacts. Measuring wider social impact is more difficult and may come later. As the figure below shows, companies in the oil and gas business, for example, have widely different levels of external impact.

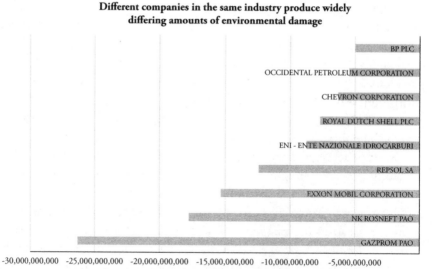

Different companies in the same industry produce widely
differing amounts of environmental damage

Aggregated amount of environmental damage
(expressed as negative US$ impact)

Source: Data from Harvard Business School. Impact-Weighted Accounts.

It is this realization that has driven the emergence of the ESG investment market. Given the increasing focus on environmental issues, any reasonable investor would see a different amount of risk associated with investing in BP as opposed to Exxon Mobil, given their respective earnings performance is dependent on different amounts of environmental damage. That is, of course, if one were investing in oil and gas companies at all.

The exact size of the ESG market is difficult to estimate. Research firm Opimas estimated its size at around $40 trillion in 2020. According to Bank of America, in 2021, a third of all global equity inflows went into ESG funds. There is little doubt that this represents the future growth market. The COVID-19 pandemic too has served to concentrate minds.

The 2020 HSBC global survey on sustainable finance and investing showed that 41 per cent of the issuers questioned felt that the pandemic made them believe even more strongly that becoming sustainable is important. For an additional 38 per cent, the pandemic made them think that the social welfare component of sustainability is more important than they thought before. Among investors, the corresponding figures were 29 and 24 per cent respectively, with an additional 24 per cent saying that they had re-evaluated how they think about ESG issues.[29]

Perhaps not surprisingly, in an environment roiled by a pandemic, significant economic stress and a prolonged period of low returns, investors' perspective on the importance of ESG issues have somewhat decreased as they become ever more preoccupied with investment performance. On the other hand, issuers' concerns with these matters continue to increase.

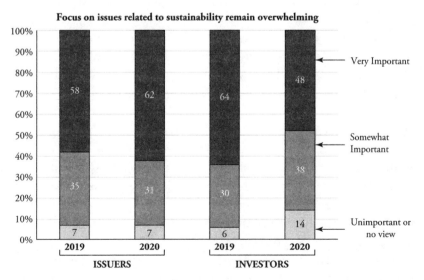

Source: HSBC Sustainable Finance and Investment Survey, 2020.

As a result of this new political movement, we are seeing a significant shift in corporate focus and behaviour. Maybe even more notable is that social impact is rising up the corporate agenda following several years where environmental issues, and particularly climate change-related ones, had dominated the agenda.

Tacking to an uncertain destination

As always with political issues, we will not be moving to a clearly defined destination in a neat straight line. First, the destination itself remains uncertain. While social and environmental issues take centre stage, what that means in practice for corporate behaviour is still being understood. Different companies will face different challenges and opportunities and they will handle them differently. The only option that is not available to those who wish to continue thriving is to ignore these issues.

Secondly, companies will tack this way and that, driven by market and regulatory developments, customer pressures, inevitable tensions in balancing these new imperatives with maintaining acceptable levels of financial performance during the transition and the availability – or not – of investible projects that are truly ESG compliant. For instance, BlackRock, in spite of the ambitions verbally declared by Larry Fink, has come under increasing criticism that it is not walking the talk:

> A year [after Mr Fink's 2018 letter], it had become clear that his were words empty of any meaning other than marketing... green ETFs only represented 3 percent of the firm's assets under management... It turns out, however, that these green funds are anything but. Scratch off the greenwash and you will find investments in coal, pipelines, oil, and gas.[30]

It is to be expected that a company like BlackRock with trillions under management will take time to change its investment model. It is a journey and every activist will believe that progress is too slow. And it may well be too slow in the context of pressing issues like climate change. But maybe more important is that we understand the broad shape, if not the detail, of the end destination and the institutional changes necessary to approach it.

Neither is BlackRock alone. JPMorgan Chase committed to facilitating $200 billion in clean financing between 2016 and 2025.

Bank of America has committed to mobilizing an additional $300 billion in capital through its Environmental Business Initiative between 2020 and 2030. Société Générale has committed to raising €100 billion in financing for the energy transition between 2016 and 2020. But the World Resources Institute reported that 57 per cent of banks making such commitments failed to disclose their accounting methodology and that it was difficult to assess whether these commitments were translated into real action.[31]

Some are more scathing. *'These commitments are just nonsense,'* according to one former head of sustainable finance. *'You don't run a bank that way – putting out a notice that you're going to finance $150 billion or something in renewables. Finance is driven by the credit people.*

'I guarantee at monthly meetings these targets aren't being checked. It's just a number these banks know they're going to meet because the renewables industry is growing. In addition, people doing the work in sustainable finance are often isolated from the boards making these sweeping statements.'[32]

It may be right to be realistic about how broad statements end up being operationalized in large and complex organizations. For instance, two years after JP Morgan Chase announced that it would no longer finance the private prison industry, it emerged that funds tied to the bank had the largest position in a bond issued by CoreCivic, a company that runs prisons and detention centres in the US.

Additionally, there is the question of supply and demand. Currently, demand for ESG compliant investment is outstripping supply with the inevitable consequence that many investments labelled as ESG compliant only make the cut because investment houses are desperate to offer such products not because the companies involved are convincingly compliant.

The temptation to mount campaigns to make corporations appear greener and more socially responsible than they actually are is probably irresistible to many. For investors, *'It begs the question as of whether some financial products are designed for a virtue-signalling investor audience.'*[33]

But an inability or unwillingness to follow through does not remain hidden for long these days. It is also right to be dubious about commentary from never-can-be-satisfied activists. It's a journey full of twists and turns but the direction of travel seems clear.

Rather than focusing solely on these operational questions, it might be worth also considering the bigger picture.

Is finance fit for purpose?

The finance sector does not operate in a vacuum. Practices have developed in response to how the market is structured and the incentives created. That market structure is a result of public policy choices. Can finance really transform itself on its own without a significant change in market structure? It's unreasonable to expect companies to develop new practices that do not fit with market structures and incentives thereby putting them in jeopardy. They will need public policy assistance coordinated with industry expertise if we are to see the desired transformation. That sort of cooperation is what political capitalism is all about.

Investors have, for decades, built their business models on the Anglo-Saxon model of capital markets and the publicly quoted limited liability private corporation. Essentially, the narrative was a simple one. Capital markets are there to provide capital for industrial development. The shareholder model keeps management from making off with the money and generates a good return for investors. Business would thrive to the benefit of everyone. What we are seeing today is that this model is shaky and may no longer be fit for purpose in the twenty-first century. We all know the drivers of that breakdown – I'll just mention some here.

Businesses today need less capital for investment than they did. Stock markets no longer make their money by intermediating the provision of capital. They now make most of their money by selling data. The 'shareholder first' model of the joint stock corporation has resulted in tremendous industrial development but, over time, in disastrous social, environmental and – let's not forget – political consequences. Financial markets have morphed from providing the life blood on which industry is built to being, overall, extractive systems that take rents out of the real economy rather than putting money in.** Over the last two decades, less money has been raised on the stock markets of Britain and the US than has been taken out through acquisitions for cash and share buybacks – '*The modern finance sector, and especially the parts of it that have grown most rapidly, is less and less related to the needs of the non-financial economy*'.[34]

** Of course, very many transactions continue their productive capital provision function. It is the system as a whole that has become extractive in nature.

In addition, the inequality consequences that are baked into our twentieth-century model of global financialized capitalism have come back to bite us. As a result, faith in the system is crumbling. The COVID-19 pandemic has seen state intervention at a level that I don't remember in my lifetime. With people everywhere seemingly liking it rather than arguing – as they would have done in the 1980s and 90s – that it's a disaster and the private sector holds the answer to all problems. All of this raises some fundamental questions for financial markets and investment institutions such as pension funds and others. Questions we have only just started to address.

I'll put it this way: are the issues we are all aware of truly solvable by putting what are essentially ESG plasters on the existing system (which is what these seemingly significant commitments to fund ESG-compliant projects amounts to)? Will market forces, the glorified agents of the late twentieth century, *on their own* really be able to drive the changes needed in our societies? Or are we seeing a slow transformation that is systemic in nature and will over time upend how we approach industrial investment going forward – and the whole business model of investment institutions?

In other words, is the narrative here really that all we need to do is to keep doing exactly the same stuff in the same way but be a bit nicer about it? That companies should now have purpose. That we should introduce more ESG transparency and reporting. That corporate governance should make more of a nod to other stakeholders. That business should keep doing their stuff but in a more socially responsible way. That banks and investment firms should remain in steady-as-she goes mode but funnel a few more dollars to what they themselves decide should fall into ESG-compliant categories.

Some argue that the question is one of better understanding 'risk'. Of course, risk is a difficult word to define as all actors rightly have different perceptions of what risk looks like from their own particular perspective – including different time horizons over which 'risk' is relevant. The narrative is growing that 'ESG' (whether it's climate, natural capital, social capital, or anything else) should be taken seriously because it's a matter of financial risk that is unaccounted for. Others argue that this simply embeds the culture of financialized thinking. It reinforces the idea that the only thing that matters remains the balance between financial risk and financial reward. That the real task is not to pander lazily to that thinking but to change the narrative so that business and financial activity have to start proving their worth to society in a much larger framework than financial performance metrics.

The two positions are complementary. As the socio-political culture changes, as society increasingly demands a broader view of the role of business, activities and business models that conflict with that evolving culture cannot be expected to do well.

In an age of financialized capitalism on the Anglo-Saxon model, financial markets take centre-stage in the economy which is why so much activity focuses on how financial markets end up allocating resources. But financial markets are made up of a number of individual actors (*see below*) each of whom has a different perception of risk, is acting in their own interest, is subject to different financial and non-financial incentives, and has different time frames for assessing success.

Simplified model of actors in the investment system

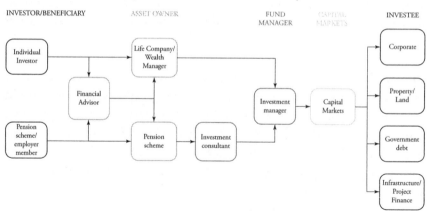

Source: Ashok Gupta. Reproduced with permission.

This brings to mind what is called the fallacy of composition. The idea that if everyone in a system does their own job well, then the system as a whole will function well. This fallacy ignores the complexity view of systems – the fact that the way that different parts of the system interconnect is just as important as how the individual parts are behaving. What is true of the parts (everyone doing their own job well) is not necessarily true of the whole.

And those operating within one part of the system are likely unaware of what is going on elsewhere. Gillian Tett relates how, when trying to understand the financial system in her early days at the *Financial Times*, she discovered how, despite all the expensive and sophisticated digital technology, different desks in banks had little idea about what was happening on other desks. Nobody on the ground really understood how the whole system fit together. Everyone was incentivized to deliver on their own targets.[35]

With everyone focused on their own set of incentives, the financial system as currently structured, while remaining vital to our prosperity, does not deliver enough of what society wants and needs.

Taking a whole system view leads us to a different narrative. That the traditional dominance of the Anglo-Saxon model of financialized capitalism as the benchmark for all else is ageing. That what we are looking at is a wholesale change in capital markets, the balance of private vs public capital, the emergence of fundamentally different types of corporate structures with different incentives, an increased interest in state involvement and, above all, a re-structuring of the rules of the game in financial markets to drive them towards adding social value and the kind of political economy that we need. In other words, the thread that connects the whole system is the socio-political and public policy environment within which all the different actors operate. All of which necessarily makes everything much more political in nature.

Larry Fink was right to title his 2018 letter to shareholders 'A fundamental reshaping of finance' rather than, say, 'business as usual with an ESG overlay'. How, and how fast, such a transformation takes place will depend on an interaction between policy intervention and changes in the way private financial institutions run their business. It cannot, and will not, happen solely through internal efforts by financial system players. Public policy will need to be part of the drive for change. It is, and will remain, highly political. And it is as well to realize that it is likely to be as much 'small p' political as 'big P' political. In other words, the socio-cultural momentum behind these changes will be big and consistent drivers of change maybe irrespective of party-political considerations.

Texas is a Republican stronghold in the control of a party that has traditionally resisted diving into climate-friendly policies. It is home to an economically important oil and gas industry that has significant political power. Texas is also flat and windy. As a result, and in spite of its 'big P' political bent, it produces the most wind power of any

US state. If Texas were a country, it would rank fifth in the world in installed wind power.

In another 'big P' political development, in 2020, under the Trump administration, the Office of the Comptroller of Currencies (OCC) proposed a 'Fair Access to Financial Services' rule designed to stop banks from limiting lending to companies on the basis for non-financial (or what were described as political) reasons. The rule required them instead to offer financing services equitably based on impartial risk analysis excluding any factors that could be considered political. The main effect of such a rule tended to be the opposite of that desired. It focused attention on the fact that social and environmental considerations are matters of long-term financial risk. That the socio-cultural momentum towards dealing with these externalities was such that those companies that failed to address them represented a less sound financial investment than those that did. In other words, the banks were led to argue that they were not withholding finance for political reasons but for reasons of financial risk consequent on political developments.

Take, for example, SSAB's proposed purchase of the Tata steel plant in the Netherlands. In January 2021, SSAB announced that it had abandoned the transaction. Why? '*We cannot align Tata Steel Ijmuiden with our sustainability strategy in the way desired,*' according to Martin Lindqvist, President and CEO at SSAB. '*The transition to fossil-free steel is a top priority for SSAB,*' he explained.[36] Tata's seemingly inadequate efforts on sustainability made its Dutch plant less attractive to potential buyers. Management had been too slow to read the runes and make the investments necessary to adapt, leaving them with a potentially unusable and unsellable 'stranded asset'. These are real financial risks that investors legitimately need to account for.

This is, by and large, where it is all going. But not completely.

Many banks had stopped or curtailed lending to private prison operators associated with President Trump's much-condemned immigration policies. The GEO Group, a private prisons contractor with sound finances, wrote to the OCC supporting its planned rule. In it, the company complained, '*The effort to politically deny banking services has now been "privatized" where political agitators have fought to redline the "undesirables" ... the need to restore the protections Americans have traditionally enjoyed is not only necessary but imperative.*'[37]

Here, I won't get into the merits and demerits of GEO's position or that of the banks' lending practices. Simply to point out that the debate put banks and other financial institutions in the lions' den of competing political positions. Overall, most seemed more sympathetic to the general cultural mood than they did to the proposed new OCC rule, recognizing that the long-term trends were not going to be stopped or reversed by a rule hastily drafted in the dying days of one administration. *'Banks are certain to be caught in the middle of a moral authority fight,'* according to The *Financial Times.*[38]

As these examples show, businesses assessing the potential impact of political action on their operations look at the world through a socio-cultural lens – 'small p' politics. Often 'big P' political action is in line with those trends. Some, however, try to push against the tide for ideological reasons. It rarely succeeds. As one government minister put it to me: *'If your policies do not match the mood, you'll find that you are pulling on a policy lever that is not connected to anything. Nothing happens and you've wasted your time.'*

Central banks, public policy and financial markets

Since the 2008 financial crash, central banks' outsized role in public policy and financial markets has become much more visible. In spite of being agents of the state, these institutions have, for a long time, tried to be seen to keep out of the political fray. They were positioned as purely technocratic institutions not subject to ever-changing political winds. Some like the Swiss National Bank and, before the introduction of the Euro, the German Bundesbank have jealously guarded their independence from political interference in monetary policy decision making. And both have benefited from a large degree of confidence by the population – greater confidence, in fact, than in their legitimately elected governments. Others like the Bank of England and the US Federal Reserve have always been subject to discussion about the nature and limits of their distance from politically driven public policy, though they, too, have guarded their monetary policy independence as much as possible.

Central banks are unusual and powerful institutions. They can move markets with simple utterances. Many combine the functions of financial regulation subject to political accountability with responsibility for monetary policy decisions that are meant to be focused on maintaining price stability unaffected by political considerations. Balancing these roles within the same institution has always been challenging. It is particularly challenging for entities like the European Central Bank (ECB), an institution that has no government to answer to and whose mandate is defined by stuck-in-time treaties of the European Union. Its mandate is to maintain price stability with due consideration for the economic policies in the Union. But the Union is made up of 27 states, all of which have different economic needs at different times. Making monetary policy decisions within such a political framework is a difficult and taxing task even at the best of times.

The financial crisis drew central banks (CBs) into implementing massive monetary operations that came to be called Quantitative Easing (QE). In effect, CBs used the unlimited power of their balance sheets to provide liquidity to financial markets and, let's be honest, monetary financing of government expenditures, by making massive asset purchases on the open market. Initially seen as temporary measures, they were still in operation 12 years later when the COVID-19 pandemic hit the world. CBs redoubled their efforts rather than winding down their asset purchases. The sums involved are eye-watering. Fitch calculated that global QE asset purchases reached US$6 trillion in 2020 alone – more than half the cumulative total of assets purchased over the whole period between 2009 and 2018.

It has always been obvious that there is no such thing in the world as a technocratic decision that is not based on fundamental social and political values or that does not create winners and losers. Even when CBs' monetary interventions were limited to moving base interest rates up and down, they either favoured savers (high interest rates) or borrowers (low interest rates). But these interventions were seen as important in order to maintain price stability since inflation/deflation themselves affect different people in different ways.

In an age of massive policy intervention using what have become known, rather inelegantly, as 'conventional unconventional policies' the distributional consequences of monetary policy became much starker. It became much clearer that, in effect, CBs were making some people wealthier, others relatively poorer. Whether technocratic bodies should have the power to do that without oversight and consultation with legitimately elected governments became a point of public debate.[39]

But things went further. Activists started pressing CBs to skew their asset purchases away from 'brown' and towards 'green' assets. In other words, they tried to push for policy-directed monetary interventions. CBs were now in an uncomfortable position. The previously accepted narrative of a clear separation between the technocratic and the political was being publicly challenged. How can it be, people argued, that CBs can be allowed to implement monetary policies that go directly against government policy – whether that be the desire to reduce wealth inequality, or to fight climate change, or, potentially, in several other policy areas? This was a Pandora's Box that many would rather have remained tightly shut.

Recognizing the difficulties with this approach, some climate activists changed tack. This was not about CBs taking policy direction from government, they argued. It all had to do with financial risk on CBs' balance sheets. They claimed that the market was mispricing climate risk and that CBs therefore had a duty to take that into account and shun the holding of climate-unfriendly assets on their balance sheets.

But this created even more problems. If CBs were to come out with a statement that pluralistic financial markets were no longer effective price-finding mechanisms for market assets and that they themselves had superior knowledge to the whole market as to how to price risk (with the implication that there is only a single perspective on what constitutes risk), it would undermine the whole concept of market pricing, potentially throwing financial markets into a tailspin. We would have been back to 1970s ideology, where the state or its agents should be the ones to set prices rather than market mechanisms. Even in markets that are pluralistic, highly competitive and not monopolistic as would be the case, for example, with public utilities. It would also have called into question the competence of CBs and other financial regulators in regulating the market appropriately so that risk pricing was reasonably reliable.

I address these issues with CBs here not to come up with a definitive answer, but rather to point out that any attempt at drawing clear lines of separation between the political and the technocratic is futile. Economics is, and always has been, a branch of politics. Economic decision-making flows from the prevalent political ideology, not the other way around. Because economic analyses and economic decisions have to be based on a set of underlying social values. As I explore later, they cannot be value-free, as so many try to claim.

Some CBs managed these conflicts skilfully. The Swiss National Bank, for instance, did exclude certain types of assets from its purchasing policies. It was framed like this:

> Since 2013, we have already been excluding investments in companies that cause severe environmental damage, violate human rights or produce condemned weapons. With these exclusion criteria, we ensure that our investment policy reflects the fundamental and broadly accepted values held in Switzerland. We are now expanding the exclusion criterion pertaining to the environment by additionally taking climate-related issues into consideration. In Switzerland, a broad consensus has formed in recent years in favour of phasing out coal. We have therefore decided that we will from now on exclude all companies primarily active in the mining of coal from our portfolios.[40]

The Swiss National Bank is operating in a relatively small country with a high degree of shared values and social cohesion. It has framed its policy as being in line with those values (i.e. small p politics), while avoiding being seen as responding to big P politics and taking government direction in monetary policy affairs. There may not be many other CBs that can easily take the same route. Nevertheless, the SNB's position that it should be acting in line with the prevalent social values is absolutely on point. And holds just as well whether such actions arise from a CB's own assessment of the prevalent social mores or if they are the result of political direction.

Transparency of values in our systems
I am not particularly mathematically minded. When faced with a long equation, or even shorter ones for that matter, my eyes glaze over. I simply don't understand that language. This led me to have a number of robust discussions with many economists over the years. When they presented me with their mathematical equations and models, I always used to ask the same question: what social values are hidden away in your black box models and unintelligible equations? Because unless we can explore and discuss openly the social values on which your whole analysis is based, then it is useless at best, deceitful at worst.

Many used to stare at me with wide-eyed incomprehension. They truly believed that theirs was a technocratic exercise unconcerned with social values. Some got angry, thinking that I was trying to undermine their work.

One example is the use of economic analyses of healthcare interventions. It has become standard in many countries to undertake health technology assessments to evaluate whether medical innovations provide good value for money and therefore should be paid for by healthcare payers. One metric that has become popular is the cost per Quality Adjusted (or Disability Adjusted) Life Year gained. In other words, how many more years of 'good quality' life does a new technology provide for what cost.

One can immediately see the values embedded in such metrics. It favours the young as opposed to the elderly since the latter have fewer remaining life years to be saved. It assumes that quality of life (QoL) is something that can be evaluated numerically across the whole population, whereas we know that perceptions of QoL differ across individuals with similar levels of disability. In other words, it discriminates against the disabled and, within that group, against those who cope with their disability better than others. And the overarching underlying assumption is that medical technologies should be evaluated on the basis of measurable medical outcome rather than perceived need. Research has shown that these assumptions may not accurately reflect the social values prevalent among the population.

Of course, all of these biases and partially hidden values can be overcome because they can easily be made obvious and transparent and therefore subject to political scrutiny. Ultimately there are viable processes whereby societies, through the political system, can decide which values and biases should be accepted and which rejected. But we are now entering an age of non-transparency where nobody may know any longer the underlying values on which decisions are being based.

This is the age of so-called 'Artificial Intelligence', machine learning and decision-making by automated and self-evolving algorithms. Delegating power to algorithmically based systems has inevitable social costs. Particularly so when we end up having little understanding of the inner workings of these algorithms or how they have self-evolved over time as they process more and more information, are constantly altered and massively scaled without much human oversight. Such algorithms may end up driving life-changing decisions – be they in financial services, medical decision making, access to products and services including public services, and very many other aspects of people's lives and livelihoods. In other words, we can end up with seemingly 'precise' decisions being spat out of algorithmic systems while having little or no idea of the basis of those decisions or the social values on which they were based.

Do the algorithms have inbuilt processes that systematically discriminate against certain individuals or groups? Do they violate basic human rights? Do we have a forum where we can understand and debate the values on which the decisions are based and subject them to democratic accountability? How is this algorithm defining what is considered 'fair' and what is not? Who is accountable for algorithmic decisions that may have adverse life-changing effects on people? Do we even know the extent to which decisions are algorithmically based or human judgement based?

While AI, machine learning and all the rest can improve efficiency, lower costs and provide many other benefits, lack of transparency and accountability may lead to a world where we no longer have any idea of the basis on which decisions about our lives are being made. Where our social values and political beliefs may be brushed aside without us even knowing it. That would be a truly dystopic outcome. But it is quite possible, maybe even probable.

And the fact that the results have been spat out of some 'highly sophisticated AI machine' may make us believe them and act on them even when the most appropriate destination of such outputs might well be the garbage bin. It is reminiscent of a line in the movie *Sleepless in Seattle* when the young boy was covertly booking an airline ticket and inputting a false date of birth so he could fly without a guardian. His friend said that they would never believe he was that age. His retort: 'If it comes out of the computer, they'll believe anything.'

All this may well bring to mind the kind of science fiction movies we have all watched, where humans create smart machines that eventually break from any form of human control to cause devastation. It further highlights that it is simply impossible to separate commercial activity from the political and social framework in which we would like to live. The development of AI within a narrow commercial perspective but without transparency, accountability and politically legitimate oversight could be disastrous. Putting such oversight in place effectively will be a huge political and business challenge. Currently there are already over 160 voluntary AI ethical principles. Some argue that '*this maelstrom of guidance, none of which is compulsory, serves to confuse, as opposed to guide*'.[41] No kind of orderliness will be achieved if politics and commerce pull in opposite directions – with potentially grievous consequences for us all.

Some of the issues were highlighted when Timnit Gebru, then co-lead of Google's AI team, was reportedly forced out of the company because of a paper she co-authored with external researchers. The paper raised ethical issues with language models trained on incredibly large amounts of text data. One issue was the environmental cost of these energy intensive models. The researchers found that training one language model one time based on neural architecture search methodology produced carbon emissions equivalent to the lifetime emissions of five American cars. And such models are typically trained over and over.

Another issue was the models' inability to detect evolving nuances in language such as, for instance, the evolution of non-racist language. Also, the models obviously only process language found on the internet, thereby skewing the results in favour of the wealthiest countries and those groups with widespread digital access while excluding those with a smaller digital footprint.

Finally, because the training data sets are so large, it is impossible to audit them and check for bias.

Google claimed that the paper 'didn't meet our bar for publication'. Gebru and others believe the resistance arose because the paper raised uncomfortable questions about a core line of the company's research – and key to future revenues. More than 1,400 Google staff members and 1,900 others signed a letter of protest in Gebru's support.

Take these sorts of issues and translate them to all types of businesses – from banks, to insurance companies, to credit rating agencies, to healthcare companies, to many others, and one can start to see the potential impacts on our societies and all our lives.

Not to mention the impact when these systems infect public decision making.

In the Netherlands, public spending cuts, a never-ending search for 'efficiency', and an enduring belief in the virtues of automation led the government to substitute human judgement with semi-automatic algorithms in the handling of its tax system. This led to tens of thousands of families being singled out and blacklisted for 'benefits fraud' often on the basis of their ethnic background. A multi-year scandal that eventually caused the government to fall.

WHAT TO DO ABOUT IT ALL

3M is a highly respected company. One of the products in its 60,000 product line up is the N95 face mask (or respirator). When the COVID-19 pandemic hit, its mask immediately turned into one of the most-wanted products on earth. 3M responded with vigour, mobilizing spare capacity, ramping up production to 100 million units a month, re-organizing its distribution system to send masks to health workers rather than construction firms – its normal market – and took down tens of thousands of price-gouging websites fraudulently claiming to be 3M distributors. It did everything right.

None of that stopped the company from getting drawn into a political firestorm. Reports that it was refusing to divert millions of masks made in Asia to the US drew the ire of President Trump, who expressed disappointment with 3M that they were not taking care of their own country – the America First platform. In American eyes, 3M was hovering between hero and villain.

Mike Roman, 3M CEO, said, '*We learnt that the spotlight on leadership in this pandemic really had additional expectations... The learning from me was we really had to step up our leadership, not just in manufacturing.*'[42] Which 3M did, with improved communication, learning how to manage the difficult politics of the situation and building a rapport with the administration.

For 3M, that change in focus was forced on to it by the politics of a pandemic. But for all companies, learning how to manage in an era of political capitalism is now an essential part of good leadership.

There are three components to successful cultural leadership in an age of political capitalism.

Business is political
First is an acceptance that business has an important role in society
that goes far beyond financial performance and shareholder returns. A
2018 study published in the *Harvard Business Review* concluded, '*Most
businesses focus on serving customers, owning resources, being efficient and
growing — but the Centennials don't. Instead, they try to shape society
and focus on getting better not bigger.*'[43] The authors define Centennials
as corporations celebrating their 100th birthday and looking like they
could be with us forever. As opposed to the 76 per cent of companies
that have disappeared from the FTSE 100 over the last 30 years. Or
those in the S&P 500, where the average corporate lifespan has fallen
from 65 to 15 years.

In trying to 'shape society', these Centennials do not go against the
grain of cultural and social mores – the politics of our societies. Rather,
they surf each wave effectively. And, just like surfers, they recognize
when it's time to get off the wave that is about to crash and to spot the
indistinct onset of the subsequent wave that they can ride to their next
success. Organizations that do this successfully have what I like to call
well-developed cultural and political antennae. They are able to read the
political runes and focus on adapting to and even driving further the
emerging political direction rather than mounting rearguard actions to
preserve the status quo.

None of this is rocket science. The capabilities are relatively
straightforward to develop – if management has the mindset to do so.
But not all corporations are interested in doing more than giving lip
service to such capabilities.

A research study conducted by my colleague Ron Soonieus with
Professor N. Craig Smith at the INSEAD business school examined
how seriously board directors took the clear and unstoppable focus on
ESG issues in their work.[44] They found that they could group directors
under five archetypes: the deniers, the hardheaded, the superficial, the
complacent and the true believers. The study showed that there is wide
variation in the degree to which corporate behaviours match the rise of
political issues, even those that now stare us all in the face.

Looking from the outside in
The second skill is the ability to look at one's organization from the
outside in rather than the inside out. Sometimes I think of most of us

as being just like the prisoners in Plato's cave; prisoners chained so they could only see the wall in front of them. The world outside was passing by the cave and all they could see were the distorted shadows of that reality cast on to the wall. They came to believe that those shadows were reality.

So it is in many organizations. Distorted shadows are brought to us through third-party research studies, the results of which are filtered and re-filtered before the findings make it to senior management in sanitized form and massaged to fit within the organization's internal culture and expectations. Leaders then tend to interpret all this information through the operational lens of their own organization. We end up spending much more time looking at spreadsheets, PowerPoint presentations and perfectly presented reports rather than at the realities faced by ordinary people in the real world and the attitudes, cultural norms and beliefs spreading outside the walls of our own organizations.

Not to mention how little time most senior executives spend with their customers – real people with political belief systems that drive their behaviours and expectations. In the age of financialized capitalism, many CEOs see financial analysts on Wall Street and the City of London as their primary customers. Those who have an impact on their stock price performance rather than those buying their products and services. The net result is that the world is filtered through increasingly opaque organizational lenses. As in Plato's cave, what we see are merely distorted shadows of the real world.

Political capitalism requires us to look from the outside in. To see ourselves and our organizations as embedded in a socio-political ecosystem that is organic, fluid, dynamic, unpredictable, driven by political rather than commercial logic, led by a culture that is changing at a revolutionary rate and populated by human beings who in no way fit the economist's fantasy of 'rational actors'. In other words, a system that is primarily human, not financial. Gaining these different perspectives requires building socio-cultural-political antennae into the DNA of any organization.

The approach is illustrated in the figure below. While, when presented in such simplified graphics, the change may seem minor, the net effect of adopting this different perspective is immense. Businesses will find themselves in fundamentally different places depending on which approach they choose.

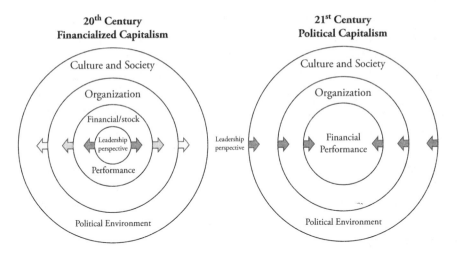

From consumers to citizens
A while back, I was kindly invited to speak at a meeting of senior executives. Before I started, I asked my host to tell me a little about the audience. He explained what I already knew – that the participants were mainly chief financial officers at major corporations. Everyone nodded.

I started by asking everyone, if they could, whether they would be kind enough to stop thinking about themselves as CFOs for the duration of the session. Could they please shed that coat for a moment and shift back into feeling what they truly are at core: people, loving fathers and mothers, sons and daughters, voters, taxpayers, part of their communities, volunteers, whatever.

The session was focused on some of the topics in this book. I knew that if the participants were in CFO mode, they would look at it through the lens of financialized capitalism and would not necessarily empathize with the discussion. There would be resistance and pushback. The shutters would come down. Old habits and years and decades of established ways of thinking would prevail. However, if I could get them to feel and think of themselves as citizens – human beings living in a society – then more of this might make sense. For organizations that succeed in the new age, executives need to think as citizens – not just about themselves but about their customers and everyone else they do business with.

The post-war world saw a period of huge industrial development largely driven by an explosion of consumerism. Today, when many think about their business, customers (i.e. people) are reduced to shaded segments of pie charts representing the abstraction of 'the market'. And people are most commonly described as 'consumers'. It is as though the only value that human beings have in this world is to consume, and consume, and consume ... preferably ad infinitum.

One way of moving towards a new culture is to stop calling our customers 'consumers' and start thinking of them as citizens. People who are a part of our complex societies, who have deep-seated values and belief systems. In whose life there are more important things than a series of purchases. For whom, in fact, habits of consumption may increasingly be driven by their perspective as citizens – as we shall see later.

Let's take Mars Inc., a traditional, family-owned company that thinks long-term and is purpose driven. Examples can be found on its web site: '*The long-term future of our business and the planet depends on us to stand for more and take bold action. That's why we take every opportunity to make a positive impact in this ever-changing world by leveraging our guiding philosophy that has always differentiated us.*' Going on to its Five Principles, Mars makes these statements: '*Purchases [of our products] are often among the smallest a consumer makes. We depend completely on our consumers to build our future.*'

While recognizing its own larger role as a corporation, Mars still describes its customers as consumers while readily acknowledging that its products are largely irrelevant to people's lives. Of course, it takes skill to prosper when your products are among people's least important purchases but apart from striving for excellence in product quality, Mars does more. It works hard to improve working conditions in its supply chain, reduce environmental waste and much more. Yet even Mars continues to describe its customers as 'consumers'. There seems to be a degree of disconnect between its commendable corporate philosophy and how it sees and relates to its customers.

If, at this point, you're convinced that I've lost my mind and am taking things to a laughable extreme when suggesting that any of this is relevant to a company that makes something as mundane as candy, the case study of Tony's Chocolonely in the next chapter (*see also* pp. 220–4) might start to change your views.

The opportunity – and the challenge – for businesses is to move beyond consumer to citizen thinking. Where would your business take you if you were to stop thinking of its primary function as encouraging consumption by your customers but instead started thinking about how your business could enhance your customers' role as citizens – people who want more meaning to their lives than offered by the next purchase, who want to live in a better society, who have small p political belief systems that guide who they are?

That this kind of thinking would lead one to very different places is evidenced by the differences one sees in market research done by companies and polling done by political parties or public policy think tanks. Although respondents are often the same people, they are looked at through fundamentally different lenses. Putting the two side by side, it is difficult to believe that one is talking about the same individuals.

Of course, each approach is trying to do a different job. But in the age of political capitalism, the overlap between the two is ever-increasing. Businesses would benefit from starting to look at their world also from different angles: 'the market' is also 'our society', 'consumers' are also, maybe primarily, 'citizens'. In fact, I suggest that simply starting to use that sort of language will go a long way to broadening perspectives with positive results.

For decades, Western culture has focused on individualism and instant gratification as the driving forces for humanity. A perspective given rocket boosters in the late twentieth century. Maybe all of it a slow burn reaction to highly prevalent nineteenth century thinking that argued that human existence was meaningless except as part of a society. But nothing is either/or. As humans we live in constant tension between our two simultaneous lives: our life as individuals and our life as citizens in a society. It is this balance between individualist gratification and customers' self-image as citizens which is constantly changing, and which businesses will need to master maybe more than was needed in the recent past. And it is also this tension between our freedoms and our needs as individuals and how to ensure that, as individuals, we can live in a functioning society that defines what politics is mostly about. Yet more that business can learn from political thinking.

WE ALWAYS LIVE WITH CHANGE

I was reading somewhere how different small businesses in a community responded to the dislocations caused by the COVID-19 pandemic. Many restaurants, bars, pubs and other hospitality venues shut their doors. Many of them folded in spite of government help. But some adapted. There was the Turkish restaurant in London that, overnight, converted itself from a restaurant to a grocery store with the added advantage of also offering cooked meals to take away. The restaurant, like all restaurants, already had a fully established supply chain for food products. All it had to do was to change the face it offered to the public. As a food store, it also avoided having to shut down like other restaurants had to.

Then there was the German brothel that started making sausages as the world's oldest profession came under strain. And many others – businesses large and small – that changed and adapted to the new reality.

By and large, businesses adapt to changing circumstances. Some do not. They stick with their old business model even as they face decline. Some maybe have little option. But the pull of sticking with what we know, what we have become comfortable with, that with which our ego and perception of self-worth has become inextricably entangled, is strong.

In this chapter I have tried to outline the shape and nature of the massive and rapid cultural changes we are living through. Social changes driven by many different factors but all of which point in the same direction – people who are increasingly aware of the political nature of human beings and the societies in which they live. And the relentless rise of political beliefs as drivers of behaviour.

As Aristotle put it, *'Man is by nature a political animal.'* By which he is thought to have meant that humans live in a society – a polis – and that the affairs of that community – its politics – are of prime concern to the citizen.

Business is an integral part of those societies and is therefore inherently political. He who declares himself apolitical is, again in Aristotle's words: *'the "Tribeless, lawless, hearthless one," whom Homera denounces… he may be compared to a bird which flies alone.'* And flying alone may, indeed, be the fate of those who close their eyes to the rapidly changing cultural framework in which we live and the implications for continued relevance and success.

Like the Turkish restaurant-cum-grocery store, the changes necessary to adapt to this evolving social environment may not be groundbreakingly radical, though they become ever more challenging the larger the business. With the right leadership and mindset, most companies can adapt. It remains to be seen which business leaders will show both the willingness and the ability to make these necessary changes.

I realize that many have an in-built allergy to the word 'political'. Call it what you will – cultural, social, whatever makes you comfortable. But whichever words one picks, the implications are exactly the same.

All businesses have to understand their socio-political environment in a level of detail that may not have been necessary in the past. They also need to come to terms with the fact that socio-political views are always contested. It is therefore impossible to pick a political position that satisfies everyone – or, at the very least, upsets nobody.

Delta Airlines CEO Ed Bastian:

'The visible role of the CEO…as an advocate for who their brand is, what their employees think, what we believe in – has taken a greater resonance and responsibility…We've been trained in the business world to not upset anyone. We want everyone to love us. But unfortunately, in society today, that's not always possible.'[45]

The alternative – abstention – which has been the preferred option for so many businesses in order not to alienate any potential customers, is no longer viable. These statements are no less real because they are uncomfortable.

Maybe nowhere does the rubber hit the road more clearly than is the case with brands. Brands are about creating belief systems around a product or service. Belief systems that, for many, may have little to do with functional value but more with what the brands they buy say about themselves and their place in the world. How brands deal with the emerging era of political capitalism is the subject of the next chapter.

6

The Political Brand

'A brand's strength is built upon its determination to promote its own distinctive values and mission.'

Jean-Noël Kapferer
Emeritus Professor of Marketing
HEC Paris

Image courtesy of Benetton Group. Photo Oliviero Toscani

BENETTON

Perhaps Benetton can be described as the ultimate political brand. Set up in 1955, this family business initially focused on various forms of apparel and later extended to cosmetics, accessories, etc. Until the 1980s, Benetton's approach to advertising was pretty standard – focused on its products and logo. That raised awareness but did little to differentiate the brand in what is essentially a market of largely undifferentiated products.

In the early 1980s, Luciano Benetton hired renowned photographer Oliviero Toscani to head the company's advertising department. Realizing that differentiating an essentially undifferentiated product line could not be achieved by doing the same old stuff that everyone else was doing, the duo came up with the idea of positioning Benetton as a 'lifestyle accessory' rather than a clothing brand. What this was to mean would evolve over the subsequent years.

Their first out-of-the-box ad appeared soon after Toscani joined. It used Benetton's already established reputation for producing clothing in a wide array of eclectic and ever-changing colours to build a social message. United Colors of Benetton was born in an ad featuring teenagers and kids from a wide variety of ethnic backgrounds promoting an image of racial harmony and world peace. The first step into advertising with an explicitly political message with clear links to a core brand attribute – colour – had been made.

The theme was carried through for many years. Two black boys kissing each other, one with a US flag and the other with a Soviet flag; a series of adverts featuring countries locked in political battles – the UK and Argentina, Israel and the Arab world, Iran and Iraq. The theme was consistent as expressed in one of the taglines: 'All colors are equal, just as all men are equal.'

It is not surprising that, carried too far, the peace and harmony theme can soon start to feel corny, illusory and somewhat disconnected from the real world. A hippie-ish love and peace mirage in a world that had become increasingly individualistic and roiled with issues and conflict.

To move forward, Benetton stuck with its political imagery but took it further. Ads became edgier and more explicit. The imagery was, to some, more disturbing. The nun and priest kissing, shown at the start of this chapter, drew the ire of the Catholic Church. Striking journalistic images focused on the AIDS crisis, environmental damage, political violence, war and so on. Images featured a dying AIDS victim, an African guerrilla holding a Kalashnikov and a human leg bone, an overcrowded refugee boat, death caused by Mafia bombings and many more. In 2000, its Slow Death campaign featured prisoners who had been condemned to death.

Toscani put it like this:

> Unlike traditional adverts, our images usually have no copy and no product, only our logo. They do not show you a fictitious reality in which you will be irresistible if you make use of our products. They do not tell anyone to buy our clothes, they do not even imply it. All they attempt to do is promote a discussion about issues which people would normally glide over if they approached them from other channels, issues we feel should be more widely discussed.[1]

For Luciano Benetton: '*Using these images in this unconventional way is an effort by Benetton to break through the complacency that exists in our society due to the constant flow of even the most horrendous realities communicated through conventional media such as the evening news or the morning paper.*'

The campaigns were met with endless controversy and condemnation from many quarters ranging from the Catholic Church to governments, to many of its own customers. All of which served to amplify awareness both of the brand and its social messaging. Newspapers refused to print its ads. Benetton retailers complained that the campaigns were, at best, useless at selling product, at worst they drove customers away. Some sued the company for its advertising practices.

But the campaigns created an image of a company that was edgy, contemporary, unconventional, not afraid of controversy. A company with a social mission. Loyal customers felt empowered and energized. The more the mainstream complained, the more its relatively young customer base felt empowered as though they themselves were taking on the establishment institutions that seemed incapable of tackling the big social issues of the day.

Toscani's view was that advertising had lost its way, that it was lagging behind social trends but was '*so rich and powerful that it is very difficult for it to change*'. He had no time for campaigns that tried to tart up undifferentiated products by wrapping them in irrelevant accessories (female models sprawled on sports cars) or offering the false hope of personal transformation if one bought a particular product – the con that '*if you buy a certain brand of sports shoes you can play like Ronaldo, even if you can't kick a ball.*' Toscani's view was that traditional advertising tapped into people's sense of guilt and inadequacy rather than giving them the sense of empowerment he hoped his campaigns would create.

Of course, it is legitimate to question whether this approach is genuine. Whether the Benetton campaigns were truly driven by the desire for citizen empowerment. Or whether they were simply a clever method of product and brand differentiation. Most likely, as always, it was a bit of both. They were certainly powerful brand differentiators in an industry where such differentiation is difficult. But tapping into a sense of citizen empowerment, even if instrumental in nature, still increases awareness of social causes and maybe encourages some to become active around those causes.

Few companies would have the courage, the chutzpah and, frankly, the skills to embark on the same journey as that explored by Benetton and Toscani. Rather than fearing anything that smells vaguely political, Benetton made politics the defining feature of its brand, grabbing controversial political issues by the neck and thrusting them in our faces in the most visually arresting and disturbing way possible. It is one of the few examples, maybe the only one, where advertising truly was a form of art, validating Jacques Barzun's statement: '*Who more aggressive than the artist when he shatters our habits of eye and ear as a means to violate our minds?*'[2]

In the end, Benetton wobbled. Toscani left the company in 2000 amid controversy created by the Death Row campaign. Benetton retreated into a conventional approach: '*By picturing our stylish clothes, we will attract more business. Consumers want to buy our clothes because they are attractive and have a high-quality reputation.* It was a statement that could have emerged from any clothing company on earth, offering nothing distinctive. Attractive clothes claiming to be high-quality are commodity products. And it is notable that the statement once again starts referring to customers as 'consumers' – quite different from Toscani's philosophy of creating empowered citizens who would be energized by feeling a part of standing up for the world's rampant injustices.

Maybe realizing the blandness of its new approach, Benetton's retreat did not last forever. Social justice issues came back into play, albeit with imagery not quite as arresting and disturbing as Toscani's – at least for a while. In 2011, Benetton launched its UNHATE campaign featuring world leaders kissing each other on the lips. President Obama was kissing President Hu Jintao of China in one ad and Hugo Chávez of Venezuela in another. Chancellor Merkel was kissing President Sarkozy. An ad of the Pope kissing Ahmed Mohamed el-Tayeb, Imam of the Al-Azhar mosque in Cairo, was withdrawn following widespread protest. Benetton seemed back in full political art form. It had something to say and people to upset. Albeit only in selected campaigns among many that adopted a more mainstream approach.

Of course, positioning oneself as a social justice warrior has its perils. Controversies arose over Benetton's purchase of land in Patagonia and dispossessing the traditional Mapuche people; being targeted for purchasing wool from farmers who practised mulesing; having to deal with the collapse, with over 1,000 deaths, of one of their factory buildings in Bangladesh. Edizione, Benetton's holding company, also controls the company that operates more than half of Italy's road network, including the Ponte Morandi in Genoa that collapsed in 2018, some claim due to poor maintenance. None of this fits the social justice image the company has built over decades. It all highlights the challenges associated with taking explicit political positions when one also has to deal with operational issues spanning the globe. Some would be less forgiving, arguing that these events demonstrate outright hypocrisy. A company that presents itself as standing for social justice while, in effect, acting with a relentless focus on optimizing financial returns whatever the social cost.

Whichever view one takes, what is indisputable is that Benetton waded into political issues as a way of creating brand differentiation. A distinctive approach in a near-commodity market.

PATAGONIA

Yvon Chouinard founded Patagonia in 1973. Chouinard was an accomplished rock climber and started in business in 1957, making hardened steel pitons for rock climbing in the Yosemite Valley. With his business partner Tom Frost, he expanded into making crampons and ice picks, which launched the new sport of ice climbing.

Chouinard soon realized that his very popular pitons were causing damage to the rocks in Yosemite. He and Frost designed new aluminium equipment that was not damaging and in the early 1970s launched a campaign for a new style of 'clean climbing'.

In 1970, during a climbing trip to Scotland, Chouinard noticed that rugby shirts made good climbing garb because the substantial collars provided neck protection from the climbing sling. He began buying the shirts and re-selling them. Patagonia was eventually born as an outdoor sports apparel and equipment company – a good business perfectly in line with Chouinard's personal passions.

Chouinard's switch from steel pitons, his biggest-selling product, to aluminium chockstones was the first indication that he did not want to be part of even the most minor damage to the natural environment. When an environmental audit in the early 1990s revealed the heavy environmental footprint of corporate cotton, Patagonia switched to organic cotton. The company has been on a steady journey to limit its environmental footprint ever since.

But Patagonia went much further, running regular events in its stores focused on environmental issues and supporting the production of activist films. It obsessively focuses on reducing its environmental footprint from how it manages its supply chains to a focus on the durability of its clothing to reduce over-purchasing and consequent waste and resource use – a stance that is, or at least was, nigh on heretical in the fashion business. It has launched a programme called 'Worn Wear', encouraging customers to buy used clothing rather than new and offering to fix worn clothing for free to discourage people from buying new. It also runs a programme that connects its customers to environmental groups. At one point Patagonia refused to sell its clothing to corporations that did not prioritize the planet. Doing all of this did not dent the company's sales which continue to grow steadily.

In 2002, the company announced its '1 per cent for the planet' – devoting 1 per cent of its worldwide revenues to environmental causes. On its own, this would probably not have meant much. After all, there are endless corporations devoting some proportion of their profits to good causes. But for many, such an approach feels superficial. Cynics see it as writing a cheque as a way of avoiding the hard work necessary to revamp the business model. For Patagonia, it only forms one part of a jigsaw that builds environmentalism into the whole business model and the brand's identity.

Patagonia's environmental focus is built into its DNA and is easily distinguishable from those corporations for which environmental concern is a thin veneer. While being probably one of the most advanced in terms of reducing its footprint, it is modest about its achievements while recognizing that it's on an endless journey. As CEO Ryan Gellert put it to me, '*We know that we still take out of the planet more than we put back in. We are working to change that, but it's a long journey.*'[3] Contrast this with the hyperbolic claims of fantastic progress on sustainability found on some websites but which lack quite the same degree of substance.

As a result of its brand profile, Patagonia has built a strong following among those dedicated to environmental issues. If you like, its customer base has more of the spirit of a private club or a community of shared ideals (some used to call it 'Fratagonia' because it felt like a frat house) than a transactional retail business. No doubt, many just casually walk into Patagonia stores without knowing much about the brand except that, for some, it's a cool brand ('Patagucci' used to be another moniker), purchasing its products simply because they like them. But the core of its business is built on a loyal long-term customer base, a large following of citizens committed to environmental protection and recovery. The brand identity is environmentalism and responsible, safe yet stylish enjoyment of nature and the outdoors. A perfect reflection of the personal identity of Yvon Chouinard: '*Communities form not around a logo, or a clever social media strategy, but a shared set of passions or ideals.*'[4]

Patagonia is also a certified B-Corporation: '*Certified B Corporations are a new kind of business that balances purpose and profit. They are legally required to consider the impact of their decisions on their workers, customers, suppliers, community, and the environment. This is a community of leaders, driving a global movement of people using business as a force for good.*'[5] In this, it is helped by having remained a privately-owned company that is not subject to the pressures of capital markets.

At one point I came across a short Patagonia-produced video clip where Chouinard was arguing for the preservation of protected natural areas. It was a good video clip. The ending was, however, strange: it made the statement that the video was not intended to be political. What is environmentalism if not a political movement? What is Patagonia if not a corporation that has chosen to immerse itself in that political issue?

The 'apolitical' fantasy was soon shattered in 2017 when President Trump decided to shrink the size of natural areas protected under the Obama administration, an action that would result in the largest reduction in US protected areas in the country's history. The company's website was changed to feature upfront an explicitly political statement, 'The President Stole Your Land'. In response, the federal government effectively called for a boycott of the company's products: 'Patagonia: Don't Buy It' was, remarkably, the subject line of an email sent out by the US House Committee of Natural Resources. Chouinard fought back: '*We're losing this planet. We have an evil government. And I'm not going to stand back and just let evil win.*'[6] This is as political – and politicized – as it gets. And, of course, intensely ideological, some would say hugely divisive, to the degree that alternative perspectives to one's own are described as 'evil'.

During the 2020 US election campaign, Patagonia doubled down on its political assault on climate deniers by adding labels to one line of shorts stating: 'Vote the Assholes Out'. The tagline was not new for Patagonia, but it had particular relevance during the 2020 election. Pictures of the hidden label went viral on social media and the politically labelled shorts proved a sellout.

Patagonia is a political brand. Its focus has been narrow – the politics of environmentalism – compared with Benetton's broader engagement with a range of social justice issues. But political nonetheless. And only by being explicitly political and building its focused stance into every nook and cranny of its business has it created a brand that builds a community of supporters and customers who buy into what it stands for – and those who do not.

In 2021, Patagonia stepped beyond its environmental focus to take up further political positions. It joined others such as Coca-Cola and Delta Airlines to condemn a voter restriction law passed by the US state of Georgia. Ryan Gellert penned an open letter to business leaders urging them to '*Join us in taking three steps to support our employees and our communities – fund activists, call Congress, stop future restrictive voting laws.*'[7] The statement was accompanied by a $1 million donation split equally between the Black Voters Matter Fund and The New Georgia Project. It remains to be seen how widely Patagonia's political activity spreads over time beyond its traditional environmental focus, and whether such a spread will enhance or dilute the strong, environmentally-focused brand identity it has patiently and successfully built over decades.

NIKE

No stranger to political controversy, Nike is one of the companies most often mentioned in surveys about politically involved brands. In 1991, activist Jeff Ballinger published a report alleging poor working conditions and low wages at the company's suppliers in Indonesia. Nike had recently moved production to Indonesia, China and Vietnam after costs had risen in Korea and Taiwan. A further Ballinger article in 1992 told the story of an Indonesian worker earning 14 cents an hour, below Indonesia's minimum wage, while documenting other abuses.[8]

The 1992 Barcelona Olympic Games saw protests against Nike's supply chain issues. Media attention to the problems continued for some years. Boycotts of the company's products were organized.

In 1996 Nike set up a department to look into labour practices in its supply chain and, in 1997, the company commissioned diplomat and activist Andrew Young to examine the issue. The ensuing report was reasonably favourable. Critics, however, widely panned it as being a whitewash and Nike's attempts to publicize it were met with even greater backlash and derision. By 1998, the controversy was hitting Nike's popularity and financial performance. It had to make workers redundant and, five years after the start of the initial controversy, there was a realization that change was necessary.

In May 1998, Nike CEO Phil Knight gave a speech: '*The Nike product has become synonymous with slave wages, forced overtime, and arbitrary abuse. I truly believe the American consumer doesn't want to buy products made under abusive conditions.*' Nike started the process, long and difficult, of cleaning up its supply chain and tried to draw other brands in to do the same by creating the Fair Labor Association.

In 2001, MIT computer scientist Jonah Peretti heard about Nike's new programme that encouraged people to personalize their shoes by having a word of their choosing sewn onto the shoe. In a moment of boredom and taking a break from writing his Master's thesis, Peretti applied to have the word 'sweatshop' written on his shoes. Nike rejected the order, claiming the word represented inappropriate slang. A rather amusing chain of email correspondence between Nike and Peretti ensued. In the end Peretti collated all the emails and sent them round to a few friends for their entertainment. What he did not expect was that the emails would spread like wildfire, ending up in the inboxes of millions of people. Peretti ended up on the *Today Show* with Nike's head of global PR and Katie Couric talking about sweatshop labour.

Following this experience, Peretti went on to found the highly successful site BuzzFeed. For Nike, it was yet another headache. It seemed that the sweatshop issue was never going to go away.

But Nike seemed determined to change its business habits. Between 2002 and 2004, it audited over 600 of its suppliers. In 2005, it became the first to publish all the factories with which it had contracts. A 2005 report revealed labour conditions in its supply chain and acknowledged widespread issues still remained.

Over time, Nike developed one of the best global supply chain monitoring systems of any company. But not a flawless one as that is an impossibility. Yet it came at a cost. An internal assessment concluded the cost per shoe of the supply chain monitoring programme exceeded the cost of the materials needed to make the shoe. How was Nike to deal with embedding such a cost disadvantage compared to competition?

It was clear that the brand could not afford to dial back on its commitments. There seemed to be only one viable solution: finding ways to ensure that detailed and effective monitoring of supply chains became standard across the industry. This could be approached through two routes simultaneously. The first was the voluntary approach as embodied in the Fair Labor Association. The second was to press for regulation that compelled others to abide by the same standards.

And it is here that small p politics meets big P politics. What started out as a grassroots campaign that forced Nike to change its habits became a political campaign to raise standards across the industry. We shall come back to that progression, and what it means, in the closing chapter. But it illustrates an important issue – public policy should not allow companies and brands that do 'the right thing' to be placed at a competitive disadvantage. Public policy intervention is essential to supporting those companies that are in sync with the times and with the political direction rather than, largely through inaction, ending up stacking the deck in favour of the laggards.

While having shown commitment and made tremendous progress, the Nike brand found it difficult to shake off its sweatshop taint. Compare this with our previous McDonald's story where, in spite of the issue, McDonald's was never painted with the animal cruelty brush to quite the same extent as Nike was with the sweatshop brush. Why?

There may be many reasons. Fixing a US-only supply chain is an achievable task. Flawlessly repairing a globally scattered supply chain where local producers can easily run rings around inspectors is not. Yet another political issue associated with global supply chains. McDonald's also got on with the job rather quietly and without much fanfare. It did not try prematurely, and counterproductively, to mend its image by publicizing questionable reports early on in the process when it was simply not credible to pretend that the issues had been fixed. Such an approach only makes activists double down on activities to disprove the claims. And the costs to Nike of cleaning up its supply chain and, maybe more importantly, to monitor its suppliers constantly, were much higher than those incurred by McDonald's. The balance between cleaning up and remaining price competitive was much trickier.

One of Nike's founding principles was that it would make its shoes outside the US. Low-cost production and scattered supply chains were an integral part of its business model. While that may have seemed reasonable at the time, it did not survive the rising political tide against unacceptable labour practices. The cost advantage the approach was supposed to deliver turned into an uncompetitive burden as well as a reputational snare. In other words, Nike built into its DNA a business model that became politically obsolescent. A sharp contrast to Patagonia that built in a political issue that became ever more politically relevant.

In 2021, Nike and other brands such as H&M, adidas and Uniqlo declared that they would stop buying cotton from the Xinjiang region of China due to the human rights abuses against the Uighur population. The backlash from the Chinese regime was swift and a boycott of the brands was encouraged. Others, such as Muji, Fila China and the Chinese operation of Hugo Boss, gave testimonials on Chinese social media that they support Xinjiang cotton. Hugo Boss has since recanted and the others have issued statements of concern about forced labour in Xinjiang. All these brands are caught in a political bind that forces them to choose between their position in the Chinese market and catering to Western citizens concerned about Chinese practices. A policy of trying to dodge the issue and stay away from the political fray is unlikely to work.

And the regulation that Nike pushed for is coming. Under the European Union's new Green Deal, companies and financial entities will need to undertake human rights due diligence for any good or service to qualify as 'sustainable' – a label that is becoming increasingly necessary to compete in the world of political capitalism.

One might have thought that the sweatshop experience might have put Nike off getting involved in any kind of political issue. Not so. Nike is one of the companies whose business became intimately involved in the Black Lives Matter movement; maybe the company most visibly involved.

In 2018, Nike mounted an ad campaign featuring Colin Kaepernick, the San Francisco 49ers quarterback who had gained notoriety by controversially not standing up and, later, taking the knee while the national anthem was being played before match play started. Kaepernick was protesting against racial injustice. His protest ignited a political firestorm and was followed by claims that NFL teams colluded to keep him and his colleague Eric Reid off the playing field. A lawsuit was eventually settled with the NFL paying $10 million to the players. After Kaepernick left the 49ers at the end of the 2016 season, he remained unsigned by any other team.

In 2017, President Trump condemned Kaepernick's and others' action, claiming that it had nothing to do with injustice but rather showed disrespect for the country, the flag and the national anthem. He called for a boycott of NFL games. Many agreed with his perspective. Many others condemned it and doubled down on the protests. It all mushroomed into yet another highly divisive issue in US politics.

Nike decided to wade in. Its campaign featured Kaepernick and the statement, 'Believe in something. Even if it means sacrificing everything'. It had taken an explicitly political position which, as always, did not turn out to be plain sailing. Many supported the Nike campaign. Others posted videos of burning Nike products on social media and called for a company boycott. All of them kept the Nike brand in the news.

In 2019, Nike celebrated Independence Day by launching a shoe carrying the Betsy Ross Flag – for some a symbol of resistance against King George III. Kaepernick objected, saying that he and others saw the flag as a racist symbol associated with slavery. Nike withdrew the product, drawing condemnation from various quarters for inappropriate 'political correctness', critics pointing out that no significant number of Americans saw the flag as racist. By using an athlete to front its campaign for political reasons rather than athletic prowess, Nike had, to some extent, become captive of Kaepernick as activist rather than Kaepernick as quarterback.

The whole racial justice issue was given fresh momentum following the murder of George Floyd in May 2020 by a policeman in Minneapolis during his arrest after he had been accused of passing a counterfeit $20 bill to a retailer. Floyd's death unleashed a wave of social unrest across the country, stoking further social division. Nike launched an ad campaign with the slogan 'For Once, Don't Do It'. A plain video with white lettering on a black background appeals to viewers:

Don't pretend there's not a problem in America.
    Don't turn your back on racism. Don't accept innocent lives being taken from us. Don't make any more excuses.
    Don't think this doesn't affect you. Don't sit back and be silent.

Finishing with the appeal '*Let's all be part of the change*'.

Nike also pledged to spend $40 million over four years to support organizations focused on social justice, education and racial inequality in the US. Nike subsidiary Jordan Brand would donate $100 million over the next ten years to those causes.

Of course, it is to be expected that such a clear stance against racial discrimination would lead to activists examining whether Nike lives by its own words. In 2018, a management shake-up followed complaints that Nike had a poor workplace culture that failed to encourage and promote women and minorities. In 2019, Nike stated that Black vice presidents represented 9.9 per cent of its US total in 2019 and 21 per cent of VPs are from underrepresented groups.

In 2020, Nike launched an anti-racism campaign in Japan titled *Keep Moving: Yourself, the Future.* Nike sponsors mixed-race tennis star Naomi Osaka, who features briefly in the commercial. Within a couple of days, the campaign had generated some 50,000 likes and some 30,000 dislikes on Nike's Japan YouTube channel. Some praised it, others saw it as anti-Japanese. Not only did the campaign focus on an issue that is considered almost taboo in Japan, it was also launched by an American company leading some to feel that the time when Americans marched in and told the Japanese what to do and how to run their lives was well and truly over. *'Endemic racism is going to be a sensitive topic in any culture. But Nike should not think, as a foreign brand, that it is appropriate for them to point it out to their hosts,'* according to Steve McGinnes, author of *Surfing the Asian Wave.*[9]

Nike's experience teaches us some lessons about involvement in political campaigning. First, campaigns can be, and likely will be, divisive. Taking a political stance will please some and infuriate others. It moves a brand from being a consumer brand, marginal in people's lives and differentiated from competition on aspects that are not that important, to a citizen's brand that taps into strongly-held beliefs, feelings and emotions.

Nike can also be described as having jumped on a bandwagon. Its reasons for doing so will likely remain obscure. Some claim that it was a purely commercial decision for a company whose customer base is skewed towards black customers, others that it was a useful tool to deflect discussion from the whole sweatshop debate. Others still, probably including Nike itself, will claim that it is a reflection of the company's belief system as with Patagonia and its environmental activism. Of course, Nike came late to the party. Its racial justice belief system does not have the same claim to authenticity and being embedded in its DNA since the day it was founded, as was the case with Yvon Chouinard. That does not necessarily mean it is not genuine, but it naturally raises suspicions of opportunism.

One can also reasonably question whether its branding advisors could have gone further. The racial justice debate as currently framed is highly divisive, an us-versus-them framing has taken hold. Nike jumped on to one side of that debate. With some deeper work, could Nike have done even better? Could its agencies have come up with a way of changing the nature of the discussion to frame it all in a less divisive fashion, to create a sense of greater unity in adversity?

That would have required a much more nuanced, multi-layered approach rooted in a comprehensive understanding of how politics and political debate works. It would also have been pushing against the instant gratification of outrage and anger. But, had such an approach been tried, and been successful (by no means certain), it would have shown the difference between jumping on a bandwagon that already has its own momentum and taking a hot political issue of the day and re-framing it to make a bigger contribution to our societies.

Of course, in a world of the social media anger machine, there is much to be gained by tapping directly into grievance – at least in the short term. But corporations need to think of the long-term durability of their brand positioning. As Nike itself found out, the cost advantages gained from widely distributed supply chains eventually transmogrified into a political and branding burden.

The politics of racial justice

In diving into the politics of racial justice, Nike plunged into one of the most difficult areas of political branding. In that, it was followed by others in the wake of the George Floyd killing. For many, the question arises as to whether they had thought it through.

Google, Amazon, Facebook, DoorDash, Reddit, Uber, Nextdoor, Lyft and many others issued statements of support along the lines of 'we stand with the Black community'. Many ended up accused of hypocrisy. Amazon was taken to task for its aggressive stance on labour relations and the firing of a black employee for trying to organize workers, an allegation Amazon denies. Luxury brand Celine, part of the LVMH group, stated, 'Celine stands against all form of discrimination, oppression and racism,' leading Hollywood stylist Jason Bolden to claim that the brand didn't dress black celebrities unless they have a white stylist. For L'Oréal Paris, 'Speaking out is worth it' was the slogan until model Munroe Bergdorf accused the company of dropping her from a campaign in 2017 for speaking out against racism. L'Oréal apologized and re-hired the model. Sainsbury's, a British supermarket chain, launched an ad featuring a black family. It pleased nobody. On the one side were racist remarks such as 'You may as well rename yourself Blackbury's'. On the other, a tweet saying, 'Shame that Sainsbury's has zero per cent black people on their board and executive leadership teams. The game . . . is the game.' Sainsbury's meets the minimum standards on racial diversity according to a Parker Review report.

All of this opens companies and brands up to obvious accusations:

> Thus, to the venerable traditions of corporate pink-washing, greenwashing, and ethics-washing their deplorable practices, we can now add another: Black Power-washing, wherein companies issue essentially meaningless statements about their commitment to Black folks but do little to change their policies, hiring practices, or ultimately their business models, no matter how harmful to Black people these may be.[10]

All of which points to the wisdom that a friend of mine, a strategic communications professional, offered to one of his clients who approached him stating that he wanted his company to do something positive about the Black Lives Matter movement. The advice – first, make sure you get your own house in order before starting to spout what risk coming across as meaningless platitudes.

TONY'S CHOCOLONELY

Maurice Dekker is a TV producer and developer of *Keuringsdienst van Waarde*, a Dutch consumer protection TV show. In the early 2000s, Dekker read a book titled *The Black Book of Marks* – an exposé of unscrupulous practices by the world's leading brands. The book got little or no public attention, much to Dekker's frustration.

Among other things, the book claimed that most of the chocolate we all happily consume has slave labour embedded in its supply chains. Articles that appeared at around the same time revealing the story of missing kids in Mali who had probably been pressganged into working in cocoa plantations in Côte d'Ivoire similarly went by largely unnoticed.

Dekker decided to investigate further for his TV programme. Heading up the investigative journalism was Teun van de Keuken. As part of the investigation, Teun phoned confectionery giant Nestlé and asked about child slavery in its supply chain. He was told that 'slavery' is maybe too big a word. 'Do you agree that child labour exists on a large scale in the industry?' he asked. 'Yes' came the answer from Nestlé's head of PR. 'Let's say that slavery exists because they are so desperately 'poor' was the position of the company. 'Is that because they don't get paid enough by Nestlé or by the companies they work for?' asked Teun. The head of PR hung up.[11] A response that ensured that Teun would be encouraged to dig further.

Eventually, Teun found that none of the chocolate manufacturers that had signed the Harkin-Engel Protocol committing to producing 'slave-free chocolate' were doing much about it. There are an estimated 2.3 million children working on cocoa plants in Ghana and Côte d'Ivoire – almost all illegally. The protocol had committed to eliminating child slave labour by 2005. The World Cocoa Foundation, to which major manufacturers belong, now claims that it will take until 2025 – a full 20 years after the original deadline – having reached only 20 per cent effective monitoring by 2019. In October 2020, 15 years after the original deadline to abolish slave labour, the World Cocoa Foundation stated, '*Companies are already ramping up their investments to fight child labor.*'[12]

As a journalist, Teun was fully aware that publishing facts and figures is not an effective way of raising awareness. Campaigning is a performative art. He therefore filmed himself eating 17 bars of chocolate and then took himself to court for 'knowingly purchasing an illegally made product'. The Dutch attorney general dismissed the case as being out of the jurisdiction of the Dutch courts. But the campaign had started.

Having failed to get any of the major chocolate manufacturers to get on board with the campaign, Teun and Dekker produced and launched their own brand. Tony's Chocolonely was born with the brand standing on the promise of 100 per cent slave-free chocolate and fully compliant with Fairtrade conventions. The 'lonely' part of the name reflects the fact that Teun (Tony) and Dekker felt all alone in trying to tackle this issue in the chocolate-making industry.

To achieve its aims, the brand does not source cocoa beans from the commodity markets, instead working directly with dedicated farmer co-operatives. A digital platform used by all players in the supply chain creates an auditable 'bean to bar' system. Tony's Chocolonely (let's call it Tony for short) pays a premium for its beans, establishes long-term, reliable and co-operative rather than transactional relationships with his suppliers, and has established a system of continuous improvement.

But the brand promise of 100 per cent slave-free chocolate did not sit well with the mainstream manufacturers. Bellissimo, a Swiss brand, sued the company for making false claims maintaining that producing 100 per cent slave-free chocolate was simply impossible. That in itself, of course, says much about chocolate production.

While Bellissimo no doubt thought they were defending their brand, the suit was a gift of massive free publicity and bringing to public attention Tony's primary mission – to raise awareness of slave labour in chocolate supply chains – in a way that no amount of paid for advertising could ever have achieved.

In 2007, the Amsterdam courts rejected Bellissimo's claim.

Tony was starting to have an effect on the industry, slowly. Following discussions with Tony, Verkade, a major chocolate brand, decided to go Fairtrade. Tony shared its know-how and helped them along the way. When Verkade made the relevant press announcements, there was no mention of Tony or the help provided. Again, they underestimated Teun's skills in thinking politically, his journalistic background and his performative skills. When Verkade organized an auction to launch its first Fairtrade chocolate bar, Teun was there and bought the first auctioned bar for €15,800. The newspaper headlines followed. Yet more priceless publicity.

Tony's skills for publicity and brand communications range into the playful. Open a Tony's bar today and you will not find it divided into neat, corporate, equal segments. Instead, it's highly asymmetric with segments of different shapes and sizes. It's impossible to share a bar equally among different people. You never know how big a chunk you're going to break off. Why? It's a statement to remind us that life isn't fair, and that the chocolate industry is unevenly divided. The segments also loosely reflect the shapes of the countries from which cocoa beans are sourced.

The brand has been a commercial success. It took some time to make any money at all. But it is now the leading chocolate brand in the Netherlands and selling in 20 or more countries. It has revenues of the order of €55 million and is profitable. But commercial objectives were never the brand's purpose. The objective was a social mission: bring attention to child-slavery, show that it can be avoided, push the major producers to change by challenging them in the marketplace.

The brand is now managed by Henk Jan Beltman, who is also the main shareholder. That Tony's continues to look at the world differently can be seen from its annual reports. Having greater commercial success is presented as an opportunity finally to be in a position to pay employees a thirteenth-month salary. The company proudly claims that employee benefits as a percentage of revenues was up from 9.5 to 11.6 per cent. That the company was able to pay €2.3 million in Tony's premium (the price paid to cocoa bean farmers over and above the Fairtrade price) in addition to the €1.23 million paid as a Fairtrade premium. Contrast all this with the average annual report that mostly vaunts an ability to reduce employee and supply chain costs.

Tony's Chocolonely is a political brand. Its reason for existing is purely political. Commercial viability is simply a necessary condition for achieving its political objective. This turns on its head what most brands are really about – primarily being commercially driven with, for some few, mission-driven objectives layered on to that primary objective – sometimes thickly, sometimes as a very transparent veneer. Even those brands that portray themselves as mission-driven are not that at their core – at least not when compared to Tony's model.

Tony's is a product of the twenty-first-century era of political capitalism. As similar brands sprout and succeed, the pressures on those who maintain the late twentieth-century financialized capitalism view of life will increase. As will public policy pressures when it becomes clear that there is another way. Of course, there will always be a market for the lowest-cost product, but it remains to be seen just how much society – be it through regulation or public pressure or customer choices – will continue to accept for the benefit of the lowest-cost production, higher margins and greater shareholder returns.

Tony's also illustrates the difference between the compliance model and the mission-driven model. The former is about maintaining one's core business model but working hard to minimize the damage being done – whether environmental or social – to fall in line with the prevailing social and regulatory goals. For some, additional expenditures go to support 'good causes' – even though in so many cases such expenditures could be better structured to enhance brand reputation. The latter is about making one's political mission the reason for existing at all and constructing one's business model accordingly.

In the US, lawsuits have been filed against leading chocolate manufacturers on behalf of children who claimed they were forced to work as much as 14 hours a day, given only scraps to eat and were severely beaten or tortured if they tried to escape. The suits have been making their way up and down the US legal system for years and will likely hinge on a legal technicality – whether corporations are liable for actions committed outside the US. The fundamental claims in the lawsuits are not in dispute.

While Tony's is a mission-driven brand, it remains to be seen how effective it can be at driving change across the industry. Its sourcing model is difficult to scale. Corporations such as Nestlé and Mars operate to a totally different scale and probably cannot avoid buying cocoa in the commodity markets – especially as demand for cocoa beans is outstripping supply. Once again, evidence that the option, whether by choice or through necessity, to be dependent on globally scattered supply chains is inevitably associated with having to bend to practices that managements may find unacceptable – and the consequences that may bring in an age of political capitalism.

Maybe the best larger corporations can do is to overlay onto their business practices philanthropic efforts to help deprived cocoa farmers. Will the commitments enshrined in the Harkin-Engel Protocol ever come to pass or will it remain a hollow aspiration? Will our societies and our political system continue to tolerate embedded child and slave labour in these products? If not, what is a viable route to change at scale? The answers to all these questions will emerge in time.

Some have also argued that Tony's commercial success and change in management will lead to a dilution of its mission. As the brand grows and requires ever more cocoa beans, will it also succumb to sourcing product from the commodity markets, thereby essentially abandoning its founding mission in order to continue its commercial growth? Or will it find another way. Some have claimed that it is already diluting its mission and compromising its sourcing practices. My attempts to speak to the company to explore where it's at have failed.

THE LUXURY BRAND

Luxury brands occupy a special place in the pantheon of leading brands. First, their appeal rests on being exclusive. You can only access the real thing if you are relatively wealthy – a tricky position in an age where wealth inequality is one of the leading political issues. Second, they claim to be 'better' than anything else one can buy. This raises expectations as to what they are and who they are as well as the quality of their products – expectations that are not always met. Next, luxury brands are used to creating around themselves an indefinable aura that appeals to our deeper sense of self. There is little difference in the functional quality of luxury vs high-quality brands – certainly not enough to justify the eye-watering price premium. But people are buying something other than functional quality. Finally, luxury brands are the embodiment of what American economist and sociologist Thorstein Veblen defined as conspicuous consumption in his most famous work, *The Theory of the Leisure Class*.

In his treatise, Veblen argued that social status is earned by individuals' visible patterns of consumption. Such consumption is a signal of social power and prestige. Over-consumption and the ability and willingness to pay prices that far exceed a product's functional value are all interpreted as ways to gain and signal status. Veblen argued that conspicuous philanthropy was also a form of status seeking. Board membership of the Whitney Museum of American Art in New York comes with an annual price tag of around $100,000 in 'donations', higher than that for New York's Metropolitan Opera. Those, too, are luxury brands.

While we're talking here about luxury brands, it needs to be borne in mind that status is relative. Conspicuous consumption is not limited to the wealthy. The less wealthy, too, use patterns of consumption to indicate status. Hence the infamous appeal of Nike's Air Jordans, where people were spending large amounts to acquire the shoes even when they could not afford to pay their rent. Or, worse, the crime waves associated with youngsters who would do anything to get their hands on a pair of the new sneakers.

Consumption is about status. And nowhere more so than in the case of luxury brands.

Or at least it has been.

How does all this map on to the newly emerging political culture where waste is frowned upon, where the environmental consequences of over-consumption are an increasing cause for concern, where flashy displays of wealth simply fuel the political debate about inequality and the evils of our current form of capitalism? Of course, brands are adapting. Most now have their own corporate social responsibility initiatives and are working to bring down their environmental footprints. A quick browse through a number of luxury brand websites is sufficient to show that such activity is widespread. But it also raises further questions.

The first is that excess and display of wealth is what luxury brands are about. Overlaying that with different forms of socially responsible behaviour is welcome but does not address the fundamental meaning of these brands in an age where such meaning may become increasingly challenging to sustain. It's a little bit like the previously mentioned case of fast fashion – an industry built on cheap production and waste – where decreasing the amount of chemicals used in the production process does not address the fundamental issues.

People also expect more from luxury brands than they do from others. Yet reviewing the social responsibility pages of leading luxury brands it's impossible to distinguish what they are doing from what hundreds and thousands of other, less glamorous businesses are also doing. True, the videos on the websites may be better and more elegantly produced. But the content, welcome though it is, is generic. When we look, for instance, at the environmental activities of a luxury brand, should they be indistinguishable from what, say, Walmart and Aldi are doing? Or do we expect that indefinable specialness also to carry through to such activities? Should they be following the same script recommended by the same CSR consultancies that have, only yesterday, implanted the same programme at the Gap?

It is possible that many of the customers of luxury brands are less conscious about these changing social trends. Or, even if they are conscious and maybe even activist around these issues, a degree of cognitive dissonance from which we all suffer means that it does not affect their purchasing behaviour when it comes to such luxuries. And it is also possible, maybe probable, that such customers' purchasing behaviours will be fundamentally different to what they might profess during market research surveys where many might feel it is more appropriate to express great concern about these issues while not, in the end, doing much about it. Aren't we all somewhat guilty of that?

If all that holds, even small and generic attempts at social responsibility programmes could be sufficient to salve customers' consciences and provide enough psychological cover to purchase luxury brands.

Or maybe not. At least in the long term.

One example that might be worth recalling is the animal fur industry. It took years of aggressive activism to bring political attention to the use of animal fur in clothing. The nude, blood-strewn campaign mounted by People for the Ethical Treatment of Animals (PETA), with its tagline of 'I'd rather go naked than wear fur' ran for 30 years, was supported by multiple celebrities and shook people's consciousness. Many continued to argue that the anti-fur craze would pass. It didn't. Retail sales of fur products fell 50 per cent between 2006 and 2018. Brands like Prada, Burberry, Chanel and others removed fur from their product lines.

The animal fur industry is trying to recover lost ground. While arguing that declining sales are not due to public opposition but rather to economic factors (hmmm), it has, nevertheless, adopted a new tack. Animal fur is now being promoted politically as a 'sustainable' and 'natural' alternative to faux fur and subject to detailed certifications on everything including animal welfare standards. For many, this will seem too little too late.

It remains to be seen where all this will go. One thing is, however, undeniable. No person walking into a room wearing a real fur coat can, today, expect the universal looks of admiration that were once so readily available. They may still expect to be conspicuous but maybe not quite in the way desired. People's belief system has changed and there is no return to the past.

Then there is the question of regulatory intervention. Some 20 years ago, the UK became the first country in Europe to ban fur farming. Following Brexit, there is a movement afoot to implement an outright ban on all fur sales.

It is also worth noting the dearth of luxury brands that have attempted to make sustainability and other socio-political issues a core part of their brand identity rather than an overlay. There are good reasons for this. The environmental movement has, for decades, associated itself with a hairshirt, self-deprivation culture. Social justice warriors are all about inclusivity and the fight against excessive wealth and inequality. All of this is anathema to the very soul of the luxury brand. It will take a while to find ways to square those circles. Some brands, like Stella McCartney, that are native sustainability brands and whose mission statement declares, '*We are agents of change. We challenge and push boundaries to make luxurious products in a way that is fit for the world we live in today and the future: beautiful and sustainable. No compromises*', reputedly have difficulty turning a profit. It is debatable, however, whether that is a function of its sustainability mission or a result of the many other factors that determine success in a difficult and highly competitive industry. Or due to the fact that the Stella McCartney brand has not managed to embody its social mission firmly enough in its brand identity (the website does not make the blood boil, for instance).

Since 2019, the Stella McCartney brand now operates in partnership with LVMH – the French luxury brand. This may be an opportunity for the brand to act as a catalyst and help LVMH further its sustainability credentials and operational activities, as, for instance, happened when Unilever acquired brands like Ben & Jerry's and Innocent. It might also be an opportunity for LVMH to bring its branding skills to bear and use the brand as a petri dish of how to make a focus on sustainability an effective core attribute of the Stella McCartney brand. On the other hand, it is also possible that the partnership might increase earnings pressures on the brand and the temptation to cut corners.

Yet even luxury brands will, over time, be unable to dodge the new age of political capitalism. The industry does not yet have the answers and it will take time to find an appropriate approach that can work. Even if it had answers, it's also a question of timing. Go too early and business will suffer, leave it too late and brand value gets degraded.

But movement is clear.

In March 2021, Gabriela Hearst made her debut as designer for luxury brand Chloé (also part of the LVMH stable). She got hold of 50 second-hand versions of the brand's once-popular Edith bag and reworked them by hand into eclectic one-of-a-kind items. She used scraps of materials from previous collections, giving the bags an artisanal feel rather than the machine-produced feel associated with so many items.

The bags sold out in a flash – with prices around €3,000 each. Chloé's wealthy and image-conscious customers bought into the 'less waste' message and happily shelled out not inconsiderable sums for what would previously have been dismissed as 'second-hand items'. Hearst has now committed to making 80 per cent of her products from reused materials by the end of 2022.

Luxury brands are trendsetters. If some of them manage to find a new way forward, the impact on our social consciousness will be substantial. Their ability to change the weather should not be underestimated. The question is how? And when?

Facebook, Twitter, et al.

What legacy do people like Mark Zuckerberg, Jack Dorsey and others wish to leave in this world? Will they be remembered as the people who gave us the gift of global connection and granted a voice to those who were previously unheard – spreading previously concentrated power to the masses? Or might they end up being remembered as the people who destroyed our societies and enabled the undermining of democracy itself? What will their brands – both personal and corporate – be seen to stand for, five or ten years from now?

I mentioned earlier that Facebook (and Twitter) can now be considered primarily political corporations. They move elections. They spread political discourse – whether true or false, harmless or harmful. They have political power, including the ability to favour one type of political ideology over another (although they deny doing so). They shape our social norms.

The political nature of social media was brought home graphically on 6 January 2021 when a group of armed insurrectionists, convened on social media and, encouraged by President Trump's social media posts, marched on the Capitol in Washington, DC. They entered and largely took over the building, forced lawmakers into hiding, caused five people to die and delayed by a few hours the certification of the 2020 presidential election. The insurrection failed to stop certification of the election results but the event shocked America and the world.

In a highly political act, Facebook and YouTube (owned by Alphabet) followed Twitter in blocking the US President's social media accounts, an action meeting with approval in some quarters, condemnation in others, and doubts in yet others. Steffen Seibert, spokesperson for German Chancellor Angela Merkel, put it like this: '*The right to freedom of opinion is of fundamental importance. Given that, the Chancellor considers it problematic that the President's accounts have been permanently suspended.*'

Social media platforms were in an invidious position: damned if they did and damned if they didn't. Jack Dorsey on Twitter:

I do not celebrate or feel pride. I believe this was the right decision for Twitter. We faced an extraordinary and untenable circumstance, forcing us to focus all of our actions on public safety.

Offline harm as a result of online speech is demonstrably real, and what drives our policy and enforcement above all.

Having to take these actions fragment the public conversation. They divide us. They limit the potential for clarification, redemption, and learning. And sets a precedent I feel is dangerous: the power an individual or corporation has over a part of the global public conversation.

Apple, Google and Amazon followed with actions of their own. They banned Parler, an alternative platform, and others from their own app sites, generating yet more controversy.

The Capitol attack was far from the first time that social media platforms were in the political limelight. In fact, it's now hard to remember a time when they were not. But these brands represent something very different to the ones described earlier – brands that enter the political space as part of what they choose to stand for. For Facebook, Twitter and others, politics is deeply embedded in their business model. They are political corporations and deeply political brands.

Thierry Breton, the European Union's Commissioner for the Internal Market, wrote in an opinion piece: '*The fact that a CEO can pull the plug on POTUS's loudspeaker without any checks and balances is perplexing. It is not only confirmation of the power of these platforms, but it also displays deep weaknesses in the way our society is organized in the digital space.*' He goes on to argue that the events should dispel any remaining doubts that these companies '*have become systemic actors in our societies and our democracies.*'[13]

This has huge implications. For social media brands, it is not a question of pulling a controversial advertising campaign or presenting themselves differently in some way or other. Neither, as Mark Zuckerberg seems sometimes to suggest, is it a question of tacking on some regulation to direct what Facebook should and should not allow on its platform. Or hiring ever more sophisticated lobbyists to press their case. Or continued obfuscation so that they can preserve their dominance and revenues while tinkering a little bit around the edges. Neither are the issues solvable through ever more sophisticated algorithms as some who think that technology is the solution to everything seem to believe – and as Zuckerberg himself has suggested in testimony to Congress.

What is in question is the continued viability of their whole business model. For political reasons.

And it's not an easy problem to solve. Those who rail against uprisings should remember that it is not that many years ago that so many were praising the social media platforms for their role in the Arab Spring – an insurrection against authoritarian regimes. The reality is that the features of the social media business model that give us all so many benefits are exactly the same features that cause the problems. Even their overwhelming market dominance provides us with benefits through network effects. Finding ways to avoid throwing the baby out with the bathwater will not be an easy task.

From a societal perspective, Dorsey's question as to how much private companies should have control over global public conversation is highly pertinent. It reflects repeated comments by Sir Nick Clegg, Facebook's global head of public affairs, that many decisions should not be left in the hands of private corporations: *'Would it be acceptable to society at large to have a private company in effect become a self-appointed referee for everything that politicians say? I don't believe it would.'*

Is it an argument that essentially shifts responsibility for making such decisions onto regulators rather than the companies themselves? Or, carried to its logical conclusion, does it suggest that the political position of social media brands in the public discourse is now so wide and embedded that they have power over 'everything that politicians say' and should therefore be treated more like public utilities than commercial entities? And, if so, how would such public utilities be regulated in a politically neutral way?

Mark Zuckerberg described Facebook as being something between a newspaper and a telecoms company. It is, in fact, much closer to an online newspaper than it is to a telecoms company. Like all major platforms, Facebook has developed increasingly sophisticated mediation processes that remove, as much as is possible given the volumes involved, content considered unacceptable or illegal. The platforms also ban certain users. Just like newspapers, they are, in effect, acting as editors and it may well be that they will be forced to carry the same responsibilities and liabilities. Looked at through this lens, the differences between Facebook and, say, the *New York Times*, is that editorial decisions are taken after the fact of publication rather than before and that the volume of material to be filtered is a huge multiple of what a newspaper has to deal with. But these are operational matters that are a direct consequence of the business model that these companies have themselves chosen, not matters of fundamental principle.

Another major difference is social media brands' ability to target content not just advertising. Everyone operating online targets advertising, but the front page of the *New York Times* is exactly the same for everyone who accesses it. My Facebook and Twitter feeds are fundamentally different from yours, leading to a lack of transparency as well as the previously mentioned problems associated with echo chambers (*see also* pp. 163–4).

Comparisons to telecoms companies are less pertinent. Users of telecoms infrastructure do not have the ability to broadcast what is said in phone conversations to hundreds of millions of people the world over with little effort. Neither do telecoms companies have the ability to collect vast amounts of personal data and analyze content, make their own algorithmic choices as to who can listen into our phone communications, or to base their business model on advertising revenue based on content-based customer targeting. Which is why, though we have all had telephones for many decades, the arrival of social media empowered people to organize quickly, cheaply and on a large scale – for good and for ill. Historically, only the printing press generated the same type of disruption.

The political and societal impact of the social media concept is further questioned by the findings of a study by researchers from MIT, who analyzed a data set of 'rumor cascades' on Twitter between 2006 and 2017, finding that *'False news reached more people than the truth; the top 1 per cent of false news cascades diffused to between 1000 and 100,000 people, whereas the truth rarely diffused to more than 1000 people. Falsehoods also diffused faster than the truth.'*[14] All of which casts somewhat of a shadow on the effectiveness of social media platforms' moderation capabilities. And simply labelling content as being contested doesn't work – 68 per cent of Republicans and 28 per cent of the whole US population continued to believe that the 2020 presidential election was rigged.

It is pointless to look backwards at previous forms of media regulation and try to shoehorn versions of old regulatory approaches to what is a totally new issue. Everyone will have to think afresh and with imagination. And regulators, politicians and political parties everywhere need to accept a fair chunk of the blame.

Regulators were asleep at the wheel, stuck in outdated ways of thinking, when they allowed acquisitions like that of WhatsApp and Instagram by Facebook (among its 80+ acquisitions since 2007) and the 241 acquisitions made by Alphabet (previously Google) in ten years. Acquisitions that increased these companies' dominant position with debatable benefits that are meaningful to the users themselves. The companies' promises that data would not be shared across the platforms were, predictably, soon jettisoned. It's not clear why anyone, anywhere, ever believed those promises.

Politicians and political parties, now complaining about misinformation on social media, have themselves been complicit. A study by the Oxford Internet Institute reveals that '*organized social media manipulation campaigns operate in 81 countries, up from 70 countries in 2019, with global misinformation being produced on an industrial scale by major governments, public relations firms and political parties.*'[15] Coupled with the fact that, in many countries, political messaging is not regulated for content nor subject to any kind of advertising standards, it's not all down to the social media companies to sort out.

Finally, there is the question of money. Facebook chose to take the fight to the Australian government over legislation that forces the social media company to pay for having information from traditional media sources in its feeds. Facebook is, of course, right to argue that traditional media companies encourage sharing of their content on social media platforms to give them access to a wide audience they would be unable to reach otherwise. It's a two-way commercial relationship and far from clear where the balance of financial value flow lies.

New Zealand publishing house Stuff has walked away from using Facebook to promote its content. It did not see any decline in traffic and has, instead, gained benefits that may be even more valuable – huge public support, growth in trust and happier newsroom staff, who are no longer being trolled in unruly Facebook comment sections. For brands, it's not great to be in a position where customers breaking away from your platform generates widespread support.

It is fair to ask whether Facebook's confrontational approach before reaching agreement with the Australian government – and its botched initial blocking of multiple pages that had nothing to do with the issues under discussion – have served to enhance its brand reputation among citizens and governments – whatever the rights and wrongs of the underlying dispute. Australian Prime Minister Scott Morrison clearly stated that social media companies '*may be changing the world, but that doesn't mean they run it.*' The former Facebook Chief Executive for Australia and New Zealand put it like this: '*a standoff between Australia and Facebook could be a catalyst for genuine global reform...the moment the world sat up and started to take serious action on making Big Tech accountable to society.*'[16] Is this a battle social media platforms really want to fight so publicly? Do they believe they can win if they turn this into a public political battle? And even if they could 'win', is such an all-out fight in the wider interests of our societies?

Saving the brands

Is it possible to save the good name of these social media brands, retain the advantages and avoid or minimize the harms? It should be in all our interests to find ways in which this can be done but it is far from straightforward. Apart from the socio-political impacts we have been talking about, continued stories about industrial-scale tax avoidance as part of tech companies' business models don't do much to enhance these brands' image among the public.

In the closing chapter of this book, I shall explain more clearly the principles and practicalities of political capitalism. Here, suffice it to say that it is a system of political economy where all players in the polity travel in broadly the same direction – and assume their respective responsibilities to do so. Companies' statements that it is up to regulators to sort it out, or regulators stating it's up to the companies to sort it out are equally hollow. We all have some role to play and it's up to everyone working together to navigate what will be a difficult path.

Through the Digital Services Act and the Digital Markets Act (still in discussion at the time of writing), Europe has started to explore new regulatory paths. The Act would pose an obligation on companies to undertake risk assessments of their moderation systems as well as their algorithms and advertising platforms. Such assessments have to consider potential negative effects on civic discourse and electoral processes. It remains to be seen whether such legislation moves forward quickly, whether it meets with co-operation or resistance by social media companies, and whether any of it will work. Some have argued that '*neither regulatory package is properly designed to address the digital media's problems or police abuses by the major platforms.*'[17] There are no easy answers to a fiendishly complex set of issues but it might be worth posing a set of questions that, I'm sure, leaders of social media brands have been tussling with.

The first is whether the current social media business model renders impossible the 'first do no harm' principle? It may well do. In which case the question then arises as to how much of the benefit we gain is worth preserving and, as a society, what degree of societal harm we are prepared to accept for having those benefits. It is going to be hard to sell the idea that societal breakdown is a price worth paying so that we can all share cat videos. Eventually the discussion will boil down exclusively to political benefits traded off against political harms. The non-political (and that includes Facebook's and others' earnings outlooks) will become utterly irrelevant.

Second, is there a desire on behalf of these brands to move into the age of political capitalism or will they remain stuck in the dying age of financialized capitalism? Zuckerberg, Dorsey and all the other leaders involved are rich well beyond most people's wildest dreams. One could therefore speculate that accumulating more wealth for themselves is not a primary objective. However, in an age of financialized capitalism quarterly earnings and stock price performance take precedence over everything else. It's easy for such metrics to become a proxy for leaders' competence, spirit and mettle. Not so in an age of political capitalism where social impact becomes the primary driver. So, which is it for the leaders of social media platforms? Will they continue to eye any proposed change and reform through the lens of quarterly earnings, stock price performance and market domination, or are they willing to take a broader view?

Third, what do they see their business as being for? Why do they exist? What is the social impact they are wanting to create? And is it possible to do so with the current business model?

The Facebook website states: '*We build technologies that help people connect with friends and family, find communities, and grow businesses.*' What this means in practice is fleshed out in the many pages of terms of service, community standards and commerce policies that prohibit all sorts of activity from terrorism to the sale of items ranging from alcohol to body parts and healthcare products, to a nuanced policy on the sale of firearms, to very many others. Yet, the practicalities of actually implementing these policies are not only huge, they are insurmountable. As is recognized by the company itself: '*we may not detect content and behavior that violates these standards.'* While the intentions are good, the practicalities of the chosen business model make reliable implementation impossible. Unsurprising given some 100 billion posts per day that appear on Facebook. As they say, the road to hell is paved with good intentions.

All these difficulties will be hard to resolve. Nobody knows how to do it. But resolving them is an imperative if these brands – as well as the whole of our digital world – are not to become forever associated with social breakdown. We shall see in the next chapter what that outcome could look like – a world that is technologically shiny but socially anarchic.

Mark Zuckerberg in a written testimony to Congress suggested that regulation should not be focused on outcomes but process, while also recognizing that the business model means that undesirable content will always be with us: '*Platforms should be required to demonstrate that they have systems in place for identifying unlawful content and removing it. Platforms should not be held liable if a particular piece of content evades its detection—that would be impractical for platforms with billions of posts per day—but they should be required to have adequate systems in place to address unlawful content.*'[18] In other words, as long as we try our best, it shouldn't matter if it works. This is the same approach widely used in industry, where a standard defence of bad outcomes rests on companies having followed 'industry best practice' – irrespective of the outcome. It is, of course, also transparently self-serving. Facebook is one of the platforms with enough heft and resources effectively to define what such industry standards should be. It would put any start-up competitor at an almost insurmountable disadvantage while, as admitted by Zuckerberg himself, not resolving the core issue. Bad content will still be among us. Facebook is essentially promoting an idea where the company itself has a large, possibly decisive, role in determining the standards for process-based regulation while having no responsibility for the eventual outcome.

Zuckerberg also focuses exclusively on 'unlawful content'. What of all the content that is highly harmful but not unlawful?

It's a little like saying that banks should design their own compliance and risk management procedures free of regulatory intervention. That such procedures should be determined by the biggest banks. And that even though they know full well that they are not internally enforceable, then it's OK if they bring the world economy to its knees again. As long as they have the written procedures and they've done what they themselves consider to be their level best, then they should not have any further responsibilities. How many of us would be happy with that?

Attempting to resolve these difficult issues will continue to make brands like Facebook, Twitter and others fully political brands, having to participate in processes and make decisions that are deeply political – and explicitly so. Neither will pressures on these brands come solely from regulators and civil society. Apple is creating pressure on Facebook and others by making user privacy one of the pillars of its business model, limiting how Facebook and others can access user data and what they are able to do with such data.

'It is long past time to stop pretending that this approach doesn't come with a cost of polarization, of lost trust, and yes, of violence. A social dilemma cannot be allowed to become a social catastrophe,' said Tim Cook, Apple CEO, speaking about social media platforms in a speech in January 2021.[19] Facebook's Mark Zuckerberg hit back, claiming that Apple's actions had little to do with social responsibility and all to do with profit seeking – seemingly failing to realize that, in an age of political capitalism, the two are becoming ever more intimately interdependent.

In short, social media brands illustrate in the clearest possible way that, in an age of political capitalism, the politics of brands is not simply a matter of presentation, slogans, operational tweaks and boundless geeky faith in algorithms. It touches on the very fundamentals of the business models on which brands are built. For brands like Facebook, their political nature is built into all aspects. They are the oligopolistic carriers of political discourse and political messaging. How they carry those messages and who they serve them up to has political implications. They are also moderators of political messaging which inevitably opens them up to accusations of direct political action and potential political bias. Whether they themselves believe that to be true or false is largely irrelevant. The issue lies in the fact that they have that power and they can never wield it in a way that satisfies everyone within their current business models.

APPEALING TO HIGHER VALUES

So, how can brands in general think about their value to our societies and how social value fits in to their brand equity?

> Social missions far transcend traditional ESG values like sustainability and are increasingly integrated into Customer Value Propositions as new-game branding shifts from trying to sell products to standing for causes customers care about.

That is the view of my long-time friend, Dr Lynn Phillips, formerly professor of marketing at Stanford Graduate School of Business. I first met him when attending one of his executive education courses where, for the first time, I grasped what 'marketing' was really all about – or should be about. In his successful ongoing consulting practice, Lynn observes that a number of his clients have transitioned to a new approach to brand building. They are now trying to build brands that stand for the causes that their customers care about. This reflects his longstanding view that innovative thinking around Customer Experience and Customer Value Propositions is what drives sustainable advantage.

Consultants at Bain & Company have developed a scheme to illustrate the evolution (see figure, p. 239).[20] It progresses from basic functional value to the emotional value associated with most brands through to perceived life-changing impact, through to what they describe as 'self-transcendence' that makes social impact core to the brand identity. Self-transcendence is, at its core, about rising above the self and relating to that which is greater than the self. In simpler terms, it is the realization that, as individuals, we are one part of a greater whole and acting accordingly.[21] This goes beyond self-actualization, previously the highest order in Maslow's hierarchy of needs.

In other words, customers as citizens come to see themselves as part of their community and their society, as well as being individuals focused on their own self-interest. The idea that people are exclusively focused on their narrow economic self-interest – economics' *homo economicus* – was always a fabrication, as everyday human behaviour shows. As outlined earlier, people have always taken an interest in the workings of their society – the polis. The rise of this broader interest as an important factor determining people's choices is what the new age of political capitalism is about.

Different brands will choose to combine different elements of value in different ways to create their overall brand identity in ways that are viable, affordable and appeal to their chosen customer groups.

The Elements of Value Pyramid

Products and services deliver fundamental elements of value that address four kinds of needs: functional, emotional, life changing, and social impact. In general, the more elements provided, the greater customers' loyalty and the higher the company's sustained revenue growth.

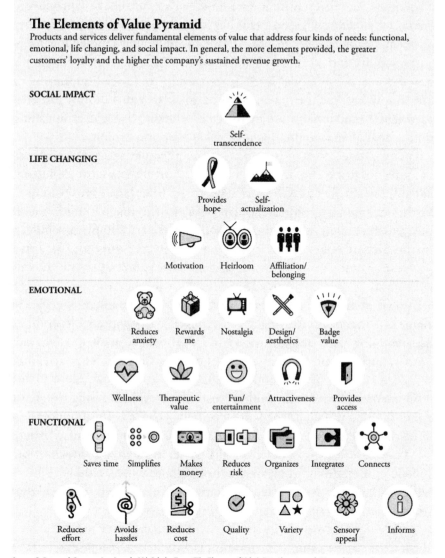

SOCIAL IMPACT

Self-transcendence

LIFE CHANGING

Provides hope   Self-actualization

Motivation   Heirloom   Affiliation/belonging

EMOTIONAL

Reduces anxiety   Rewards me   Nostalgia   Design/aesthetics   Badge value

Wellness   Therapeutic value   Fun/entertainment   Attractiveness   Provides access

FUNCTIONAL

Saves time   Simplifies   Makes money   Reduces risk   Organizes   Integrates   Connects

Reduces effort   Avoids hassles   Reduces cost   Quality   Variety   Sensory appeal   Informs

Source: © Bain and Company Inc. Icons by Nik Schulz. From: 'The Elements of Value', Eric Almquist et al, Harvard Business Review, September 2016. Reproduced with permission

Most brands are good at communicating functional and emotional value. Some include 'life-changing' elements by creating a sense of belonging, providing hope and motivation. This is what some brands aim to achieve when they strut their sustainability credentials, talk about their social programmes, etc. Yet, when they communicate these credentials in purely utilitarian terms (we've ticked the appropriate boxes, we've reduced carbon emissions by X, here is our sustainability report and a pretty video to go with it, we're number Y on the Dow Jones Sustainability Index), their efforts tend to slip back in people's minds into the lowest functional level. Sustainability and social responsibility can simply become the new normal of doing business. A now essential part of the functional value of the brand rather than a distinguishing feature that gives brands an additional sphere of meaning.

Few manage to include social impact through self-transcendence as a meaningful element of brand value. And it's not easy. Benetton, Patagonia and Tony's Chocolonely, three brands I have examined in this chapter, are on that journey (or, in the case of Benetton, it was until Toscani was removed and replaced with plain vanilla). In the case of Nike, it was clear that simply fixing its supply chain problem would not achieve it. It was just patching up what was wrong rather than creating additional value for its customers. A fight for racial justice has a bigger chance of adding a self-transcendence element – for some customers. For Patagonia, its approach combines life-changing, self-actualization and self-transcendence elements. Tony's, business model clearly targets the self-transcendence attribute as a core element of its brand appeal.

Elements of brand value build on each other. Which is why the above figure is titled 'Elements of Value', building blocks that all have to fit in place like a jigsaw puzzle to create the overall brand identity desired.

Many of the factors listed in the lower tiers of the pyramid are generic commodities. They are what one has to deliver simply to be in business. It is only as one includes elements further up the pyramid that sustainable competitive advantage can be created.

People's engagement with brands will be a complex mix of all the above elements of value. The question is whether, as people everywhere become increasingly politicized, the social impact and life-changing elements of value will become increasingly important drivers of customer choice. Whether brands can use these elements more effectively for competitive advantage. And whether, if they choose to ignore these elements as part of their brand identity, they will simply become attached to them through the activities of others.

It's not a linear hierarchy, it is best understood using complexity theory as a guide to brand strategy. This treats the citizen-customer landscape as a complex adaptive system where individual and collective behaviour changes over time and, maybe, with each individual purchase, in response to an unorganized collection of events and the unruly and untidy nature of socio-political evolution. It also calls into question the idea that customer behaviour is predictable – one way or the other. In a politicized world, many may well disapprove of some corporate activities while still happily buying the brand. What has been called the de-coupling between separate spheres of meaning that co-exist. In a 'moralized brandscape' individual brands can encapsulate many meanings that can be contradictory, allowing customers to justify their purchasing behaviours by selectively picking that meaning which suits them at the time.[22]

Some will argue, maybe correctly, that we are still in the relatively early stages of seeing these changes play out on a massive scale. The politicization of the investor outlined in the previous chapter is more advanced than the widespread emergence of the citizen customer – though that in itself is due to social pressure. Yet the trend is clear and accelerating even if the pace of change is up for discussion.

What is almost certain is that there won't be many brands that can afford to continue to ignore the moral and political characteristics attached to them. No brand will remain apolitical for long. Some will choose to make political meanings more of a core brand characteristic, as we have seen in the examples quoted. Others will weave it skilfully into the web of meanings represented by the brand. Yet others, through inaction, will find that political meanings become attached to their brands from the outside, thereby ceding to others some control of an area of increasing importance to brand identity while limiting their own influence on the moral meaning of their brands.

It is also likely that regulatory intervention will increase. Customers can make choices but there is an information asymmetry between brands and their customers in that customers are unable to test the veracity of those meanings that brands develop for themselves – as we have seen with Volkswagen's supposedly 'clean' diesel technology (*see also* pp. 56–9).

Some suggest that continuing disillusionment with the traditional political processes will drive further acceleration: '*The call for politicians and governments to take responsibility nationally and worldwide has not yielded sufficient response. No wonder the market is once again politicized and a site of citizen action. Worried, conscientious people use the marketplace to vent their frustration, take responsibility concerning global injustices, and as a way of initiating discussions and standard-setting for global economic regulation.*'[23]

It used to be the case that being a political brand was a matter of choice – as with Toscani and Benetton. By far the great majority of brands steered well away. We have now entered an age of greater political awareness and progressive politicization – and polarization – of the citizen customer. Over time, no major brand will escape moral and political characteristics being a part – small or large – of its web of meanings. The question is to what degree such characteristics will be driven by brands themselves or become attached to them from the outside.

7

The New Political Capitalism

'What collapsed on September 15, 2008, was not just a bank or a financial system. What fell apart that day was an entire political philosophy and economic system, a way of thinking about and living in the world.'

Anatole Kaletsky
Economist
Author *Capitalism 4.0*[1]

Capitalism has been the only successful and lasting system of political economy. Before those of a certain political bent start howling in protest, let me first explain what I mean by capitalism.

Capitalism is a system that recognizes private property and privately owned capital. It relies on well-structured, well-regulated, pluralistic markets as the best price-finding mechanism. Using that definition, there is no country in the world today that is not capitalist in one form or another, though to a greater or lesser extent. Even North Korea has started to recognize private ownership as a – still tiny – part of its political economy.

The only alternative to capitalism is communism – the idea that everything should be collectively owned, or rather owned by the State (which is not the same thing). It has been an abject failure. Not only could full State ownership of everything not be implemented in practice, the political, economic and social consequences of communism proved to be disastrous – a system that could only be maintained through ever-increasing and ever more brutal authoritarianism before it collapsed under its own contradictions.

CAPITALISM – THE EVOLUTION

There is far from one form of capitalism. As with everything else, and as Darwin explained in the context of nature, what determines capitalism's long-term resilience is its ability to change with the times.

'What is capitalism?' has been the subject of much study and academic debate. I do not pretend to resolve the question here. For the purposes of this book, I have taken what might be called a maximalist view of capitalism. In other words, I am considering 'capitalist' all structures of political economy that contain a meaningful component where private capital is deployed to fulfil market needs and generate profit. Such a definition includes what are known as 'mixed economies' and also assumes a market in other inputs such as labour.

Whether agrarian or feudal systems can be considered truly capitalist is up for debate, seeing as there was no true market for labour. Nevertheless, feudal systems were characterized by private ownership, albeit one held in very few hands while most of the population was held in serfdom to the owners of property. Power was dispersed among the various landowners, usually nobility, and centralized government was dependent on, and could only function with, their support. Feudal capitalism (if one accepts that moniker) was the dominant form for centuries – from England to Tsarist Russia, China and Japan.

The expansion of trading activities and, particularly, the development of international trade led to what can be called mercantile capitalism from the sixteenth century. French historian and Annales School leader Fernand Braudel argues that this was the first emergence of capitalism as traders were, for the first time, able to gain surplus monetary value. In mercantile capitalism, merchants became the new aristocracy, gaining surplus financial wealth, contributing to the national coffers through a positive trade balance and getting political power in return – as, for instance, in the case of the regents of Amsterdam during its seventeenth-century golden age. Protectionism was a hallmark of the mercantilist perspective of a zero-sum economy.

The eighteenth century saw the emergence of industrial capitalism. Industrialization created much financial wealth and, eventually, spread private ownership more widely across the population. Coupled with an increase in global trade, largely through colonialism, some countries became much more broadly prosperous. Starting in Great Britain, the protectionist policies associated with mercantilism were slowly abandoned. Politically, the spread of wealth and education across broader sectors of the population came together with the class conflict between capital and labour to underpin the evolution of Western democracy as we know it today. A wide segment of the population became emancipated and wanted a meaningful say in how they were governed. The market in political ideas continued to grow.

With notable exceptions, Western democratic capitalism built on industrialization came to be seen as a system of political economy to which many aspired. China, Russia, the Arab states and others did not embrace democratic capitalism and went their own way, in the process creating less wealth that was less widely spread in a political system that was centrally controlled.

The West also benefited from first mover advantage. It captured foreign markets, acting to suppress endogenous industrialization processes in the global South and East while exporting its own systems. Colonialism provided another obstacle to more widespread industrialization, as did the failure, at least until the early-to-mid twentieth century, to produce working classes with sufficient purchasing power to create the necessary demand.

Several other different forms of capitalism have evolved. From plutocratic capitalism, where power is vested in the wealthy, to oligarchic capitalism, where wealth and power are controlled by largely unaccountable political leaders and those close to them as, for instance, in today's Russia and some former Soviet states.

The twentieth century also saw the emergence of socialist capitalism (aka socialism) based on ideas that became more fully developed in the nineteenth century. This sought to alter the balance of power between capital and labour, between private and public ownership, the power of the State relative to private enterprise and increased levels of redistribution through the tax system. But in continuing to recognize the legitimacy of private ownership, private assets (not least people's ability to own their own homes), the legitimacy of generating monetary surpluses and the value of markets, albeit in more limited form, socialism is still a capitalist system that stops short of the alternative – communism.

Post-war, consumerism became the dominant characteristic of capitalist societies. The continued refinement of mass production techniques lowered production costs and also employed large numbers of people bringing the purchase of many goods within their reach. Post-war stimulus created the perfect combination of mass employment and increased earning power for an exploding middle class. Demand for goods and services soared, further powered by the keeping-up-with-the-Joneses social culture that became prevalent. The age of consumerist suburbia was upon us.

The late twentieth century saw the emerging dominance of financialized capitalism on the Anglo-Saxon model. As outlined earlier, financialized capitalism puts finance at the centre of economic activity. Economic activity based on industrial and human development becomes secondary to the creation of wealth through the financial system. Wealth and prosperity are defined solely in financial terms. Financial engineering becomes a widespread way of creating financial wealth even as it becomes increasingly dissociated from underlying economic, social and human development. The financial sector becomes an ever more dominant part of the economy and with that gains more political power. The extent to which we have been taken over by financialized capitalism can be noted by the fact that, today, when people ask: 'How are the markets doing?', everybody understands that one is talking about the capital markets rather than what most people used to understand by markets – places, real or virtual, where people exchange goods and services. What we now call the real economy to distinguish it from the economy of international finance.

Financialized capitalism was given rocket boosters by the abandonment of the gold standard leading to fiat money underpinning the new monetary system and by the abolition of capital controls which enabled finance, and financialization, to spread like wildfire across the globe. It also appealed to the political notion of libertarianism. Buccaneering, financially-driven activity in the hands of privateers unconstrained and unencumbered by the messy hand of the State.

The era of financialization was given a boost by what became known as the 'neoliberal' political philosophy most prominently expressed by Ronald Reagan and Margaret Thatcher in the 1980s. It was a period where private enterprise and 'the market' were seen as providing the answer to all ills and where *'Government is not the solution to our problem. Government IS the problem'* in the words of President Reagan's inaugural address. Deregulation became the mantra of the day – not least the deregulation of the financial sector itself. In the UK, finance deregulation came with a Big Bang on 27 October 1986, paving the way for the City of London to become one of the top two financial centres in the world.

Finance is the lifeblood of any modern economy and financialized capitalism was accompanied by economic development and increases in financial wealth. As private banks could create money more or less at will, and collect largely risk-free rents for doing so, credit boomed, as did the explosion of multiple financial instruments, each more complex and less transparent than the previous one. The short-term consequences were positive, both for the financial sector itself that accumulated much financial wealth, and for industry that could make investments that promised to generate a financial return – even if not a positive total return. The amount of risk capital available for new business ideas soared, leading to multiple waves of innovation.

As we approached the twenty-first century, the weaknesses of the twentieth-century combination of consumerism and financialized capitalism had started coming into view. By limiting our definition of wealth to financial wealth, we were rapidly destroying all other forms of value that are important to our well-being, to our social cohesion and to our very survival as a species. As Mark Carney, former governor of the Bank of England, put it in his 2020 Reith Lectures:

[Adam] Smith's moral sentiments turned into market values. Society's values became equated with financial value. This contributed to this century's crises of credit, COVID and climate.

The focus on financial capital had all but eliminated any attention being paid to social capital, natural capital and the very many things that form an important part of being human, of our overall prosperity, and even our long-term survival. In fact, wealth was, and had been for some time, taken away from all these other sources and converted to financial wealth. We have seemingly forgotten that which we had all known for some time – money is a poor measure of value.

Another way to look at it is that businesses utilize and generate various forms of capital: social capital, environmental capital, natural capital, financial capital, knowledge capital, political capital, and so on. Business is only valuable to society when it generates a net gain in these various capitals through its activities. When it adds net value to the totality of its capital networks. Money, in and of itself, is not 'capital'. It only becomes so when it is put to good use.

Financialized capitalism has misled us into believing that money = capital and further narrowed our perspective that it is the only capital that matters. Corporations have thereby reduced their role to funnelling money to shareholders and others in the mistaken belief that such activity, in itself, constitutes the creation of value.

To be a useful part of society, and to be sustainable, a corporation must have knowledge of the capitals it interacts with, relies on and serves; evaluate whether these interactions have led to an improvement of those capitals or not; and have the ability to observe whether critical thresholds are being approached beyond which capital provision might collapse (e.g. through environmental degradation or societal breakdown).[2]

Neither should we fall into the trap of trying to convert all these forms of capital into money for them to matter and to be taken into account. Many of these different forms of capital need to be embedded as *values* that corporations live by rather than as *numbers* on a spreadsheet. They are valuable even if they cannot be measured accurately or monetized. We need to break out of the idea that only that which is measurable in numbers is valuable. The most valuable things in society, as in life, may neither be easily measurable nor convertible into money as a universal measuring stick.[††]

Financialization also encouraged industrial consolidation and monopoly power. Merger and acquisition activity grew on the back of large transnational financial flows and encouraged by the lucrative nature of such deals for the financial services industry. Many deals were exercises in financial engineering designed to push up stock prices and short-term shareholder returns rather than follow any industrial logic (anyone remember Enron?). As a result, the big, who could access any amount of finance, became bigger, eroding the pluralistic and competitive markets on which a thriving market economy depends. This was particularly the case in financial services themselves and in the tech industry, where network effects multiply the benefits of scale and reach. But consolidation was everywhere and competition authorities were asleep at the wheel. Still in thrall to *laissez-faire* and mired in an outdated competition policy framework. It was all reminiscent of Braudel's view of the state, through action and inaction, becoming a guarantor of monopoly and concentrated power rather than a protector of pluralistic, competitive markets.

[††]Received wisdom is that if you can't measure it you can't manage it – a thought attributed to W. Edwards Deming. What Deming actually said was: *'It is wrong to suppose that if you can't measure it, you can't manage it – a costly myth.'* Or, as Einstein put it: *'Everything that can be counted does not necessarily count; everything that counts cannot necessarily be counted.'*

Many other characteristics of financialized capitalism also became visible. The financial wealth being generated was far from broadly spread. The post-war period of industrial development had created a thriving middle class. Financialized capitalism was creating a class of the super-wealthy, many, though by no means all, in the financial sector itself, while a large swathe of the population saw declining or, at best, stagnant levels of income and wealth. Even a cursory systems-level evaluation makes it obvious that concentration of wealth is built into the very fabric of financialized capitalism. 'Trickle-down', the predominant belief system of the 1980s, became seen as an utter fiction in a financialized system.

As a successful and highly agile financial sector continued to grow, it became increasingly difficult to create a regulatory framework that ensured stability, oversaw the multiple financial products that were being developed, dealt with increasing financial crime and money laundering, and worked to align the activities of the financial sector with the needs of broad and balanced economic development. It soon became clear that a complex, multi-layered but increasingly consolidated financial sector had accumulated challenging conflicts of interest. When every actor within the system is, not unreasonably, acting to maximize their own gain, the system does not end up delivering what is needed for the overall political economy absent a solid framework within which that system operates.

Prominent economists and central bankers started to argue, '*We need to re-examine our all-too-easy assumptions that a large financial sector invariably benefits the real economy. We have to acknowledge that the financial sector, not to mention some of its components, may sometimes become "too large". It can end up posing a threat to both economic and financial stability.*'[3]

There were also political consequences. As covered in the section on globalization (*see also* pp. 91–139), the free flow of global capital combined with technology to fracture the concept of a political economy. While politics, political legitimacy and political accountability lay largely at the national or sub-national level, transnational business and finance worked globally, enabling business to undercut national sovereignty and political accountability through arbitrage in investment, taxes, employment and regulation. Legitimately elected governments seemed increasingly powerless in the face of transnational economic forces – with potentially corrosive consequences for democracy. This fuelled the rise of what became labelled 'populist' political forces. Political movements that ran on a platform of tearing down a system that many believed was not working for them. It fuelled Brexit and other separatist movements, all part of a plummeting faith in globalization and a perception that the polity had been taken over by financial forces.

There were two deeply wounding blows to financialized capitalism – blows that, over time, will become fatal. One is gradual, the other rather sudden. The steadily festering wound comes from the fact that, except for the need for relatively modest amounts of start-up capital, today's businesses no longer require the large amounts of capital investment that was necessary for the industrial era corporation. This makes the role of mega-finance ever less relevant to the development of the real economy. In fact, rather than providing finance for industrial development, capital markets have become a situs for some founders, executives, investors and shareholders to extract surpluses from our industrial base for their own remuneration, leading to an ever-shrinking proportion of surpluses being re-invested for future development (cf. the Boeing example, pp. 47–54).

Some still deem capital markets to have a stewardship function to perform, '*supervising incumbent management's competence and integrity, and acting when necessary to effect changes*'.[4] Many believe that capital market players are not discharging this role adequately. If capital markets do, indeed, end up failing, their future looks bleak. They will have very little reason to exist in their current shape and scale.

The more sudden blow to financialized capitalism came on 15 September 2008. Lehman Brothers declared bankruptcy. The Dow dropped more than 200 points. The whole financial system was threatened with collapse due to lack of liquidity and evaporating confidence. The financial system had collapsed under its own weight. It was a classic Black Elephant event, a term first defined by former head of the Singapore Civil Service Peter Ho as a problem that is actually visible to everyone, but no one wants to deal with it, and so they pretend it is not there. When it blows up, we all feign surprise and shock, behaving as though it were a black swan.

That day and subsequent events crystallized the weaknesses of financialized capitalism. It resulted in what Anatole Kaletsky described at the start of this chapter: the collapse of an entire political philosophy and economic system, a way of thinking about and living in the world. That system was deregulated financialized capitalism.

The change to come was also recognized within parts of the business community. '*The interaction between government and business will change forever. In a reset economy, the government will be a regulator; and also an industry policy champion, a financier, and a key partner,*' according to then General Electric CEO Jeff Immelt in his letter to shareholders in the GE 2008 annual report.

After 2008, it became fashionable to blame the whole mess on 'greedy bankers' – an easy and popular target. And doubtless there were practices that many would consider unethical and irresponsible. But bankers were part of a system and were operating within the culture and incentives of that system. It was the system that was broken because it had been pushed too far – a poor system structure with even poorer levels of supervision relative to the complexity and agility of the system that had been created.

A NEW SYSTEM EMERGES

Systems do not die suddenly. They lose their lustre and eventually, over a period of years, decades, or even centuries, become replaced as something new emerges – slowly and usually painfully. One characteristic of dying systems and civilizations is that they end with a last hurrah – a period of uncontrolled excess, hedonism, anarchy and the throwing off of any kind of moral or social constraints. This is what I was reminded of when, in April 2021, I read the story of a delicatessen in Paulsboro, New Jersey that has annual revenues of some $14,000 and a stock market valuation of some $100 million. Coming hot on the heels of a 1,500 per cent rise in the stock price of GameStop, a low prospect video game retailer that became, for a period, a 'meme stock' driven by nothing other than social media buzz, and a 15,000 per cent surge in the value of Dogecoin, a crypto launched as a joke, it's easy for all this to suggest a financialized capitalism in its Bacchanalian end of times.

Following the Great Financial Crash that started in 2008, the late President Reagan would have had to eat his words. Because government became the only solution. Pumping money into the financial system to maintain liquidity and bailing out large numbers of financial firms. Not least in the US under a Republican administration.

Less than a decade later and we were all reeling under the effects of the COVID-19 pandemic. Once again, governments were the only game in town, hosing the whole economy with money to save businesses large and small, maintain employment and support some modicum of economic activity until vaccination could be deployed on a massive scale – vaccination developed by the private sector in collaboration with public research institutions, paid for and deployed by governments.

Those two events will come to be seen as the period in which political capitalism started seriously to take over from financialized capitalism. I define political capitalism as a resilient capitalist system that is in tune with political and socio-cultural mores and works to deliver sustainable long-term benefits for society as a whole. Where private and public sectors are aligned in delivering to common socio-political objectives.

Political capitalism is what emerges when the externalities of financialized markets become so visible and large that market actors can no longer ignore them. Where divisions and inequalities in society have come to bear directly on the structure of markets and opportunities to run successful businesses. Where businesses themselves become increasingly reflexive about their political roles.[5] All these conditions are in place today.

Maybe one form of political capitalism or, more accurately, politically controlled capitalism (as we shall see later) is that which originated haltingly in China in the post-Mao era from the late 1970s. The change was not initiated by Beijing but rather was a grass roots movement of private enterprise that was economically and politically marginal and therefore allowed to go forward by the central authorities. Regional competition followed. This forced reforms to create what was effectively a Chinese single market to prevent fragmentation between competing regions. Privatization of state-owned enterprises started in the mid-1990s. This all unleashed a competition for investment from regions, towns and villages – in effect, a giant set of disparate economic experiments that led to widespread industrialization. Today's China is a state-directed market economy.

As China transformed itself economically from a communist state to a capitalist one, political control was not relinquished. Private enterprise was explicitly expected to work in the interests of the State in line with the ideology of 'what is under heaven is for all', leading to what has been called the 'party-corporate conglomerate'. In that sense China is socialist in that its rulers still believe, or at least publicly maintain, that the interests of the State and the interests of the people are one and the same. It is not clear how many Chinese people believe it. As one diplomat in the Chinese foreign ministry once, undiplomatically, put it to me, 'The rulers in Beijing look after their own interests first, the interests of the people come second.'

In their book, *How China Became Capitalist*,[6] Ronald Coase and Ning Wang argue that, while China has developed a market for goods and services, it still lacks a market for ideas. China still, in effect, clings to a politically controlled form of capitalism subject to a single, unchallengeable political philosophy and tight central rule. Neither have Western assumptions that China would develop a thriving private sector subject primarily to commercial logic come about. The country's businesses are still seen, and used, as an extension of the Chinese Communist Party.

China, of course, has also been drawn into some aspects of financialized capitalism. Shanghai and Hong Kong are two world-class financial centres doing their thing in much the same way as London and New York. And with similar consequences.

China's growth has been far from even in spite of the central direction and control. All regions have benefited from the extraordinary growth the country has enjoyed. But the difference in GDP per capita between the poorest and the wealthiest parts grew from some 60,000 yuan in 2010 to 135,000 yuan in 2019 (*see* figure below). Increasing differentials are also reflected in China's Gini Coefficient.

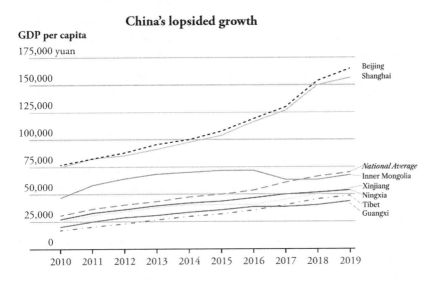

China's lopsided growth

GDP per capita

Note: 1,000 yuan = $153
Source: National Bureau of Statistics.

By 2020, China had created some 800 billionaires (the most anywhere in the world) while 17 per cent of its population (some 240 million) still lived below the poverty level of $5.50 per day. In spite of its direct central control, China has seemingly been unable, so far, to prevent unequal growth. Maybe a lesson for those who believe that state control is the answer to everything.

To date, the Chinese model continues to prioritize central control over other factors. In 2020, the authorities intervened to stop the Initial Public Offering of Ant Financial – a private enterprise that seemingly got too big for its boots. Fearing power that is not under its control, as well as the potential threat to state-owned enterprises, the regime embarked in a 'rectification' drive to bring the Alibaba Group, Ant's parent corporation, to heel. Other major interventions followed. Private educational businesses were essentially obliterated. A clampdown was initiated on Chinese companies with foreign listings. Between February and July 2021 Chinese shares listed overseas lost some $1 trillion in value, with Western investors the biggest losers.

The West has developed a love-hate relationship with the Chinese model. Western corporate leaders focus on its market potential. Western governments can see the advantages of China's ability to marshal both private and public resources to drive its economic development and its projection of power – for instance, through the Belt and Road Initiative. Its readiness to step in to fill the vacuum left by Western disengagement in certain parts of the world. Yet they are repelled by the Chinese top-down, authoritarian model with robust and ruthlessly enforced political direction, human rights abuses, manipulation of international trading norms, abuse of intellectual property rights, illegal military expansionism, widespread environmental destruction, its seemingly general disdain for the rule of law and international conventions, and more.

China illustrates the dangers of political capitalism taken to authoritarian extremes. It remains to be seen whether that system will prove sustainable, it is certainly not a model suitable for democracies. At the time of writing, China is doubling down on central control having already reversed previous liberalizing reforms of State Owned Enterprises. An approach that may not form the best substrate for sustained innovation and original thinking. We shall have to wait and see whether China's economic success to date will be sustained.

What is less often talked about, and what the West would do well to parse, is the difference between China's economic ethos and the political system used to deliver it. China's economic ethos – or culture – does not prize profit maximization. Rather, social stability, steady production growth and cost reductions through learning and new technologies are the driving forces.[7] It is by no means inescapable that such an economic ethos needs authoritarian means of enforcement, though it does require a different approach to public policy. One that achieves socio-political imperatives without over-burdening regulation and central diktat that stifles innovative enterprise. A difficult but essential balance to strike. One that both policy makers and business leaders will have to work together in good faith to explore and construct.

The twenty-first-century challenge for democratic countries is to evolve their own distinct model of political capitalism. One that captures the advantages of being able to mobilize all to achieve, jointly, national and trans-national social, political and economic objectives without falling into a heavy-handed or even authoritarian model.

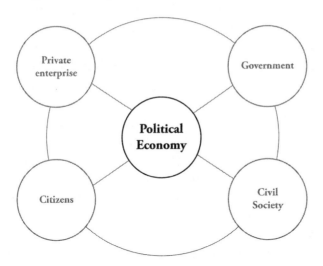

As opposed to autocracy, in democracies the political weather is created by the interaction of multiple players in the market of ideas (*see figure*), not by an all-powerful politburo accountable only to itself. In political capitalism the aim is aligning commercial business and economic activity with the wishes and broad direction of the polity. In democracies that process is messy, even chaotic at times, since it is achieved through a process of relentless contestation and constant adaptation.

In such a complex adaptive system, multiple endogenous control mechanisms emerge to act in much the same way as our bodies' homeostatic control system – that which causes us to sweat to cool down when we get too hot or shiver to warm up when we get too cold. Such social homeostatic mechanisms are in a process of continuous evolution. Government is just one component of the homeostatic system and is best thought of as the means through which individuals solve collective problems.[8]

Just as systems don't die suddenly, new systems do not appear overnight. Neither are they carefully planned by some all-knowing beings. They emerge over time. Countries like France, Germany, Japan, South Korea and others have long believed in a greater alignment between their societies' political and social goals and the nature and shape of economic activity than, say, the UK or the US. The degree to which that alignment was achieved changed over time as did the methods used. In some cases, as outlined in the Samsung, Wirecard and Volkswagen cases earlier, the relationship between politics and commerce became far too close, leading to inadequate supervision, the tail wagging the dog, and outright corruption. France has, in recent years, moved from more to less state involvement in commercial matters but the revolving door (or *pantouflage*) of the French elite between business and government remains. Yet, even those countries had become seduced by the promise of financialized capitalism and slowly adopted more of the Anglo-Saxon model. Sometimes with unpleasant consequences for some of their own businesses. Germany, France and the Netherlands also started to compete to attract a bigger financial services sector post-Brexit.

Be careful what you wish for.

The term 'political capitalism' is itself not new. It was almost certainly coined by Gabriel Kolko in the 1960s. In his reading, political capitalism was an economic system in which business controls government more than government controls business. In this book, I suggest that plutocratic capitalism may be a more appropriate term for such states.

The thesis of this book is that the new political capitalism is very different from that which Kolko described. In an age of widespread communication, greater transparency, competing interests pulling in different directions and the empowerment of citizens and civil society, crony capitalism may hopefully become progressively less viable. Instead, private enterprise is seen as one part of the polity. Playing its important role in affecting the political weather but no longer able to control it in quite the same way as in previous eras.

The new political capitalism offers big advantages to private enterprise if business plays its part in making it work effectively. It could blunt the politics of extremes. At one end the idea that social and economic prosperity lies in a freewheeling business culture with a narrow focus on short-term financial performance to the exclusion of all else. The Milton Friedman doctrine that has been utterly and irretrievably discredited by its very visible adverse consequences. At the other end, the idea that the only way forward is by bringing private enterprise to heel through socialist capitalism that lionizes the benefits of heavy-handed state intervention and runs on the pretence that the interests of the state and the interests of the wider polity are one and the same. That people value being made wards of the state more than they value their own freedom and the dignity and sense of self-worth that goes with the ability to stand on their own two feet.

For decades, our politics has swung between one extreme and the other. As each has failed, the pendulum swings back to the other. The outdated political competition between the traditional right and the traditional left – obsolete concepts both. The rise of Bernie Sanders and his followers in the US, and their persistent influence in the Democratic Party, is one such swing. The election of President Trump and the rise of nationalist forces in Europe and elsewhere are also political manifestations of the failure of financialized capitalism. In Europe, they have led to Brexit and to increased tensions within EU member states. In France, as in the US, both nationalism in the form of Le Pen's *Rassemblement national* and socialist capitalism in the form of Jean-Luc Mélenchon's *La France Insoumise*, made a run for it. The UK's brief dalliance with the socialist capitalism of Jeremy Corbyn crashed and burned.

This widely swinging political pendulum does not benefit anyone, least of all private enterprise. It does not provide the relative political stability on which businesses thrive. And it is dangerous for business leaders to assume that every so-called 'anti-business' political force is forever destined to fizzle out – as is not uncommon for those whose way of thinking developed in the 1980s and 90s.

The version of political capitalism I envision recognizes that the innovative energies of private enterprise operating within competitive, well-structured and well-regulated markets is vital to progress. It also recognizes that 'progress' means creating a better society. That the purpose of private enterprise is also just that – creating a better society.

And that the definition of what constitutes a better society is what emerges from the market of ideas debated across the whole polity with elected governments having the final say as the only institutions with the democratic legitimacy to do so.

Businesses that are successful in this era of the new political capitalism are those that, first of all, understand they form an important part of the polity and abandon the idea of being apolitical. Second, they learn to be successful by reading the political weather, moving with it and improving their performance by providing broad social value to the whole of society and adding net value to their whole networks of capital rather than pushing against the socio-cultural winds in pursuit of narrow, short-horizon self-interest evaluated exclusively in financial terms.

Businesses also need to be wary of the type of external advice that they seek and follow. The previously mentioned $600 million fine paid by McKinsey & Co. for the firm's advice to Purdue Pharma on how to 'turbocharge' sales of OxyContin (*see also* p. 23) illustrates the dangers of narrow financial focus to the exclusion of social impact. The description of 'high abuse-risk patients' as 'opportunities' in the firm's reported advice to Johnson & Johnson,[9] another opioid manufacturer, suggests a loss of moral compass. As do the same firm's woes in Saudi Arabia and South Africa, where, in the latter case, the firm's top executive reflected, *'To be brutally honest, we were too distant to understand the growing anger in South Africa.'* In other words, a lack of political antennae and a seeming inability to look at the world through a political and human lens rather than an exclusively numbers-driven lens landed the firm in hot water.

There are neurobiological reasons as to why this happens. As outlined earlier, many business leaders and their advisors like to live in an analytical world where they believe that they are making 'rational', data-driven decisions. The political lens is, on the other hand, focused on empathy, moral choices and human values and feelings. Neuroimaging studies have shown that the activation of those neural networks associated with analytical reasoning leads to the actual suppression of brain activity associated with social, emotional and moral cognitive processes.[10] These findings are supported by behavioural data and by further imaging data that suggest that over-reliance on analytical, non-emotional forms of reasoning results in dehumanization and a suppression of the ability to connect with the human side of moral dilemmas.[11] It is therefore unsurprising that an analytical culture inevitably creates large blind spots when it comes to the political framework in which businesses are operating.

THE JOURNEY

In Chapters 5 and 6, I sought to provide some ideas on the skills, capabilities and attitudes that can be built for businesses to succeed in this evolving environment. It is a journey without an end point.

Simon Zadek has provided a framework for what that journey entails and the stages that it will go through (*see* Figure below).[12] This provides a good model as to how the new political capitalism is emerging.

At the stage of maturity collaborative and public policy solutions become essential

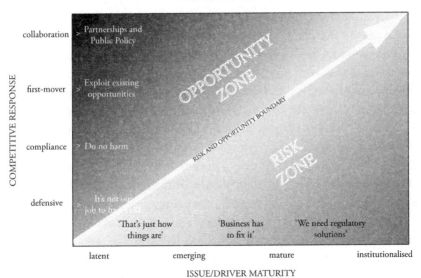

Source: Zadek, Simon (2019), 'Pathways to Corporate Responsibility – Revisited', in G.G. Lennsen, N.C. Smith (eds.) Managing Sustainable Business, *Springer Science + Business Media BV. Reproduced with author's permission.*

On the horizontal axis are the four stages of maturity. Initially the issues are latent. We are well past that stage in most developed countries. 'That's just how things are' and 'There is no alternative model' are words that are no longer on the lips of any thoughtful businessperson, serious politician or any significant number of citizens. Then the new approach starts to emerge. Its exact shape and nature remain shrouded in mist, but its silhouette and the general principles are clear and readily visible. Some look at the ill-defined silhouette and interpret it by looking backwards – at that which they have known and become comfortable with throughout their careers – seemingly unable to accept obsolescence and imagine the new. But emergence of the new is unstoppable and its exact shape eventually will be determined through public debate.

In time the new form becomes clear – the stage of maturity. Finally, the emergent system will become embedded in institutional structures, both private and public. The new political capitalism is on that journey. It is clear that the era of financialized capitalism is dying and the new era of political capitalism is emerging but not yet mature. How long it will take to reach maturity and then institutionalization is unclear. My personal bet is that progress will be relatively quick. Those who would slow down progress in the interests of the status quo are losing the battle at an ever-accelerating pace. Let me stick my neck out and take a guess that we will have reached the institutionalized stage within a decade.

What about the journey for private enterprise? Simon suggests four stages for that also.

We have all had to suffer through the first stage of denial. That it's not the job of private enterprise to fix any of the flaws in our political economy – that's for someone else to do while we get on with the job of making money. Today, few continue to cleave to that philosophy. As we have seen earlier, most leading business organizations have moved beyond that, at least in words. Translating that change to have operational meaning will naturally take longer.

The next stage is that of compliance – yes, OK, we'll go along with that and conform to the new approach. Maybe not because we like it but because we have to. Many are in that stage as they start to conform to the emerging socio-cultural imperatives. The focus on compliance with ESG codes maybe best fits here, as do efforts such as reducing carbon emissions – the 'first do no harm' principle.

As such changes become more widespread and more embedded, their ability to generate competitive advantage wanes. If everyone is doing it to a greater or lesser extent – and largely following the same playbook – it becomes the normal way of doing business rather than a way of generating advantage. A minimum requirement that some have called the licence to operate. Those who fall behind will put themselves at a disadvantage.

It is those who go further, who can go beyond merely complying but instead come up with innovative approaches to appeal to their citizen customers and stakeholders that move to the next stage of exploiting the opportunity by becoming first movers. Being a first mover and maintaining that position is hard. Few will manage it and reap the rewards. I have covered some examples of brands that have done so or seem to be moving in that direction. They are the companies and brands that choose to, and prove able to, stand out from the herd. Pulling it off takes a certain type of management culture and an exceptional management capability that some companies have and others lack. Precisely because it is unlikely to be widespread, it offers the chance for competitive advantage.

The final stage is that where public policy and private enterprise collaborate to continue to create the sort of societies, we want to live in. Simon calls that a stage of 'partnership'. It is not intended as a partnership in legal form, simply an acceptance that everyone is heading in the same direction, has the same societal goals and that those goals can be reached better and quicker through co-ordination and collaboration than through private and public efforts pulling in different directions. The path to progress becomes embedded in institutional structures.

And herein lies the paradox of political capitalism. In democracies, conflict of ideas is an essential part of progress. To some extent, such conflicts might increase as divisions open up between different views of right and wrong. If buying a chocolate bar becomes a statement of political belief rather than a matter of preference based on largely irrelevant trivialities, the potential for conflict increases. But so does the opportunity of progress through competition and market forces.

The fact remains that, as outlined above, the conditions for the emergence of political capitalism are already well in place. The trend is there – and growing. We are past the question of whether this will all emerge. Rather, the question is how to make it work well. In that, pluralistic markets catering to different views will play a central role.

For businesses, the task is to remain in the Opportunity Zone. At the very least travel along the risk and opportunity boundary and avoid falling into the red Risk Zone, where their operational practices lag behind the socio-cultural and political developments leaving them forever scrabbling to catch up as their business models risk obsolescence.

Those enterprises that have the vision and management capability to do so will live deep in the Opportunity Zone. They will be ahead of the game and use their well-developed political and cultural antennae to create competitive advantage. An advantage likely to be sustainable as their laggard competitors scrabble to catch up and some of which, including many household names, will decline and whither.

Just think of Patagonia – a company that has environmental politics embedded in its DNA and decades of experience in how to develop it further. How easy is it going to be, and how long will it take, for others to reach that same level of skill and capability to compete effectively on a similarly well-constructed platform?

Different companies will go in different directions. If we take the focus on sustainability as one aspect of these changes, one study found that 73 per cent of board members feel that a focus on sustainability is important to their ability to create long-term value. But they split in how they plan to address it. Thirty per cent intend to 'keep up with developments' – in other words, travel along the risk and opportunity boundary. A further 29 per cent, on the other hand, were seeking ways to turn it into a competitive advantage – the Opportunity Zone.[13]

As mentioned above, once certain aspects of the journey reach the institutionalized stage, the opportunity for generating competitive advantage disappears. This is where ESG is now headed. Gary Gensler, President Biden's pick to head the Securities and Exchange Commission, has made it clear that he intends to institutionalize ESG disclosure and compliance rules. Which is why I have argued that those who wish to generate competitive advantage will soon have to go beyond mere ESG compliance to do so, while failure to comply effectively with ESG requirements will become a significant drag on performance.

Of course, as Zadek points out, any two-dimensional model such as the one above is necessarily a simplification of a complex adaptive system where things don't move in a neat linear fashion. Where the interaction of many different actors within the system results in winding roads and many cul-de-sacs. Nevertheless, the overall direction is clear even if getting there will be tortuous.

As we have seen in the previously described stories, in an age of political capitalism, strong influences on corporations will come from many sides. From governments and civil society, from investors and employees, from individual customers and business customers. All will be pushing in similar directions albeit at different speeds and with varying levels of effectiveness. There will also be the competitors and innovators – increasingly social innovators as well as technological and business model innovators – who will continue to transform

markets and render obsolete previous approaches to what business is all
about. Innovators like Tesla forcing belated change in the mainstream
car industry. Showing that what was claimed by the laggards to be
impossible is nothing of the sort.

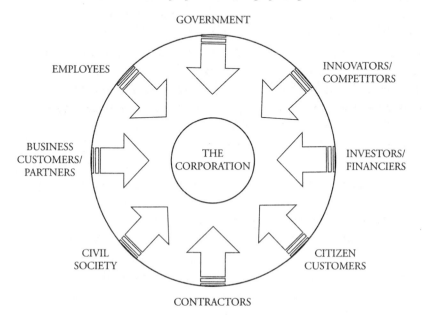

Political Capitalism: influence from all sides
The investor perspective is no longer privileged

Capabilities
In Chapter 5, I outlined some of the capabilities that can be built to
enable enterprises to thrive in an era of political capitalism. One other
question relates to the structure of boards and executive teams.

My experience of working with various business leaders is that teams
tend to be insufficiently diverse. By that, I am not referring to the usual
narrow interpretation of diversity in terms of race and gender. Some
progress in that regard has been made in many countries though, frankly,
there remains some danger that it all risks descending into tickbox
diversity. Here, I am referring to diversity of thought and outlook.

In my experience, many executive teams tend to be monocultural.
A group of people with rather similar backgrounds and outlooks. Male
or female, black, white, Asian or anything else, they tend to have gone

through similar types of education, similar career paths, have been trained to think in very similar ways, and go to the same conferences and dinner parties. In other words, they all tend to belong to the same tribe. Many reach higher levels of management because they have been good operational managers who have delivered to financial targets.

Some CEOs actively push towards uniformity in outlook because it is more efficient, decisions get taken more quickly and it avoids endless discussion on what may seem esoteric and philosophical arguments that, it might be believed, do little to contribute to increased operational efficiency. The result is that many ideas end up getting judged in terms of their short-term operational implications and how they fit with established ways of thinking. With management having to deal with often challenging day-to-day operational questions, there is little time for exploration of stuff that seems initially to be somewhat more abstract. Disruptive innovation is inevitably stifled.

Which is why the same study just quoted above, where the large majority aspire to move forward on sustainability issues, also found that:

> These beliefs and aspirations did not necessarily extend to their firms identifying the policies which need to be in place and the information required to meet environmental and societal challenges…their responses overall suggest that boards are just beginning to recognise its complexities and the difficulties companies face in gauging and integrating sustainability measures.

And the tasks associated with everyday operations tend to overshadow grappling with the complexities of the challenges and opportunities that require a new focus as well as, in some cases, structural change.

Some believe that two-tier board structures that separate executive boards and supervisory boards, as is common in some parts of continental Europe, should help. Others do not, believing that supervisory boards simply create another layer but with a culture that is largely indistinguishable. The only reasonable evidence available seems to be that family-owned companies tend to have longer-term outlooks and to address these issues more, and more effectively, than do publicly quoted companies. Another consequence of the era of financialized capitalism. This is to be expected, given the prevailing structures and incentives.

It remains to be seen whether senior management and board structures will push towards a greater diversity of thinking. Whether CEOs will start to welcome rather than shun 'trouble-makers' – directors and executives who are welcomed because they think differently, constantly challenge the conventional ways of doing things and are relentless in pushing management to consider and act upon that which needs to be done to thrive in the new era of political capitalism.

Management thinker Manfred Kets de Vries suggests that once you become a leader, you are surrounded by liars – people who only tell you want you want to hear. He argues, *'Every leader needs a fool,'*[14] by which he means the equivalent of the court jester – the only person who was protected when telling all-powerful monarchs some hard truths wrapped in humour.

Some leaders do seek out diversity of thought. *'You need new and diverse thinking to tackle contemporary challenges'*, according to Andreas Jacobs who has chaired multiple boards and is now Chair of the Board at INSEAD.[15]

WHAT DOES THE NEW LOOK LIKE?

I recall a conversation with the CEO of a major multinational I was advising. We used to talk constantly about the idea that his corporation's business model was broken and obsolete. One day, he said to me: *'We've had this conversation many times. But you'll also notice that nothing here has changed.'* I nodded, not quite knowing where he was going with this. *'The problem,'* he continued, *'is that I know my business model is broken, but I have no idea what the new one could look like. So here I am. Stuck.'*

So, this talk of political capitalism is all very well, I hear some say. But what could the new political capitalism look like? What does a 'partnership' between private and public sectors – but which is not really a partnership – actually mean? What does it look like to have government, enterprise, citizens and civil society all move broadly in the same direction without having the unwelcome heavy hand of the state intruding into everyone's lives or falling into the cosy 'I scratch your back and you scratch mine' type of conspiracy against the public?

Maybe one example of such a situation was the extraordinary efforts by both public and private sectors in dealing with the COVID-19 pandemic. There was no disagreement that getting past the pandemic was the overarching societal goal. As we have seen in the various examples in this book, private enterprise and the public sector mobilized towards that goal. Those that did not and instead used the crisis to seek their own short-term financial self-interest at societies' expense became outcasts.

Take the COVID-19 vaccination programme as just one example. It was a huge combined private and public effort. Vaccines were the result of collaborative private and public research, development and financing. They were developed in record time, rapidly approved by the regulatory authorities and drew upon a huge public and private infrastructure for distribution and actually getting them into people's arms. Some, like AstraZeneca, made their vaccine available at cost for the duration of the pandemic, making it affordable to reach billions of people.

Some missteps were, of course, inevitable – political as well as commercial. Maybe the most conspicuous were those by the European Commission (EC) and some EU member states. Plagued by botched vaccine acquisition and delivery programmes, the EC decided to pick a fight with vaccine manufacturers. Particularly, in the still emotionally raw post-Brexit stage, with Anglo-Swedish AstraZeneca. Picking fights with companies that were doing their best to overcome huge operational and logistical issues to deliver the world from a crushing pandemic was not a good look.

AstraZeneca, for its part, made communications missteps. Its management learned that providing the vaccine at cost was not a sufficient condition for protecting the company from political fallout in a highly emotionally laden political environment. The company's reputation was not enhanced by the changes, in the midst of the pandemic, to the CEO's compensation package, a move that generated controversy and which 40 per cent of shareholders voted against.

The Biden administration 'vaccine diplomacy' stance chose, at least initially, to combine retaining in-country all US produced vaccines with verbal support for discussing the potential waiving of intellectual property rights surrounding vaccine patents – a stance that I suggest was highly mistaken.[16]

It maybe took longer than it should have done, but eventually agreement of sorts was reached to mobilize resources for worldwide distribution though challenges inevitably remained around both governance issues and health care infrastructure needs in many countries.

Everyone is still learning how to deal with the new age of political capitalism and behave appropriately but, by and large, how the partnership between politics and commerce handled the vaccine programme was a huge success. And an active civil society and fourth estate did their best to bring to light instances of collusion and corruption. If we can do these things in times of war and crisis, and clearly see that everyone benefits, why can it not become the norm of how we run our political economy? Why do we have to wait for dark times before we can summon up what the British call the 'Blitz spirit' – a collaborative national and international effort where everyone plays their role as part of the bigger whole?

None of this means living in a utopian dreamworld, believing everyone's interests can always be perfectly aligned. Politics knows all too well that that is never the case. But, when crises happen and everyone pulls in the same direction, it tends to fill us all with a sense of pride, a sense of community with shared interests, a can-do spirit. We both trust and help others. We are more tolerant of inevitable missteps committed in good faith, less ready with immediate outrage. We start to examine how our own private efforts fit in with those of others and with those of the public sector. And, in the search for rapid results and fuelled by the rediscovery of mutual trust, that bureaucracy that adds little value is simply swept aside (it is as well to remember that bureaucracy is the direct result of a lack of trust and a depleted social capital). We all mobilize to a common endeavour and trust each other to do so.

And then, pfft! Mysteriously, it all fizzles out without as much as a puff of smoke to remind us that it even ever existed. We all go back to ploughing our own furrows seemingly oblivious once again to all that is around us. Having witnessed in glorious Technicolor how individualist market forces on their own and without a shared purpose and collaboration with the population and the public sector would have been utterly incapable of solving the acute crisis, we suddenly go back to our old belief systems without missing a beat or noticing our own inconsistency. When the crisis is over, we are once again treated to the same tedious arguments of 'the market' needs to be left well alone and it will solve everything, or markets and private enterprise don't work and state control of almost everything is the only solution.

Some business leaders have clearly recognized the shift towards political capitalism – and their vital role in it. JP Morgan CEO Jamie Dimon in his letter to shareholders in April 2021:

> 'The problems that are tearing at the fabric of American society require all of us – government, business and civic society – to work together with a common purpose.'[17]

Neither will the challenges of adapting to political capitalism fall exclusively on business. Politics, too, will need to adapt.

When corporations took a stand against the new, more restrictive voter eligibility law in the US state of Georgia, Senate minority leader Mitch McConnell claimed that it was 'stupid' for companies to jump into controversial political issues such as the Georgia voting law. 'If I were running a major corporation, I'd stay out of politics,' McConnell reportedly said. Of course, what we all know he really meant is that businesses should avoid taking political positions that are counter to his own. I suspect he would have welcomed wholehearted support for his own policies as he has for many decades.

Politicians will feel the pressure when corporations take stances that reflect the socio-political mood but run counter to their own positions. Maybe some will even be tempted to follow Boris Johnson and shout 'F**k business!'

McConnell also reportedly clarified that when he said that corporations should keep out of politics, he did not mean that they should stop making campaign contributions. Make what you will of that combination of statements.

Resistance is not limited to Senator McConnell. At a Goldman Sachs' annual meeting in 2021, a shareholder asked why the bank was supporting 'Marxists' against the capitalist policies that had made it such a powerhouse. The bank was accused of pandering to what some called woke capitalism (hardly the same thing as Marxism but there you go). Such questions show a fundamental misunderstanding of what is going on. The fake juxtaposition of the issues as Marxism vs Capitalism is a well-worn rhetorical device that attempts to polarize into black and white issues that are complex and nuanced.

It is highly unlikely that such transparent devices will be taken seriously, significantly change the trajectory of political discourse, or how companies respond. When JP Morgan Chase and Citigroup resumed

THE NEW POLITICAL CAPITALISM 269

political campaign contributions after suspending them following the Capitol riots in January 2021, they did so selectively. JP Morgan would not support candidates who voted against counting electoral votes in the 2020 presidential election while Citi added two criteria to its selection process: *'one based on character and integrity and a second focused on a commitment to bipartisanship and democratic institutions.'*[18] All explicit political positions that, if genuinely carried through in practice, are pretty far from what cynics suggest that corporate political contributions are all about – buying favours.

AN ALTERNATIVE FUTURE?

The new political capitalism as I have outlined it is, in my view, inevitable. There will be some for whom it represents their vision of hell. They will fight against it in the market of ideas. What sort of alternative future might they be fighting for?

One alternative is well encapsulated in a book titled *The Sovereign Individual: Mastering the Transition to the Information Age*.[19] The authors put forward a view similar to that which I have suggested about the impact of information technology, social media, global communications and the unconstrained movement of capital and business activity across the globe. But their vision of how these developments might play out is quite different. They paint an image of an age of unfettered individualism, *'the new revolution of power which is liberating individuals at the expense of the twentieth-century nation state.'*

In the book, the authors envision a collapse of democracy as we know it – a system that, after all, requires that which some seemingly despise most – a government: *'The good news is that politicians will no more be able to dominate, suppress and regulate the greater part of commerce.'* Instead, the new masters of the universe will be *'the brightest, most successful, and ambitious... those who can educate and motivate themselves.'* It is these Sovereign Individuals, freed from any form of collective responsibility, freed from belonging or being subject to any political or social constraints who will prosper and accumulate wealth and power: *'The most obvious benefits will flow to the "cognitive elite" who will increasingly operate outside political boundaries... anyone who thinks clearly will potentially be rich... The more clever you are, the less propulsion you will require to achieve financial escape velocity.'*

The authors share my diagnosis of the progressive fracture of the political economy. The separation of economic activity from any kind of political structure or democratic accountability. While I warned of the bedlam that such a continued separation threatens, they seem to welcome it. A substrate on which they build a vision of a Hobbesian world – a war of all against all. Where the clever will triumph. Where there will be no possibility of any institution to collect taxes, nor institutionalize any kind of endeavour focused on our shared interests. The welfare state will be history. The individual reigns supreme. The clever will flourish; the less clever will perish or revert to serfdom.

Democracy will cease to exist. Instead, welcome to the new feudalism – the plutocracy of the clever elite. Or, if I might be permitted to coin a word, an exypnocracy. It is an all-encompassing, globalized version of the previously quoted chairman of Dow Chemicals who dreamt of establishing the company's headquarters on an island (owned by no nation), beholden to no nation.

Here are some more of the delights we can all look forward to according to the authors:

'First in scores, then in hundreds, and ultimately in the millions, individuals will escape the shackles of politics.'

'We believe that as the modern nation-state decomposes, latter-day barbarians will increasingly come to exercise power behind the scenes. Groups like the Russian mafiya, which picks the bones of the former Soviet Union, other ethnic criminal gangs, nomenklaturas, drug lords, and renegade covert agencies will be laws unto themselves.'

'As this technological revolution unfolds, predatory violence will be organized more and more outside of central control.'

'We expect to see a radical restructuring of the nature of sovereignty and the virtual death of politics before the transition is over.'

We've seen all these fantasies before in, for instance, the *Mad Max* movie franchise. It is a vision of a lawless world. Yet one that expects business to thrive in the face of all the evidence to the contrary from current lawless states.

Dear reader, if you choose to reject what I believe is the inevitability of political capitalism, what is your proposed alternative to the status quo which, as everyone knows, never, ever lasts? *Mad Max*? Some kind of back-to-the-future process of re-discovering a nostalgia powered version of the past? Something else entirely? If so, what does that look like?

And, seeing as the future is not pre-determined by fate but rather depends on human action, which model should you and I personally be contributing to creating and making work?

WHERE TO NOW?

In this book, I have outlined my conviction that political capitalism as I have defined it represents the next stage of our development. I realize that my perspective rests on a certain underlying belief system. One that believes that democracy, messy, untidy and incredibly difficult though it is, and under challenge by a resurgence of authoritarianism in many parts of the globe, still continues to represent the preferred form of organizing our politics and our societies. That market capitalism, the right of private individuals to earn their own dignified living and own capital and assets, with, as much as is possible given human fallibility, well-structured, well-functioning, well-regulated, competitive markets representing the best price finding mechanism remains the best way to organize our economies. That the new political capitalism represents a fusion of those two structures. A state of affairs where private enterprise, citizens, civil society and legitimately elected governments – the polity – all have an important role to play in the constant contestation of *how* we can all create a better society. That the creation of a better society should be the overarching purpose for all.

We are also witnessing a massive economic transformation the effects of which we do not yet understand. Public expenditure, and, therefore, governments' role in the economy, is soaring. The Biden administration in the US has unleashed a massive stimulus programme and infrastructure plan that dwarf Lyndon Johnson's 'Great Society' programme and the military spending of the 1960s. The relationship between the politics of these programmes and the consequent shape of the economy is unknown but will certainly be different from what we have all become used to.

The emergence of political capitalism is well under way. I believe it to be unstoppable. The only questions are around its nature, the ultimate shape that will emerge and the pace of change. For business leaders, the choices are around how they respond – and how they lead.

That will depend on the nature of their business, the opportunities that change can offer and the skills and capabilities of management teams in different businesses to be early movers, go with the flow, or laggards.

A number of business leaders are taking much more time than maybe some have done in the past to lift their eyes from poring over quarterly earnings figures and have started asking themselves, what future for our society do I want to be part of making happen? In other words, they are becoming ever more political. Understanding that the time is long past when 'being political' simply meant attempting to capture state institutions to further their own interests. Realizing that their role in society is much larger and of much more foundational importance than simply 'making the numbers'.

The non-partisan turn

There is an additional welcome paradox about political capitalism. As it evolves, business will become ever more political but less partisan. The days when one side of the political spectrum wrapped itself in the mantle of being 'pro-business' and the other was labelled 'anti-business' are rapidly disappearing. Citizens are now concerned about political issues more than about political parties. Identities are shifting from allegiance to a particular political colour to identities based on which side of a particular issue one stands. Today's political polarizations are around issues, identities or personalities, not traditional party allegiances.

One such example was the Brexit debate in the UK. Apart from the Liberal Democrats with their uncompromising pro-European stance, all other parties hosted people with different views. The main parties – Labour and the Conservatives – had within their ranks pro- and anti-Brexit campaigners. Citizens' identities became defined by their pro- or anti-Brexit stance, not by which party they supported.

The same pattern is developing around climate change and environmental protection in the US. Republican voters are split by ideology, gender and age when it comes to their views on environmental protection. Conversely, a small proportion of Democrat voters (around 10 per cent) believe in the need to expand the fossil fuel economy. For many on either side, their views on environmental issues transcend party loyalty. Similarly, in the Trump-Clinton 2016 election campaign, we saw a fundamental reversal of traditional party roles. Trump became the standard bearer for the working class, Clinton the creature of Wall Street.

It's no longer about parties, it's about issues and identity and often wrapped around personalities. Although not happening by design, what is going on is reminiscent of the seventeenth-century Iroquois confederacy, where a society of village tribes (let's call them today's political parties) also built a series of clans that cut across tribal divisions. People therefore had two identities – the tribe and the clan. Conflict among tribes was minimized because other tribes had people one identified with as part of one's own clan. What we would today call large-scale matrix management – similar to the ten tribes system introduced in Athens by Cleisthenes around 508 BC.

Of course, these developments are difficult for political parties (today's tribes) to come to terms with. They, too, will need to change to flourish. But it is a welcome development for business. Businesses will need to have clear stances on the issues, but in doing so, they need not nail their colours to one or other political party tribal mast but rather to the cross-cutting clans. The key issues of our day will remain the same whichever party happens to be in power at any one time. Whatever stance is taken will cut across party lines, finding supporters and objectors in every political party. It simply becomes another interpretation of that horrible, dehumanizing concept – market segmentation – this time along political lines rather than any other. The fear that many business leaders have had of being seen to be partisan will slowly fade away.

Issues are bigger than just 'getting on with business'
There are further very large elephants in the room that will also have to be addressed in the context of political capitalism. What does the world look like when automation and digitization get to the point where our economies no longer have the capability of employing any significant proportion of the population? When the structures underpinning our welfare and pensions systems no longer work? When our current belief system around how we fund public services crumbles? When climate change, environmental degradation and biodiversity loss change everything? When it becomes clearer than it already is that our existing structures and institutions for global collaboration can no longer deal with a rapidly transforming geopolitical environment? Even taking a superficial stab at answering these questions is well beyond the scope of this book. Except to say that it will all make everything ever more political in nature.

The US National Security Council argues that the interactions between four key areas: demographics, environment, economics, and technology are '*likely to produce greater contestation at all levels than has been seen since the end of the Cold War, reflecting differing ideologies as well as contrasting views on the most effective way to organize society and tackle emerging challenges.*'[20] Business leaders, for the sake of their own businesses as well as for the sake of our societies as a whole, cannot exempt themselves from playing their part in dealing with these issues effectively. In as much as there are solutions to mitigate the negative effects of these trends, they have to be political in nature and business must play its role. A role that goes very much further than the continued parroting of obsolete narratives narrowly focused around shareholder enrichment and money creation masquerading as the creation of wealth and broad societal value.

Clayton M. Christensen was a professor at Harvard Business School. He was diagnosed with cancer and sadly passed away in 2020. In a *Harvard Business Review* article titled 'How will you measure your life?' he writes:

> I have a pretty clear idea of how my ideas have generated enormous revenue for companies that have used my research; I know I've had a substantial impact. But as I've confronted this disease, it's been interesting to see how unimportant that impact is to me now. I've concluded that the metric by which God will assess my life isn't dollars but the individual people whose lives I've touched.[21]

As we have seen throughout this book, it is no exaggeration to say that business leaders play a vital role in shaping our political economy, our societies, what lives people will have the opportunity to lead, in determining how our democracies work, even whether democracy in its real sense can survive and thrive. How business leaders choose to use their political impact is one of the defining issues of the twenty-first century.

Whatever shape of political capitalism one would like to see, it behoves us all to remember that it won't just happen by magic. We will all have our part to play in its crafting. And a positive outcome certainly cannot be achieved without the full-throated and determined involvement of a significant proportion of private enterprises.

References

Epigraph

1   Megginson, 'Lessons from Europe for American Business', *Southwestern Social Science Quarterly* (1963) 44(1): 3–13, at p. 4.

Chapter 1

1   Snow, C.P. (1998), *The Two Cultures*, Cambridge University Press, p. 2.
2   Zammit-Lucia, Joe (2017), 'Beyond Governance: Towards a market economy that works for everyone', RADIX. https://radixuk.org/wp-content/uploads/2019/08/Beyond_governance_V5_singles.pdf
3   White, Gordon (1993), 'Towards a political analysis of markets', Institute of Development Studies Bulletin 24.3.
4   Korschun, Daniel & Smith, Craig N. (7 March 2018), 'Companies Can't Avoid Politics – And Shouldn't Try To', *Harvard Business Review* online. https://hbr.org/2018/03/companies-cant-avoid-politics-and-shouldnt-try-to?autocomplete=true. Accessed 28 April 2020.
5   Jane Fraser. Citi's commitment to net-zero by 2050. March 1, 2021. https://blog.citigroup.com/2021/03/citis-commitment-to-net-zero-by-2050/
6   Peters, Tom (15 February 2021), 'McKinsey's work on opioid sales represents a new low', *Financial Times*.
7   Thornton, Mark (Ed). The Quotable Mises. Ludwig von Mises Institute, 2005, p. 176.
8   Kaletsky, Anatole (2011), 'Capitalism 4.0: The birth of a new economy in the aftermath of the crisis', Public Affairs, Kindle edition, Location 3,177.
9   Harari, Yuval Noah (2014), *Sapiens: A Brief History of Humankind*, Harper, Kindle edition, pp. 180–1.

10 Randall Wray, L. (1998), *Understanding Modern Money: The Key to Full Employment and Price Stability*, Edward Elgar.

11 Osimo, David (March 2021), 'Policy 2.0 in the pandemic world: What worked, what didn't and why?', The Lisbon Council.

CHAPTER 2

1 https://worthsharingessays1.pressbooks.com/chapter/why-its-pointless -to-argue-about-politics-or-religion/

2 Trenkner, Tina (23 March 2012), 'How Do Business Execs Do as Candidates and as Governors? Governing: The Future of States and Localities'.

3 Drucker, Peter (1977), *Men, Ideas & Politics: Essays*, Harper Colophon Books, p. 143.

4 Drucker, Peter (1977), *Men, Ideas & Politics: Essays*, Harper Colophon Books, p. 158.

5 Sandbrook, Dominic (5 April 2021), 'Prime Ministers Don't Need To Be Virtuous', Unherd.com.

6 Boswell, Christina (14 January 2020), 'What is Politics?', The British Academy. https://www.thebritishacademy.ac.uk/blog/what-is-politics ?gclid=EAIaIQobChMIjYf1stWG6QIVBap3Ch2OeQtfEAAYASAAEg KgcfD_BwE. Accessed 26 April 2020.

7 Doherty, Alex (16 May 2020), 'Has the coronavirus crisis killed neoliberalism? Don't bet on it', *Guardian*.

8 Janis, Irving L. & Mann, Leon (1977), *Decision Making: A psychological analysis of conflict, choice and Commitment*, New York: Free Press.

9 Herman Jr, Paul F. & Treverton, Gregory F. (2009), 'The Political Consequences of Climate Change', *Survival*, 51:2, pp. 137–148.

10 Coates, Daniel R. (29 January 2019), 'Worldwide Threat Assessment of the US Intelligence Community'.

11 Campbell, Peter (29 June 2018), 'Harley-Davidson boss drives Donald Trump into a fury', *Financial Times*.

12 Brown, Dana & Poole, Isiah J. (16 September 2019), The Case for a Public Option for the Drug Industry. *The New Republic*.

13 Boeing Statement on Lion Air Flight 610 Preliminary Report: https://bo eing.mediaroom.com/news-releases-statements?item=130336. Accessed 30 April 2020.

14 Been, Ryan & Suhartono, Harry (14 January 2020), 'Bloomberg. Boeing mocked Lion Air for requesting extra 737 Max pilot training year before crash', *Forbes*.

15 Bushey, Claire & Edgecliffe-Johnson, Andrew (10 January 2020), 'Damning emails threaten Boeing's reputation with the flying public', *Financial Times*.

16 https://www.koamnewsnow.com/boeing-ceo-muilenburg-wont-get-most-of-his-2019-pay/

17 Richter, Wolf (20 January 2020), 'After Blowing $43 Bn on Share-Buybacks in 6 Years, Boeing Scrambles to Borrow $10 Bn, on Top of a $9.5 Bn Credit Line in Oct, to Fund its 737 MAX Fiasco', *Wolf Street*.

18 Michaels, Dave, Tangel, Andrew & Pasztor, Andy (7 January 2021), 'Boeing Reaches $2.5 Billion Settlement of U.S. Probe Into 737 MAX Crashes', *Wall Street Journal*.

19 Tangel, Andrew & Pasztor, Andy (9 January 2021), 'Boeing's Legal, Business Challenges Persist After Settlement', *Wall Street Journal*.

20 Federal Aviation Administration (March 2017), 'A Blueprint for Air Transformation'.

21 Hawranek, Dietmar (14 October 2015), 'Volkswagen: Dutzende Manager in VW-Skandal verwickelt', *Der Spiegel*.

22 https://www.reuters.com/article/us-volkswagen-lower-saxony/lower-saxonys-new-government-says-will-keep-volkswagen-stake-idUSKBN1DM1Y9

23 Miller, Joe (18 May 2020), 'German car industry gets cold shoulder from Berlin', *Financial Times*.

24 Huggler, Justin (24 June 2020), 'Deutschland despairs and Wirecard becomes "the German Enron"', *Telegraph Online*.

25 McCrum, Dan & Palma, Stefania (30 January 2019), 'Executive at Wirecard suspected of using forged contracts', *Financial Times*. Accessed online.

26 Storbeck, Olaf (25 January 2021), 'BaFin boss "believed" Wirecard was victim until near the end', *Financial Times*.

27 Olof Storbeck. German police had close ties with Wirecard report shows. *Financial Times*, 14 April 2021.

28 Mazzucato, Mariana (2013), *The Entrepreneurial State*, Anthem Press.

29 Tett, Gillian (2021), *Anthro-Vision: A new way to see in business and in life*, Avid Reader Press/Simon and Schuster, p. XIV.

Chapter 3

1 Quoted in Gilpin, Robert (1975), *US Power and the Multinational Corporation*, New York: Basic Books, p. 136.

2 Silver, Nick (2017, first edition), *Finance, Society and Sustainability: How to Make the Financial System Work for the Economy, People and Planet*, Palgrave Macmillan, p. 63.

3 Raworth, Kate (July 2017), 'Monopoly was invented to demonstrate the evils of capitalism', *Aeon Magazine* online.
4 Hague, William (18 May 2020), 'The Right must plan now if we are to save the post-COVID world from the torment of socialism', *Telegraph.*
5 Ballegeer, Daan (9 June 2018), 'Ons huidige systeem is kapot', *Het Financieele Dagblad.*
6 Cowen, Tim (June 2019), 'Freedom to Choose: Why competition policy affects us all', RADIX paper, No. 11. https://radixuk.org/wp-co ntent/uploads/2019/08/Freedom-to-Choose-Report-June-2019_EMAIL .pdf
7 Freeman, George MP. In Goldsmith, Paul (October 2018), 'The Quadruple Helix: Tackling the issues of the left behind', Radix paper, No. 10. https://radixuk.org/wp-content/uploads/2019/08/Quadruple -Helix-E-Final.pdf
8 Keynes, J.M. (ed. Moggridge, Donald) (1972), *The Collected Writings of John Maynard Keynes. Volume IX. Essays in Persuasion*, Macmillan/St Martin's Press, 1972.
9 https://radixuk.org/video/can-democracy-outlast-capitalism/

CHAPTER 4

1 Rachman, Gideon (7 April 2008), 'The political threats to globalization', *Financial Times.*
2 González-Durántez, Miriam (2018), In 'Backlash: Saving Globalization From Itself' by Joe Zammit-Lucia and David Boyle. RADIX.
3 Miller, Joe (14 February 2020), 'Porsche rules out Chinese factory as it hails cachet of "Made in Germany"', *Financial Times.*
4 Davidann, Jon (9 February 2021), 'The Myth of Westernisation', *Aeon Magazine* (online).
5 Tett, Gillian (1995), *Ambiguous Alliances: Marriage and Identity in a Muslim Village in Soviet Tajikistan*, unpublished PhD thesis from the University of Cambridge. As quoted in Tett, Gillian (2021) *Anthro-Vision: A new way to see in business and in life*, Avid Reader Press/Simon and Schuster.
6 Veblen, Thorstein (1915), *Imperial Germany and the Industrial Revolution*. Re-published by Batoche Books, 2003.
7 Luttwack, Edward N. (summer, 1990), 'From Geopolitics to Geo-Economics: Logic of Conflict, Grammar of Commerce', *The National Interest*, No. 20, pp. 17–23.
8 Hague, William (13 July 2020), 'Too many in the West are still blind to the inconvenient truth about China', *Telegraph*. Accessed online.

9 Pratley, Nils (26 January 2021), 'Caught between China and the US, the pressure for HSBC to split grows', *Guardian*.

10 Kinder, Tabby, Morris, Stephen & Noonan, Laura (21 February 2021), 'HSBC intensifies pivot to Asia with job moves and US exit', *Financial Times*.

11 Sugiura, Eri & Iwamoto, Kentaro (1 February 2021), 'Myanmar's apparent coup rattles companies that bet on democracy' *Nikkei Asia* online.

12 Krugman, Paul (issued May 1989), 'Is Bilateralism Bad?', NBER Working Paper No. 2972.

13 How the West got China wrong. *The Economist*, 3 March 2018.

14 *Financial Times* editorial (6 August 2017), 'US should trade carefully on China trade concerns'.

15 Rodrik, Dani (12 December 2017), 'The great globalization lie', *Prospect Magazine*.

16 Lee, Kai-Fu (17 January 2018), 'China and the UK should be partners in the AI revolution', *Evening Standard*, p. 15.

17 G7 Communiqué, 13 June, 2021.

18 Hu, Fred & Spence, Michael (July/August 2017 Issue), 'Why Globalization Stalled. And How to Restart It', *Foreign Affairs*.

19 Muller, Mike (13 February 2013), 'Nestlé baby milk scandal has grown up but not gone away', *Guardian*.

20 Rodrik, Dani, 'What do trade agreements really do?' https://drodrik.scholar.harvard.edu/files/dani-rodrik/files/what_do_trade_agreements_really_do.pdf

21 Rodrik, Dani (March 2012), *The Globalization Paradox. Democracy and the Future of the World Economy*, WW Norton & Company.

22 Monnet, Jean (1978), *Memoirs*, Garden City, New York: Doubleday & Company Inc.

23 Luttwack, Edward N. (summer, 1990), 'From Geopolitics to Geo-Economics: Logic of Conflict, Grammar of Commerce', *The National Interest*, No. 20, pp. 17–23.

24 Dahrendorf, Ralf (March 1995), 'Economic Opportunity, Civil Society and Political Liberty', United Nations Research Institute for Social Development Discussion Paper.

25 Lakner, Christoph & Milanovic, Branko (12 August 2015), 'Global Income Distribution: From the Fall of the Berlin Wall to the Great Recession', *The World Bank Economic Review*, Advance Access.

26 IMF Policy Paper (10 April 2017), 'Making Trade an Engine of Growth for All: The Case for Trade and for Policies to Facilitate Adjustment'.

27 Corlett, Adam (September 2016), 'Examining an Elephant. Globalization and the lower middle class of the rich world', Resolution Foundation.

28 Beattie, Alan (19 November 2017), 'The flaws of trying to compensate globalization's losers', *Financial Times*.
29 Collier, Paul (2018), *The Future of Capitalism: Facing The New Anxieties*, New York: HarperCollins, p. 193.
30 Caliendo, Lorenzo & Parro, Fernando (2015), 'Estimates of the Trade and Welfare Effects of NAFTA', *Review of Economic Studies*, 82, 1–44.
31 Hakobyan, Shushanik & McLaren, John (October 2016), 'Looking for Local Labor Market Effects of NAFTA', *Review of Economics and Statistics*, 98(4), 728–741.
32 Krugman, Paul (March 2018), 'Globalization: What did we miss?'. https ://www.gc.cuny.edu/CUNY_GC/media/LISCenter/pkrugman/PK_ globalization.pdf
33 International Monetary Fund (14 November 2012), 'The liberalisation and management of capital flows: An institutional view'.
34 Janeway, William H. (26 June 2020), 'The Retreat from Globalization', *Project Syndicate*.
35 The Bretton Woods Project (5 April 2016), 'IMF re-opening case for capital controls?' http://www.brettonwoodsproject.org/2016/04/imf -reopening-case-for-capital-controls/
36 *City AM* (26 February 2018), 'Debate: Should tech firms be taxed on revenue, rather than profit?'
37 Bradshaw, Tim (14 January 2018), 'Self-driving cars raise fears over "weaponization"', *Financial Times*.
38 DeNardis, Laura (2015), *The Global War for Internet Governance*, Yale University Press.
39 Solomon, Erica (19 July 2020), 'German proposals for supply chain law spark fierce debate'.
40 Tett, Gillian (1 June 2017), 'Executives take a quiet turn away from globalization', *Financial Times*.
41 DHL Global Interconnectedness Survey, 2019.

CHAPTER 5

1 Sherman, G.D. & Haidt, J. (July 2011), 'Cuteness and Disgust: The Humanizing and Dehumanizing Effects of Emotion', *Emotion Review* No. 3, 245–251, p. 245.
2 Bell, Ryan (19 August 2018), 'Temple Grandin, Killing them softly at slaughterhouses for 30 years', *National Geographic*.
3 Xiuzhong Xu, Vicky with Cave, Danielle, Leibold, Dr James, Munro, Kelsey & Ruser, Nathan, 'Uyghurs for sale: Re-education, forced labour and surveillance beyond Xinjiang', Policy Brief Report No. 26/2020.

Australian Strategic Policy Institute. Available here: https://s3-ap-southe
ast-2.amazonaws.com/ad-aspi/2020-10/Uyghurs per cent20for per
cent20sale per cent2020 per cent20October per cent202020.pdf?_Yl0J
D1KRkYoOW3XyR89qC3Orjt1FZD_=

4 Sherwell, Philip & Spence, Madeleine (2 August 2020), 'Fashion firms
   to be shamed for using Xi's "cotton gulag"', *The Sunday Times*.

5 Rouch, David (2020), *The Social Licence for Financial Markets: Reaching
   for the end and why it counts*, London: Palgrave Macmillan.

6 https://www.businessroundtable.org/business-roundtable-redefines-the
   -purpose-of-a-corporation-to-promote-an-economy-that-serves-all
   -americans. Accessed 14 June, 2021.

7 Heald, Morrell (1998), *The Social Responsibility of Business: Company and
   Community 1900–1960*, Transaction Publishers, New Brunswick.

8 Zammit-Lucia, Joe (29 January 2020), 'Has the business world found its
   purpose? Trust, but verify', *CityAM*.

9 Kay, John (March 2021), 'RIP PLC: the rise of the ghost corporation',
   Prospect Magazine.

10 Boyd, Tony (20 May 2021), Lessons from forced CEO exits, *The
   Australian Financial Review*.

11 https://www.strategyand.pwc.com/gx/en/insights/ceo-success.html.
   Accessed 5 June, 2021.

12 McDougall, D. (22 November 2020), 'Anders Povlsen on his radical
   mission to "rewild" Scotland', *The Sunday Times*.

13 'Culture Wars', *The Economist*, 20 February 2021.

14 Pukas, A. (13 January 2019), 'Danone Morocco saga highlights
   enduring role of consumer boycotts', *Arab News*.

15 'Battle of the Wallets: The changing landscape of consumer
   activism', Weber Shandwick/KRC Research. Research conducted in
   August 2017.

16 Rodgers, Joann Ellison (11 March 2014), 'Go Forth in Anger',
   Psychology Today online.

17 'The Kay Review of UK Equity Markets and Long-Term Decision
   Making', Final Report, July 2012.

18 Coyle, Diane (2 December 2020), 'Taking National Investment
   Seriously', *Project Syndicate*.

19 Zadek, Simon (2012), *The Civil Corporation: The New Economy of
   Corporate Citizenship*, London: Routledge.

20 Nadella, Satya (20 June 2018), 'My views on US immigration Policy',
   Memo to Microsoft employees.

21 An Amazon Employee (16 October 2018), 'I'm an Amazon Employee.
   My Company Shouldn't Sell Facial Recognition Tech to Police', *Medium*.

22 Department for Business, Energy and Industrial Strategy (November 2016), Corporate Governance Reform – Green Paper.

23 Sinclair, Brendan (21 June, 2021), 'Activision Blizzard wins executive compensation vote', gamesindustry.biz

24 www.vlerick.com/en/research-and-faculty/research-for-business/governan ce-ethics/executive-remuneration-research-centre/our-research-output

25 High Pay Centre (November 2014), 'Performance Pay: New Ideas on Executive Remuneration'.

26 Krippner, Greta R. (2005), 'The financialization of the American economy', *Socio-Economic Review*, **3**, pp. 173–208.

27 Rappaport, Alfred (September 2006), 'Ten Ways to Create Shareholder Value', *Harvard Business Review*.

28 Haque, Umair (2013), *The New Capitalist Manifesto: Building a Disruptively Better Business*, Harvard Business School Press.

29 HSBC Sustainable financing and investing survey 2020. 'Pandemic intensifies awareness of environment and society', October 2020.

30 Eagan, Eleanor & Hauser, Jeff (26 February 2019), 'BlackRock's "Greenwashing" Threatens to Undermine Climate Action', *The American Prospect*.

31 Pinchot, Arial & Christianson, Giulia (3 October 2019), 'How Are Banks Doing on Sustainable Finance Commitments? Not Good Enough', World Resources Institute.

32 Avery, Helen (3 December 2019), 'Sustainable finance's real problems, by the people who know best', *Euromoney*.

33 John Arnesen. The rush to ESG compliance may hurt its long-term goals. 19 May 2021. https://www.pierpoint.info/post/the-rush-to-esg -compliance-may-hurt-its-long-term-goals

34 Kay, John (3 March 2021), 'RIP PLC: the rise of the ghost corporation', *Prospect* Magazine.

35 Tett, Gillian, (2021) *Anthro-Vision: A new way to see in business and in life*, Avid Reader Press/Simon and Schuster.

36 SSAB Press Release, 29 January 2021.

37 Evans, Brian R. (10 December 2020), Letter to Office of the Comptroller of the Currency.

38 Temple-West, Patrick (18 December 2020), in 'Breaking down BP's bet on carbon credits', *Financial Times*.

39 Zammit-Lucia, Joe, Boyle, David & Silver, Nick (2016), 'Quantitative Easing: The debate that never happened', Radix Paper No. 1.

40 Jordan, Thomas (17 December 2020), Introductory Remarks, Swiss National Bank, Zurich.

41 Elliott, K., Price, R., Shaw, P., Spiliotopoulos, T., Ng, M., Coopamootoo, K. & van Moorsel, A. (14 June 2021), Towards an

Equitable Digital Society: Artificial Intelligence (AI) and Corporate Digital Responsibility (CDR), *Society*, published online, https://doi.org /10.1007/s12115-021-00594-8

42 Edgecliffe-Johnson, Andrew (20 December 2020), 'A CEO's challenge to meet stratospheric demands', *Financial Times*.

43 Hill, Alex, Mellon, Liz & Goddard, Jules (27 September 2018), 'How winning organizations last 100 years', *Harvard Business Review* online.

44 Smith, N. Craig & Soonieus, Ron (19 April 2019), 'How Board Members Really Feel About ESG, from Deniers to True Believers', *Harvard Business Review* online.

45 McCartney, Scott (May 12, 2021), 'Delta CEO Ed Bastian Bets on Business Travel: Higher Prices for Better Service' *Wall Street Journal*.

CHAPTER 6

1 Genesan, Senthil (November 2002), Global CEO, pp. 53–59.

2 Barzun, Jacques (1975), *The Use and Abuse of Art*, Princeton, NJ: Princeton University Press, p. 67.

3 Personal Communication, 2019.

4 Hayward, Emily (2 July 2020), 'More people see "value" and "quality" in a brand's politics—not products—as Facebook and other companies are finding out fast', *Wall Street Journal*.

5 https://bcorporation.net/

6 Baldwin, Rosecrans (5 April 2018), 'Patagonia vs Donald Trump', *GQ*.

7 Gellert, Ryan (5 April 2021), 'Business Leaders: Actions Speak Louder Than Words', Patagoniaworks.com.

8 Ballinger, Jeffrey, (August 1992), 'The New Free Trade Heel: Nike's profits jump on the back of Asian workers', *Harpers* Magazine.

9 Harper, Justin (2 December 2020), 'Nike's diversity advert causing a backlash in Japan', BBC News online. Sanghera, Sathnam (27 November 2020), 'High time for companies to practise what they preach on racial diversity', *The Times*.

10 Gilliard, Chris (6 March 2020), 'Tech companies caring about Black Lives Matter is too little, too late', *Fast Company*.

11 Horlings, Sandra & Ind, Nicholas (eds) (2016), Crazy about chocolate, serious about people. In *Brands with a Conscience: How to build a successful and responsible brand*, Kogan Page.

12 Scobey, Richard (19 October 2020), 'Statement: Assessing Progress in Reducing Child Labor in Cocoa Production in Cocoa Growing Areas of Côte d'Ivoire and Ghana', World Cocoa Foundation.

13 Breton, Thierry (10 January 2021), 'Capitol Hill – the 9/11 moment for social media', Politico.eu.

14 Vosoughi, Souroush, Roy, Deb & Arat, Sinan (9 March 2018), 'The Spread of True and False News Online', *Science*, 359, Issue 6380, pp. 1146–1151.

15 Bradshaw, Samantha, Bailey, Hannah & Howard, Philip N. (January 2021), 'Industrialized Disinformation: 2020 Global Inventory of Organized Social Media Manipulation', Oxford Internet Institute, University of Oxford.

16 Taylor, Lenore (19 February 2021), 'Facebook is gambling Australia can't live without it. Imagine if we prove them wrong', *Guardian*.

17 Hill, Steven (25 March 2021), 'Europe's Digital Fix Is Already Broken', *Project Syndicate*.

18 Hearing Before the United States House of Representatives Committee on Energy and Commerce Subcommittees on Consumer Protection & Commerce and Communications & Technology (25 March 2021). Testimony of Mark Zuckerberg, Facebook, Inc.

19 Higgins, Tim (28 January 2021), 'Apple, Facebook trade barbs over privacy-focused business models', *Wall Street Journal*.

20 Almquist, Eric, Senior, John & Bloch, Nicholas (September 2016), 'Elements of Value', *Harvard Business Review*.

21 Ackerman, Courtney E. (10 December 2020), 'What is self-transcendence? Definition and 6 examples', Positivepsychology.com.

22 Salzer-Mörling, M. & Strannegård, L. (2007), 'Ain't misbehavin'—consumption in a moralized brandscape', *Marketing Theory*, 7(4): 407–425.

23 Micheletti, Michele, Follesdal, Andreas & Stolle, Dietlind (2017), Introduction. In Micheletti, Michele, Follesdal, Andreas & Stolle, Dietlind (eds), *Politics, Products and Markets. Exploring Political Consumerism Past and Present*, London: Routledge. Kindle Edition.

Chapter 7

1 Kaletsky, Anatole (2011), *Capitalism 4.0: The Birth of a New Economy in the Aftermath of Crisis*, Public Affairs.

2 Nico Aspinall. Public interest, purpose-driven institutions and the actuary as arbiter of the ethical process. Note based on opening remarks made in the Institute and Faculty of Actuaries' Finance in the Public Interest webinars hosted in mid-March 2021.

3 Smaghi, Lorenzo Bini (15 April 2010), 'Has the financial sector grown too big?' Speech given at Nomura Seminar, Kyoto.

4 Kay, John (3 March 2021), 'RIP PLC: the rise of the ghost corporation', *Prospect* magazine.

5 Wansleben, Leon (March 2021), Personal Communication.
6 Coase, Ronald & Wang, Ning (2012), *How China Became Capitalist*, Palgrave Macmillan UK.
7 Weber, Isabella M. (May 2021), *How China Escaped Shock Therapy: The Market Reform Debate*, London: Routledge.
8 Colander, David & Kupers, Roland (2014), *Complexity and the Art of Public Policy*. Princeton University Press.
9 Edgecliffe-Johnson, Andrew, Hill, Andrew & Kuchler, Hannah (23 February 2021), 'It needs to change its culture: is McKinsey losing its mystique?' *Financial Times*.
10 Jack, Anthony I. *et al.* (2013), 'fMRI Reveals Reciprocal Inhibition Between Social and Physical Cognitive Domains', *NeuroImage* (66), 385–401.
11 Rochford, K.C., Jack, A.I., Boyatzis, R.E. *et al.* (2017), 'Ethical Leadership as a Balance Between Opposing Neural Networks', *J Bus Ethics* 144, 755–770.
12 Zadek, Simon (2019), Pathways to Corporate Responsibility – Revisited. In Lenssen, G.G. & Smith, N.C. (eds), *Managing Sustainable Business*, Springer Science + Business Media BV.
13 Smith, N. Craig & Soonieus, Ron (Winter 2021), 'Boards and Sustainability: From Aspirations to Action', *Management and Business Review*, Vol. 1, Issue 1, pp. 101–109.
14 Skapinker, Michael (5 March 2021), 'The CEO Whisperer: "Every leader needs a fool"', *Financial Times*.
15 Soonieus, Ron (June 2021), Interview with Andreas Jacobs, *Camunico Bulletin on Sustainable Corporate Governance*.
16 Joe Zammit-Lucia. We need to support the rights of pharma if we are going to beat Covid. RADIX, 28th April 2021. https://radixuk.org/opinion/we-need-to-support-the-rights-of-pharma-if-we-are-going-to-beat-covid/
17 Jamie Dimon. CEO Letter to Shareholders 2020. 7 April, 2021.
18 Citigroup internal memo to staff as reported in the *Financial Times*, 4 June 2021.
19 Dale Davidson, James & Rees-Mogg, Lord William (1997), *The Sovereign Individual: Mastering the Transition to the Information Age*.
20 Global Trends 2040: A More Contested World. National Intelligence Council. March 2021.
21 Christensen, Clayton M. (July–August 2010), 'How will you measure your life?' *Harvard Business Review* online.

Index